RIT - WALLACE LIBRARY
CIRCULATING LIBRARY BOOKS

OVERDUE FINES AND FEES FOR <u>ALL</u> BORROWERS

*Recalled = $1/ day overdue (no grace period)
*Billed = $10.00/ item when returned 4 or more weeks overdue
*Lost Items = replacement cost+$10 fee
*All materials must be returned or renewe(

SOVEREIGNTY

AN INQUIRY INTO THE
POLITICAL GOOD

SOVEREIGNTY

AN INQUIRY INTO THE
POLITICAL GOOD

BY

BERTRAND DE JOUVENEL

TRANSLATED BY
J. F. HUNTINGTON

THE UNIVERSITY OF CHICAGO PRESS

THE UNIVERSITY OF CHICAGO PRESS, CHICAGO 60637
The University of Chicago Press, Ltd., London

*Copyright 1957 by Bertrand de Jouvenel. Published 1957
Fourth Impression 1972. Printed in the United States of America*

*International Standard Book Number: 0–226–14161–6 (clothbound)
Library of Congress Catalog Card Number: 57–9548*

To my children

ROLAND
Lux perpetua luceat ei

ANNE   HUGUES

HENRI

CONTENTS

CONTENTS

PART III. THE SOVEREIGN *page* 167

PREFACE

This book is the direct sequel to *Power*.[1] It has cost me much hard work and may, I fear, cost the reader no less. Anyone wishing to follow me will find himself engaged in a difficult piece of exploration, and I know well that I am not a good guide; but I feel strongly that this exploration is necessary and should be attempted by whoever would exercise the duties of a citizen with full awareness of what he is about. In a word, though what I say may be of small importance, the subject itself is of vast importance.

These meditations of mine, which have been taken up at intervals during the last nine years, have reverted progressively to the very heart of the problem of politics. Each of us, even if he gives no thought to it, has a political activity and exercises an authority; we should achieve awareness of this role and of the obligations which it entails and should strive to play it better. Politics as an everyday activity at once more widespread and more necessary than is commonly thought, authority as present in some degree in every man, the good to which this activity and this force, observable everywhere, should be directed—these themes are inseparable from the inquiry undertaken in this book.

The first object of this inquiry was at once too limited as to its subject-matter and too ambitious in its aim. It flowed directly from the preoccupation which gave birth to *Power*. That book described the stages in the growth of the public authority in the historical States of the West. It noted also an attendant phenomenon which may be called the moral emancipation of the public authority. Anyone harking back to the notion held of the public authority in old days finds that it was conceived as something chained to the service of a closely defined purpose; let it aim at doing more, let it succeed in doing less, it would equally meet with disapproval by reference to a not imprecise criterion. But external and internal

---

[1] *Power: the natural history of its growth* (Cheval Ailé, Geneva, 1945). Translated into English by J. F. Huntington and published by the Batchworth Press, London, and the Viking Press, New York.

causes (circumstances and ideas) have both disturbed and extended the public authority; they have shaped its course towards taking on ever wider and more numerous tasks, lacking all certain outline. So it has come about that any fixed notion of its purpose, any sure preconception of its conduct, by which to judge whether it is doing too much or too little, has been lost. And political theorists, who for so long devoted themselves to the question of what was right for the public authority to do, are now concerned only to consider what is the right manner of its formation. In the result, the only judgments now formed are on whether public authorities have a good title to act, not on whether they act well.

Originally, my objects were to tell in this book how the idea of the legitimate origin of Power has suppressed and driven out its natural fellow, that of the legitimate use of Power, and to drive home the loss thereby inflicted. But what was the good of noting and emphasising this loss if no attempt was made to repair it? So it was that my original purpose drew me on to a search for the criteria applicable in our own day to the conduct of public authorities. But the difficulty of such an undertaking is boundless. The thinkers of old could without difficulty picture clearly the ideal role of the public authority, for they thought, wrongly, that their society was static and unchanging, and that it was only a case of keeping in being a given state of things. No less fortunate were those who held the opposite conception, that there existed an ideal order which had to be installed by revolutionary means and then would run on of itself: ardent destroyers of what they found, they were already conserving in anticipation a future Utopia. But is it possible for us, who make no claim to stabilise either the present or the future, to find canons of conduct for the public authority of a dynamic society?

Reflection on this problem brought me to the conclusion that it was posed wrongly. To believe that there exists at any moment whatsoever the best of all possible social orderings, with the result that all that it is right and necessary for the public authorities to do is to bring about or maintain that ordering, is an error whose inevitable end is tyranny. On the other hand, every man who finds himself dressed in the smallest degree of authority over another (and that is the case with even the least important citizen of a republic) is bound to form some conception of the good which he hopes to achieve by the exercise of the power which is his. Will he use it, small though it may be, despotically by making the good sought only his own good,[1] or will he use it properly in the interest of a good which is in some way common?

This intellectual approach came up against two problems. First, wherein does the substance of this common good, which the public authorities are exhorted to serve, consist? It is something left undefined, so that these exhortations are of as much use to them as an unidentified star to a pilot. The difficulties of this large subject will appear in the course of our discussion; that discussion contains a vigorous warning against regarding the good of society as an intelligible whole which is, as such, suitable for the attentions of the public authority. The second problem enlarges the matter for consideration: the authorities in whom public command is vested neither are nor ought to be the only authorities which affect individual behaviours. The phenomenon called 'authority' is at once more ancient and more fundamental than the phenomenon called 'state'; the natural ascendancy of some men over others is the principle of all human organisations and all human advances. The political phenomenon is something much wider and more general than what is commonly denoted by the word 'political'.

This idea took such hold on me that in the end I came to picture the entire movement of society as an unceasing flow of authoritative initiatives; each of them comports a moral responsibility, whether consciously felt or not, and in them may be found more forms of authority at work than that represented by the public ordinances. This last is the highest in one sense but the lowest in another as being the most dependent on the force of intimidation.

I must warn the reader that he is going to find himself involved in the exploratory workings of a questing spirit. This book is not like some clearly drawn map of a familiar country; rather, it is a work of exploration, undertaken now from one starting-point and now from another. To those who think it wrong of me to have launched on the world the results of my researches in so disorderly

[1] 'The despot is he who pursues his own good.' Aristotle, *Nicomachean Ethics*, Book VIII, 1160b.

a form, I can only excuse myself by saying: *studium longum, vita brevis.*

I have been able to give this book much less of my time than I could have wished and much less than it needed. Thanks are due to various friends who have kindly discussed with me some of my ideas, sometimes as a sequel to their partial exposition in the Universities of Manchester,[1] Cambridge, Oxford, the London School of Economics, the University of Chicago and the College of St John. I also wish to acknowledge my gratitude to my friend Mr Huntington for translating this book, and for seeing the translation through the Press.

B. J.

ANSERVILLE
27 MARCH 1956

[1] Here the almost complete exposition of a first version greatly assisted me in writing a completely different book.

TRANSLATOR'S NOTE

This translation has had the benefit of revision by the author himself who has, here and there, varied or expanded the original. The last chapter was not included in the French edition and has been written in English by the author for this edition.

J. F. H.

LONDON
17 JANUARY 1957

INTRODUCTION

Who has ever come across the completely solitary man?

All that explorers (or anyone else) have ever found has been man in society, involved unceasingly in relations with his fellows. Let us try to picture these relations.

Let us represent some one individual (whom we will call 'he') by a dot; let us represent each single action, whatever its nature, directed by him at any other individual by dashes furnished with arrows pointing outwards. Even in quite a short period, a week if you like, the picture will be one of a great density of dashes linking him with a small number of individuals (these we will call 'the neighbours'), and of single dashes linking him with a large number of individuals (these we will call 'the strangers').

Now taking as our point of departure each 'neighbour' of a 'he', let us represent by dashes the actions of each which are pointed at other individuals; let us so continue step by step till we have come to the end of the 'he's neighbours'. As we thus proceed, one of two things will happen. To include the persons touched first by the actions of the neighbours of each and then by those of the neighbours' neighbours, either we must represent a rapidly growing number of individuals—an expanding picture; or else we shall find that the opposite happens, that our picture quickly reaches its limit and that the neighbours in the first degree reappear as neighbours in the third or fourth.

The expanding picture is characteristic of a social order of wide extent, such as our own. The other picture is characteristic of a restricted social order, such as that of the societies which we call 'primitive'. The series of successive 'neighbours' is divergent in the one case, convergent in the other.

Let us get back to our 'he': if we have put him in a primitive society, it is certain that his actions will touch few 'strangers'—and those but seldom—and that those strangers will quickly reappear as neighbours of neighbours; there will be no distant strangers. A social order of wide extent, on the other hand, fosters actions which touch a large number of strangers, some of them very distant; it will, in other words, take a long time to formulate by analysis the successive series of 'neighbours'. That is not to say, however, that in a social order of wide extent each individual will have numerous contacts with very distant strangers. Rather we find that a small number of individuals have contacts with a large number of others, whereas a large number have, each of them, contacts with but a few others. The 'he's' of a society can be classified by reference to the extent of the range of their contacts, by, in other words, the number of 'others' to whom their actions are addressed.

All these actions which one man directs at another make up a web of infinite complexity. The study of this web is the aim of social science. The web, be it noted, knows no frontiers. However far away from each other any two countries are on the map, there will be found to exist many contacts among their several inhabitants.

Let us now apply our minds to a particular category of actions taken by certain men: we shall find that they are regularly directed at the same recipients, among whom they bring about changes of conduct which are similar in kind. These actions are orders given by authorities to those under them. But one species of authority is especially remarkable, because it issues invariably from the same source, applies itself invariably to the same subjects and is invariably obeyed by reason of the support given it both by the feeling of moral obligation it inspires and by its own possession of means of compulsion: this authority is the public authority of a State.

Political science is in current usage the study of the relations between public authorities in a State and the State's nationals.[1] This science is normative when it considers what these relations should be and by what means they should be brought about; it is juridical when it tells us what they should be according to the constitution in being (constitutional law); it is historical when it recounts their changes over the years (history of political institutions); it is sociological and positive when it examines what they in fact are; lastly, it is naturalistic if it seeks to find in these relations conformities of a seemingly inevitable nature.[2]

[1] We shall not here discuss this usage. Personally we think that every human grouping organised for any form of regular co-operation is a body politic, and that the aim of political science is the study of what holds these bodies together, how their cohesion comes about and how it is maintained and perfected. Political science also includes consideration of the moral influence exercised on the individual by his membership of the body.

[2] If this last branch of the subject has made little advance, the reason must, we think, be sought in the failure to look for these regular characteristics in every sort and kind of organised grouping.

THE WHO AND THE WHAT

It is the fashion today to neglect the normative approach. Is this because of its practical ineffectiveness? Not at all! It has inspired and shaped all the constitutions of our western States; it has strikingly demonstrated the influence of ideas on society. We must, therefore, seek some other explanation: which is, perhaps, that what was once theory is now practice. And so one might think if one looks at the source of the taking of decisions in our own time.

The subjects of a State are affected and acted on by the decisions of the State's authorities. Whose business is it to take those decisions? Theory replies: the totality of the subjects, who constitute the Sovereign and are the supreme source of all decisions. But, as it is practically impossible for decisions to be taken in this way, the subjects choose representatives who will take all major decisions (laws) for them, and will act as overseers of the administrative services whose duty it is to execute these decisions. (This notion of 'execution' pure and simple finds expression in the word Executive.) Again for practical reasons, a large number of lesser decisions have to be taken by these administrative services in their various grades. My intention here is not to give what would be a lamentably incomplete general description of the democratic form of government, but to insist on the fact that such a regime is in essence a development of the answer to the question: 'Who decides? Who is the Sovereign?' In such a regime, properly constituted, the place of each category of decision, great or small, is exactly prescribed.

We will next observe that, when the subjects of a State complain of a decision which has been taken, what interests them much more than who took it is what it is. A decision, even though it has been taken by the competent authority (the 'who'), may still vex and revolt and scandalise: and that because of what is in it (the 'what'). Few and far between are the citizens who, if a decision handed down to them meets with their approval, ask themselves whether the authority from which it comes has not exceeded its competence. Only those who disapprove of it will raise, if they can, the question of competence. In the winter of 1950–1 President Truman, against the wishes of a sector of opinion, decided to send four troop divisions to Europe. This sector was opposed to the substance of the decision (its 'what'); its tactic was to agitate the question whether the President had the power to do such a thing (a question of the 'who').

A curious coincidence, is it not, that everyone who condemned the decision also considered that it exceeded the competence of the President, whereas nobody who approved it took this view of the constitution?

Excitement over what the decision is induces in men forgetfulness of their most cherished convictions as to who is competent to take it. How often have we seen the most ardent democrats shut their eyes to the undemocratic way in which a decision to their taste was taken!

When the importance of the problem of the 'what' is given its due weight we may well ask ourselves why the normative approach has for several centuries paid no attention to it. It has confined itself to considering where the power of decision should rest; it has been careless of the question how it should be employed. It has influenced minds as to who should decide; it has given no guidance as to what decisions should be taken.

What are the reasons for this neglect? There are three possible ones: the problem of the 'who' is first in time, the solution given to it resolves automatically the problem of the 'what', the problem of the 'what' is insoluble. Let us examine and weigh these reasons.

THE PRIMORDIAL CHARACTER OF THE PROBLEM OF WHO DECIDES

Never has there been, and never will there be a State from which frictions and internal jars are absent. Between both individuals and groups rivalries grow and differences take on an edge. These antagonisms do not, however, pull to pieces a body politic which is tied by an undisputed allegiance to a single Sovereign. He is the supreme judge, and appeal against his decisions is only to himself. So long as trust, affection and respect, or force of habit, keep subjects bound to his control, the State goes on; it falls to pieces as soon as the authority of the Sovereign loses its hold on a part of the subject mass, which bestows its allegiance elsewhere. Then, to put it bluntly, there is no longer one State but two; or, at the least, two States tend to form where there was one, and in the end one will be violently destroyed by the other. That is a terrible hour in the history of States and one which will leave behind it irreparable bitterness. Never again will all citizens join together in celebrating public festivals, for what are days of glory to one man will be days of mourning to another.

For that reason nothing matters more to the well-being of States than that there should be unchanging agreement as to the identity of the Sovereign—in other words, that a principle of legitimacy should be built up and receive general respect. Anyone seeing in monarchical legitimacy, as France knew it in past centuries, a principle fit only for primitives is making a great mistake, whether he wants to attack it as crude or to praise it as natural. The truth is that the sure and undisputed descent of the sovereign authority to the eldest of the nearest male heirs in the masculine line only was a masterpiece of political art, which came to perfection only with time and after much trouble had been taken. The first Capetian king had been installed by election; he was careful to take the chair at his son's election as heir some months after his own, and this precaution was maintained down to Louis VII, who saw to it that the future Philippe-Auguste was crowned in his presence at Rheims. Even with this precaution, Henry I had to struggle against the candidatures of his brothers. The exclusion of women was formally ordained only at the death of Louis X, and the brother who supplanted the daughter of the dead king had to pay dear for his supporters, who were at first hesitant. Indeed, the banishment of descent in the female line had not become a completely settled thing at the time of the outbreak of the Hundred Years' War, so that the claims of Edward III of England, the nearest in descent but through the female line, were not really extravagant; the exclusion of women, not only as rulers but as transmitters of the Crown, was only placed beyond doubt by the victory of Charles VII.

From then on the Sovereign's identity was settled. Observers of the monarchical era saw in the settlement an underlying cause of its brilliancy, in marked contrast to the feebleness of the States whose monarch was installed by election. This was the case with the disintegrating Holy Roman Empire, and with Bohemia and Hungary which lost their independence—a fate which also befell Poland at a later date.

If it took centuries, as it did, to place monarchical legitimacy on a settled footing, it is no matter for surprise that the transition to democratic legitimacy required in its turn so long a time. This was especially true as the new principle settled the attribution of sovereignty only to outward view, the lawful owner being merely a fictive creature who must entrust to others his right of government. This idea has justified effective attributions of the most varying kinds: sometimes we see complete delegation of powers to a single man, as in the case of the two Napoleons; sometimes complete delegation to a collegium, in other words to an elected aristocracy, which is the regime of parliamentary government in its pure form as it has time and again been seen in France; or sometimes delegated power has been fragmented, as in regimes where there is a separation of powers. So it became a matter of urgency to agree on such a development of the principle as would give the best practical results. In the end certain methods of choice were discovered comparable to the procedure in the case of monarchical heredity—with, however, this difference between the monarchical and democratic procedures, that, while both lay down the method of choosing those who shall govern, the latter, unlike the former, does not in the same breath declare their names.

Because of the importance attaching to the precise attribution of sovereign power, it is not surprising that, in the long period required for one power to take the place of another, discussion of rightful attribution preceded the study of what in fact constitutes a good act of government and by what criteria it may be known. Argument about attribution has now, however, passed into history; the transitional period is over, and all that matters now is the realistic study of the 'what'.

HAS THE QUESTION OF WHAT IS A GOOD ACT OF GOVERNMENT BECOME OTIOSE UNDER DEMOCRACY?

Some assert that the question of a good act of government has reached finality, for any act of government is good if only it has been taken by the competent authority. It is the very principle of arbitrariness that the goodness of an act is merely a matter of its conforming with the sovereign will. But it is not recognised for the principle of arbitrariness when the People is the Sovereign, by virtue of the following train of reasoning: nothing is good in itself, for goodness is a matter of subjective judgment,[1] and therefore what everybody thinks good will in fact be good—for them. Ignoring

---

[1] This is Hobbes's standpoint: 'For these words of good, evil and contemptible, are ever used with relation to the person that useth them: there being nothing simply and absolutely so; nor any common rule of good and evil, to be taken from the nature of the objects themselves, but from the person of the man, where there is no commonwealth, or, in a commonwealth, from the person that representeth it.' *Leviathan*, I, 6.

here the essential difference between unanimity and majority, let us recall that Plato said in answer to this line of argument that, however much a man is willing to maintain it in regard to the just (*bonum honestum*), it becomes absurd when applied to the merely advantageous (*bonum utile*).[1]

But we need not take part in this centuries-old debate. We know very well that democracies, like all other regimes, require of their subjects that they treat as good, in the sense that they obey it, a decision taken by the competent authorities. Democracies do not require, any more than other regimes required up till the totalitarian period, that consent in action be accompanied by approval in thought and that the citizens concur in thinking just and good the commands to which they are held in obedience. And the liberal democracies of our acquaintance are particularly generous of the liberty which they allow the citizens to propagate a personal judgment contrary to the proclaimed judgment with a view to the overthrow of the latter at some future date. Thus it is entirely lawful, even after a decision has been taken, to agitate the question whether it is a good decision.

Suppose, however, the opposite state of things. Let us postulate that the will to be at one with the body politic subdues my every other feeling and my every other thought, so much so that it is not enough for me to conform to some decision taken; I also range my heart and soul behind it, which is the demand that Rousseau seems at one point to make on the citizen.[2] Am I thereby quit of all need to consider the decision rationally? Not so. For, if I am determined to range myself behind the opinion which has won as soon as the discussion of it is over, I cannot so range myself at the moment of my participation in the discussion, when it is not yet known on which side the majority will come down and I have to express my own view on what is the right course to take.

[1] 'For these men are willing to maintain especially in regard to justice that whatever laws a State makes, because they seem to it just, are just to the State that made them, as long as they remain in force; but as regards the good, that nobody has the courage to go on and contend that whatever laws a State passes thinking them advantageous to it are really advantageous as long as they remain in force.' *Theaetetus*, 177 D.

[2] 'When therefore the opposite opinion to mine wins it shows, merely, that I was wrong, and that what I considered to be the general will was not the general will. If my own opinion had won, I should have acted against my real wish, and in that case I should not have been free.' *Du Contrat Social*, IV, 2. Voltaire called this passage, which should be read in its context, sophistry. I discuss it in my edition of *Du Contrat Social* (Editions du Cheval Ailé, Geneva, 1947).

So that, even on the wholly gratuitous assumption that the question of what decision is good is no concern of public servants and ministers, as being the executive and no more, it has still to be faced by a member of the deliberative assembly acting in exercise of the sovereignty of the People, and if—still a gratuitous assumption —we look on the member as merely our representative, then in the final analysis it must needs be faced by me as a member of the sovereign people. In the final analysis, in fact, it is the concern of everyone, as we very well know, and a contrary opinion now somewhat in vogue stands refuted. The mere fact of each man's involvement, in whatever capacity, in public affairs implies each asking himself what decision is good, hearing the arguments of others and giving his own opinion when he has formed it. How then has it come about that political theory seems so little concerned to help us form the opinion which we must give?

SUPPOSE THE PROBLEM OF THE WHAT
IS INSOLUBLE

The first two excuses produced were worthless: one became otiose with time, the other was logically inadmissible. But there is a third which cannot be dismissed so lightly.

It is, quite simply, that no theory of what constitutes good decision can be constructed. Appeal is made to the infinite variety of political decisions and their high degree of particularity. The subject is one which invites an easy irony: 'Will this general theory of yours instruct us on what was the right number of divisions for President Truman to send to Europe—eight or four or perhaps only one?' And just as easy to us is the retort that no general theory, in whatever domain of the social sciences, can bring precise answers to particular questions: it can do no more than guide the exercise of personal judgment.

This is exactly what is now thought wrong to attempt—to bring particular decisions within a general theory: such an ambition is frowned on by most specialists in political science. What yields to measurement, they say, is personal preferences, not the quality of a decision: the latter is an unknown quantity.

This argument, put forward as it is with the greatest seriousness, is in fact comic. Were it impossible to gauge the worth of a decision, you could have no preferences to be aware of, and, if you have some, the reason is simply that each of us does every day of his life what you think impossible—gauges the worth of a decision. But then it is insisted that our doing so is but the expression of a subjective and irrational preference: for the masterstroke of modern rationalism is to make all our motive forces irrational. Against this can be set the evidence furnished by self-examination. We can look inside ourselves and see our judgment forming by means of a process of thought within. If, for instance, it is a question of whether to build a dam, I shall balance the advantages for the city-dwellers against its drawbacks for the mountaineers of the neighbourhood; those who will gain are much more numerous, but the mountaineers who will have to be evicted will suffer a most cruel hardship. Into consideration too will certainly enter what the effect will be on the outward appearance of the district: the mountains will suffer, but the cities will gain, for there will be less smoke. Next the mind takes up the question of expense: assuming that the capital is available, is there some other use to which it could be put and might it not be more advantageous? These considerations and many others (labour resources, balance of payments problems, etc.) confront each other in the understanding.

Also to be noticed is the tendency of the modern mind to think entirely in terms of consequences—never of conditions. People never say 'This is impossible because a prior right stands against it'; what they say is 'This must be done to bring about some result or other'. The idea of result holds the entire field. That being so, we may picture the thought-process of appraisal as a meditation on the long chain of consequences which a decision involves. The events which will flow from it cannot be known for certain, but our appraisal will be formed by pricing the probable outcomes according to our respective sets of values.

To form an opinion, the problem before us is to calculate correctly probabilities of good and evil results; this is something which the wiser among us find difficult and the less wise can do standing on their heads. Clearly the solution of such a problem can only be found by knowing what good and evil results can be expected, who will receive which, and what weight and value is to be given to each. Whenever we give forth a political judgment, we are, all unconsciously, setting to work a whole apparatus of definitions and postulates, we are using coefficients and parameters.

It would be a great thing, surely, if each individual could be made conscious of the apparatus of thought which goes into the making of his judgments; his various judgments would then be subject to the coherence induced by one and the same structure of assumptions.

THE DANGERS OF AN AVOWEDLY
NORMATIVE APPROACH

But, I shall be told, this critique of political judgment is surprising in you who had promised us a theory of what constituted good decision. One would have thought that, to construct it, the right questions would have been to what species of good political good belongs and what are the ways to its realisation; that then these ways towards it would have to be the criteria of good decision.

But there would be grave dangers in so avowedly normative an approach as this. It would in the first place build an ivory tower which was so remote from reality that advice issuing from it would be unable to influence the citizens of the real world: so it was with Plato's *Republic*, which was built on just these foundations. Worse still, the attraction exercised by pretty pictures of this kind lures men into importing them into reality and leads them on to tyrannical actions to achieve their ideals: there is a tyranny in the womb of every Utopia.

We must consider too that, even if it was possible to define a real 'political good', such as, for instance, the cohesion of a group by reason of the good feeling among its members, every decision cannot for all that be brought to the single touchstone of this one political good, for political decisions involve many other goods: therefore there is no single criterion for basing judgments—rather we must make comparisons among several.

Perhaps it will help the reader to understand this book if he receives this 'key'. The author's essential concern is with the benefits which men confer on one another by social co-operation. Therefore, he is concerned too with what maintains and enriches this co-operation. He does not believe that it is possible even for the most powerful intelligence to envisage in advance all future possibilities of this co-operation, and he cannot for that reason take the view that it needs to be built up in successive stages from a single organising centre. The cause of its enrichment he finds in the unfailing supply of fresh initiatives taken independently; these are as seeds which cannot, however, come to flower except under certain conditions of stability. In the vast complex of revolutionary and conservative agencies he looks on the public authority as one agency among others, which, though it is the most powerful, should not consider itself the only one. Rather its part is that of grand accessory to the others.

In this study of it, sovereign authority is looked on throughout as the servant of social relationships, and these are precious for what they bring to man, who is the end to which our labours are finally directed.

PART I

AUTHORITY

CHAPTER I

THE ESSENCE OF POLITICS

1. Political science must presumably be a species of knowledge. Of what, of what order of facts? Of political facts. How defined? In order to be a true science, it must seek conformities: in the behaviour of what agents? and in what respects? To delimit the object of our study we may use one of two methods. We can start from the amorphous mass of facts which are loosely called political, and boil it down to the common denominator which earns these facts their description. Or we can start from a narrow and clear definition. This latter course involves the considerable difficulty of finding a good definition, and the great inconvenience that some things termed political may stand outside the limits of our definition. The former course, however, we have found impracticable, and the reasons are hereafter expounded.

2. The root word 'politic' is currently employed with the function of an adjective. It does not clearly and definitely designate any distinctive thing; it has no frontiers; indeed, the word 'non-political' is used merely to denote one more political attitude. The use of the word 'politic' designates not a thing, but the relations of anything with government. This assertion can easily be illustrated. There is no natural affinity between the word 'politics' and the word 'meat', but they come together as soon as it is proposed that the government should do something about meat. We call 'political' the pressures exerted upon the public authorities to bring about this or that decision desired by this or that private interest; we also call 'political' the stands taken on the matter by the parties, with a view to attaining or retaining popularity and power. Finally the line of conduct adopted in the meat issue is in most languages called a policy: in French we have no distinctive word and have to say 'une politique'.

What we have here are, clearly, things of different species. A difference of suffixes in English, of articles in French, denotes the difference existing between the tug-of-war over the formation of some decision or the seizure of some power, which comes under 'politics', and the line of conduct finally followed, which we call 'policy'.

In this way the root-word 'politic' splits evenly into two meanings in relation to some decision. 'Politics' may be taken to denote the tussle which precedes the decision, and 'policy' the course adopted. It is quite clear too that, in the tussle which precedes the decision of a large group, each little group has its policy, its line of conduct to bring about the decision it desires, and the small group's policy at this stage is not to be confused with the policy it seeks to promote. No less clearly this ultimate policy is not outside the sphere of politics, for politics go on, and the policy adopted is a factor in them.

Are valuable results likely to be achieved by the method outlined above, which consists of the progressive break-down into its elements of a vast mass of phenomena all falling under the word 'politics'? We do not think so: not a single science can be named which seeks to arrive at the simple by way of the complex.

We much prefer the opposite method, making our base a narrow meaning of the word 'politics' and building on it.

3. The conduct of a private individual, operating on a very modest scale, is sometimes called 'politic'. When is it so called? Whenever his conduct has been apt to bring about the results desired by him, has been well conceived for its purpose, has been well calculated. But there is something more than that. No one would say that Robinson Crusoe, in using his intelligence to make himself comfortable on his island, had acted on wise political principles—but on wise economic ones.

The word 'economy' is used to denote the good employment (or, more generally, just the employment) of the resources of which a man disposes. When, therefore, is it proper to speak of his private behaviour having a 'political' complexion? Whenever the help of other men is a necessary condition of his attaining his aim and object. Conduct which secures this help, and causes men to perform whatever is necessary to the realisation of the prime mover's object, is 'political' conduct, and 'political' action is action which inclines to his will the wills of others.

It is this 'politics of personal relationships' which is the great theme of Balzac. Critics have gone on saying ever since Taine (Balzac's own words authorising this view) that Balzac's monument is the description of a society in its every part—and that is what Zola, with others after him, tried to do again. But it is bad criticism:

Balzac was not a painter of society as others were painters of battlescapes. What he has painted against various backgrounds is, essentially, the individual's political conduct in society. In most of the novels of Balzac there is a goal to be reached, very often some social position, and the author's full genius appears in his description of the manœuvres which tend to advance a man socially and of the blunders and counter-manœuvres which tend to pull him down.

A man's 'social position' is analogous to his 'political position': both rest on a sufficient number of people agreeing on his importance; both are won by certain agents, whom he has been able to rally to himself, working actively in his favour. Balzac lays especial stress on the part played as 'private agents' by the 'grandes dames' whom he is for ever putting on his stage.

Developing the implications of Balzac's vision, we will advance the proposition that 'politics' occur whenever a project requires the support of other wills—to the extent to which its author sets out to rally those wills. It is a significant fact that the word 'campaign' covers strivings for very different objects, while the conditions necessary to the attainment of all of them are similar. Whether it is a man aiming at a public office or at admission to a club, or a social climber seeking an entrée into someone's salon, or an industrialist trying to put a new product on the market, not one of them, different though these ends are, can achieve his own, except by disarming hostility, rallying popularity, winning support, conciliating wills.

4. Any action tending to rally wills is, in kind, a political action, and, whatever the undertaking to be furthered, takes much the same form. Whether it is a case of securing the support of several political groups for the formation of a ministry, or of several financial groups for the start of a business, or of several social groups for some philanthropic venture, the way of approach is the same.

Must we say, then, that every human undertaking has its politics? Certainly, just as each single one has its economy as well. The entrepreneur proves himself a good economist when he makes such allocation of his means as will best enable him to attain his end; he proves himself a good politician when he enlarges his means with help won from others. We might give such a man this epitaph: 'He proved successful in the struggle, thanks to the adroit policy which brought him allies and to the prudent economy which gave him great superiority of force at the decisive point.'

Economics and politics here appear as two complementary arts necessary to efficient human action: economics is concerned with the use of resources on the spot, politics with adding to them. It also appears that, in any enterprise requiring for its accomplishment the energies of more than one man, the political aspect precedes in logic the economic aspect; how to extract the maximum of useful result from all the forces assembled is a problem later in time than that of their assembling. Take, for instance, an enterprise which is in substance economic, a matter of business: the first step in it must be action which is political in kind, a 'campaign', namely, to assemble the financial backing.

We thus arrive at a first conception, very narrow but very precise, of the art of politics: it is a technique for increasing the human energies at our disposal by rallying other men's wills to our cause.

And action falling into the category of 'political' can, we think, be defined as one which increases the sum of energy lent us by wills which are independent of our own. This definition is valuable as giving us a narrowly defined human phenomenon which occurs at all times and places; as such it lends itself to study.

5. The technique of increase is at its most primitive when the increase is needed for some *ad hoc* purpose—when, that is to say, the end in view is some 'once for all' action, enthusiasm for which on the part of the men involved comes easily, because naturally, to the boil. As, for instance, when white men are incited to lynch black men where they hate them already. But, as the action in this example is morally low, we will take another one; for we are concerned not with what is 'low' morally but with what requires a 'low' degree of political skill. Bringing neighbours together to fight a fire is also a political action, but a primitive one, since the co-operation needed is only for a short time and meets with ready acceptance from the men called on. One difference, however, we may note between these two political actions (rallying for a lynching and rallying for fighting a fire): the predisposing factor is in the one case passion and in the other a sense of moral obligation.

The technique of increase is at its highest when the increase aims, not at some 'once for all' action, but at the establishment of some permanent condition, to which the group of men who bring it about must continue loyal.

It is much harder to win the assent of men to the inauguration of some permanent condition. Men respond readily enough to a suggestion to do something which is in the line of their own inclinations. But, when the object in the promoter's mind is the establishment of something lasting, their imaginations are apt to be touched but feebly and the thing itself to make but a dull impression; even when it is something strongly desired and clearly envisaged, some of the links in the chain of actions necessary to its realisation will be weak ones, for some of the actions will be intrinsically unpopular.

But, more than anything else, it is the keeping together of a team of human beings which will present difficulties. We are thinking now of a durable combination, of an habitual running in double harness which should prove as lasting as a building. Wills are inconstant things, and anything built by them must for that reason show an innate tendency to come apart. And with enlargement of the thing built the forces making for disruption and incoherence will themselves multiply. Therefore the maintenance of the structure must proceed day in, day out: conservation is a harder task than construction. The problems thus presented are political problems in the true sense, and the labours required are political labours.

It will be convenient to distinguish by words action directed to a rallying of wills for some 'once for all' purpose and action directed to forming a durable combination: the former we will call 'additive', the latter 'aggregative'. The one, of course, shades gradually off into the other, and the two words signify no more than the upper and lower zones of a single form of action—a form of action which is everywhere present in all human formations: the activity of a boy organising a game is 'additive', that of a man organising a continuing team is 'aggregative'.

6. So far we have regarded action of a political kind as instrumental in relation to some purpose or other. Every purpose, we have seen, whatever its nature, provided only that it requires the active participation of other men, demands of its promoter some political action, and sets in motion a technique for rallying assents— a technique denoted the art of politics.

Let us now suppose that combination is no longer a means employed to achieve a given end but is looked on as an end in itself, that the promoter of the particular grouping is no longer concerned with a certain task for which he requires the energies of the group but makes the existence of the group his end.

Whenever action of a political nature has no other end in view than the formation of a group of men, it enters the category of 'pure politics'. The substance of action is then as much political as is its form. And let us note at once that action of this kind can never be merely additive. For it would be a self-contradiction to aim at a group as an end in itself and to want it only for a moment. The virtue required of it is its mere existence; this necessarily carries with it length of life. Action in the sphere of 'pure politics' is inevitably aggregative.

We may say, to sum up, that the action of forming a group of men is always political in form but that its end may or may not be political. When both the form and the end are political, when the action of combining men has no other final end than the existence of the group, then we have 'pure politics'.

Even if reality showed us no concrete instance of 'pure politics'— an analogous case would be that of a chemical element which cannot be isolated—the idea would still be not without its value. But in fact it is true that some men have been concerned only with basing, extending or consolidating aggregates (in French they are called 'grands politiques'); also there were those to whom in times of civil strife the all-important thing has been, not to take sides, but to keep the aggregate together (in French these are called 'politiques').

The characteristic activity of 'pure politics' may, therefore, be defined as an activity that builds, consolidates and keeps in being aggregates of men.

7. This definition carries, we think, many advantages. It shows us at once the nature of a political achievement—it is a closely-knit aggregate. It shows us at once the nature of a political operation— it is the formation and unending rehabilitation of an aggregate of this kind. Also we see at once that there is as well such a thing as political action of a negative kind—the kind that makes for dis-aggregation. We realise too the nature of a political force—it is one which conducts a political operation; and it dawns on us that differing political forces, even when each is positive in isolation and all alike are constructive in tendency, may have a negative effect as regards one another, with one tending to disassociate a whole which another tends to build or keep in being.

Knowing as we do that a strong internal cohesion is what gives to a political achievement its essential durability, we can now understand that an effort directed to some merely additive end, however great its immediate effectiveness, may yet prove a political action of a negative kind, destroying aggregates in being and unable to replace them with an aggregate of its own.

Now we appreciate the political battle as it really is—creators of aggregates fighting for the allegiance of the wills that go to form them. We realise too what is sovereignty—the visible sign of an inner conviction held by the members of an aggregate that their aggregate has an absolute value. So too *raison d'état* (and every organised body has its *raison d'état* or *de corps*) is seen to be what seems rationally needful to the preservation of the aggregate.

8. Our mode of presentation focuses attention on two points: the capacity to found aggregates and the conditions making for their stability. The capacity to found aggregates would be suited by the word 'authority'. But we can hardly use it because in present use it has become, alas, associated with intimidation. In our context it should mean the ability to cause others to act. An *auctor* is, properly speaking, a source, an instigator, an architect. Significantly enough, the Latin word included the idea of that which causes increase. And truly the creator of an aggregate causes an increase, for the aggregate is something more than its parts, just as the men who make it up are themselves something more than they were, materially and in most cases morally.

This power to found or initiate is the *vis politica*, the causative force of every social formation or company of men. Not for a moment must we be understood to think of this *vis politica* only in relation to states: it is at work in every co-operative aggregate.[1]

The study of this *vis politica* must form an essential part of a real political science. We may analyse it under three aspects, which are not often found together in the same operative agent: the capacity to bring into being a stream of wills, the capacity to canalise the stream, and the capacity to regularise and institutionalise the resulting co-operation. The first capacity can itself be subdivided into the faculties of initiation and propagation. The man who leads into action a stream of wills, whether he found it or made it, is *dux*, the conductor or leader. The man who institutionalises co-operation is *rex*, the man who regularises or rules. This duality of *dux-rex*, of which Rousseau had an inkling,[2] has been wonderfully brought out by Dumézil in researches which are of fundamental importance

---

[1] An example would be the formation by Mr Bevin of the Transport and General Workers Union in Great Britain, or the founding of the Congress of Industrial Organisations by Mr John L. Lewis in the United States.

[2] Cf. the observation on the names of Romulus and Numa, in a note to ch. IV, Book IV of the *Contrat Social*.

for political science.[1] Let us put it in this way: it depends on the capacity proper to the *rex* whether the additive achievement of the *dux* becomes a lasting aggregation.

Let us here throw in some remarks on the parasitic talents needed by a professional politician for personal success. Two are enough, but these he must have: a flair for recognising whatever currents of will are astir in society, that he may use them to carry him on, and, at its very lowest level, the additive talent, which enables him to dispose men favourably to his person (his one aim), so that he acquires a sort of primacy among, as it were, twigs swept along by a flood. The element of *auctoritas* (in the true sense) is here entirely lacking, for what these professionals do is substantially nothing at all, not even evil. The part played by them in the body social is that of coloured particles which make it possible to follow the directions taken by the various eddies.

9. The conditions making for the solidity and stability of an aggregate are, naturally, a chapter of major importance in political science. One thing is certain: that no aggregate can hold together if the ties which bind it are downward only, from, that is to say, the *auctor* to each participant. Let us picture each element of an aggregate as fastened to its *auctor* (founder) by a force of attraction exercised by the latter. This tie will, by hypothesis, hold only so far as the force of attraction of the *dux* holds. And it will not hold even so far as that if sufficiently powerful forces of repulsion are at work among the members of the whole.[2]

As forces of repulsion, liable to take on sudden growth according to circumstances, will never be wanting, the tie can only hold if the forces of attraction are both extremely strong and continuously operative. The study of these forces of attraction is vital to our subject. They may roughly be divided into the centripetal and the lateral. Centripetal attraction is exerted by a nodal centre, such as a dynasty, which is always visible and always operative. Lateral attraction is ensured by the links which come to exist between members of the group: that *auctor* has laid weak foundations who has not intermarried the associates. The intimacy established

---

[1] Cf. G. Dumézil, *Mitra-Varuna, Essai sur deux représentations indo-européennes de la Souveraineté* (Bibliothèque de l'Ecole des Hautes Etudes, Paris, 1940). Dumézil's thesis is in line with the comment on Rousseau in my own edition of the *Contrat Social* (Geneva, 1947).

[2] An instance of this is General Boulanger whose support was drawn from varied quarters and fell away with great suddenness.

between them must satisfy material, sentimental and moral needs. It is a condition of long duration for the structure that linkages occur among its human elements. This is sufficiently shown by the advantages which flow from a mutual adaptability of behaviours and from the warmth of friendship arising from a well-conducted neighbourliness. But the blessings of a good social feeling would not by themselves be adequate: also required is acceptance by each of the members of symbols common to all, which have become incorporated in the spirit of each and become for him the real tie binding him to the rest. The biologists tell us that in each cell of a living person the chromosomes are the same; in other words, a single operative principle brings it about that the cell is peculiar to this body and this only. Similarly, a complex of symbols brings it about that each member of a very advanced aggregate, such as an old nation, is the carrier of a complex of symbols which belongs specifically to a single nation.

A scientific study of the process of linkage has still to be made; here we can only give its merest outline. Suffice it to say that every aggregate that has in its nascent state come under our observation— a trade union, for instance—presents certain characteristic features: continuity of action on the part of the founders, a network of symbols, co-operation that has become institutionalised (organised benefits and recreation), formation of personal ties.

Let us note also that the less a particular aggregate lends itself by its nature to the formation of affective ties, the more successful it must be in conferring at all times on each of its members benefits of a material and tangible kind. So it is with enterprises of a commercial kind, which are for that reason most unstable aggregates.

10. Co-operation is the means by which a man procures himself material and intellectual goods beyond the reach of a solitary individual. Also, it is the school of his morality. For this reason aggregates must be regarded as blessings and this *vis politica*—their source—as essentially beneficent. Naturally, therefore, a great respect is felt for builders of aggregates, and sometimes this respect becomes a cult.

What we have said earlier points the way to the distinction between aggregates with one particular object and aggregates with no such single object. It is certain that co-operation for one particular object stems from co-operation of a general kind which never ceases—in short, that without life in society and general association there can be no particular associations. Hence the politically pure formation, such as the state or the city, enjoys an acknowledged pre-eminence. It is in the nature of things that aggregates formed for specific ends should always have been subjected to the condition that they have no disruptive consequences for the political aggregate, the polity.

Always and everywhere the greatest social crime has been held to be that of working against the aggregate—*perduellio* or treason: and for the horror felt for an act of treason—for, that is to say, an act tending to dissolve the aggregate—there are the best of grounds.

In every highly developed society a man forms part of several aggregates, but these allegiances of his are arranged, naturally, in a hierarchy. And serious trouble has never failed to result when there is a conflict of loyalties to various aggregates, as when a party or an empire is preferred to the state itself—two forms of solvent of a state which are often seen in conjunction.

Every aggregate, whatever it is, is kept alive by the loyalty of its members, without which it dies; in the last resort the executive power rests in the hands of individual men and women. An aggregate without adherences is a contradiction in terms. Only the unreflecting suppose that there can ever be a government of pure force, for this force must come from somewhere.

11. Allegiance, that necessary counterpart of this *vis politica*, calls for profound study. The best approach to it, no doubt, is by way of the extreme case, when a subject still acknowledges the sway of an authority which does him injury. Force of habit could not by itself keep him in obedience, were he not restrained as well by strong lateral ties, by means of which the respect given to the authority by his fellows whom it does not injure reaches him too by power of contagion. The weight of the motivated adherences carries along with it one which is unmotivated.

The capacity of an authority to work injury to some of its subjects rests wholly and exclusively on the essential advantages conferred by an aggregate. But for these advantages the authority could not continue at all. From this may be deduced a natural political ethic.

When the one aim set himself by the *auctor* (founding father) is that of making an aggregate endure—the end of 'pure politics', in fact—he must, inevitably, take care that the aggregate conduces in general to the well-being of its members. Let that condition stay unfulfilled and the aggregate is no more than a tower of Babel which in the end collapses under its own weight, as the disruptive forces grow with every addition made to it.

12. It is, then, a condition of successful 'pure politics' that an ethic finds a place in them. This ethic, it must be noted, though appropriate to a particular objective, does not necessarily comprehend all the moral ideas which are capable of attracting the mind of man. In our own time, however, it is generally supposed that the aggregates of men we see are as wax, always ready to receive whatever impress it is sought to give them.

The role played by these conceptions of what should be is an 'authoritarian' one, in the sense that they tend to create aggregates conforming to an ideal structure. But it is by no means certain that aggregates whose internal structure has been amended to order will prove durable. The study of the structure of aggregates suggests that the forms making for stability partake of necessity, not will. If this is so, though without a profound study we cannot be certain on the point, those aggregates which men have tried to make conform to shapes of their own choosing cannot survive for long; in that case these shapings themselves will be no more than 'myths', useful for demolishing aggregates in being and building others—these last, however, conforming not at all to the myth that built them.

13. A useful definition of the subject-matter of political science properly so-called would be, we think, the study of the way in which aggregates are formed and of the conditions necessary to their stability. In this way, in our view, the object of our search is clearly outlined, and it becomes possible to observe phenomena which are the same in their essential natures, though differing widely in degree of complexity and in expectation of life. One of the obstructions which has hitherto hindered the development of political science was its limitation to the aggregates called States, which are too long-lived for any summary comprehension of them to be possible. Just as genetics has greatly gained by the study of heredity as it operates over many generations of short-lived insects, so political science will gain greatly from an ability to work on aggregates that mature quickly; of these life in society presents instances all around us.

CHAPTER 2

AUTHORITY

Man is made by co-operation. To affirm this does not belittle the gifts of the Creator. He has determined, as is clear to see, that man should develop and has furnished him with the means of doing so, first among which is the sociability graven on our nature.

Every man is born helpless and wild. He wins control of himself through the education given by the group—by, first and foremost, the narrow group called the family. He wins control over his environment through the collective organisation: this control, which he can never call his own in his own right, comes to him from membership of a whole, and grows from age to age with the enlargement and improvement of the co-operative whole.

If then the individual is born of the group, if man owes to the group his moral and material condition, it is of the greatest importance to know how the group is formed. Two working models of this process hold the field in the general conception, that of voluntary association and that of domination imposed from without. We propose to show first that neither of these models corresponds to reality: having done so, we will then bring to view the true formative influence.

THE MODEL OF THE VOLUNTARY ASSOCIATION

For three centuries now the human understanding has made an ever wider and more general use of an explanation of association which we will call the classical explanation. It has had a profound influence on the public law of the West, on its civil law, its commercial law, its law of association. What is this explanation?

It is that men come together under the pressure of a purpose which each has and which is the same in each. This idea is often romantically illustrated: strong men of the woods move from different directions towards a clearing. Here they may be seen forming an assembly in whose bosom the common purpose has its origin and finds its basis. The purpose will in time take concrete form and be crystallised in a binding pact. The word 'convention' carries three meanings, each of which corresponds to one of the acts in this drama. It can mean 'to come together, to join up': that is the first act. It designates the formal assembly (we think of 'the National Convention' in France, and in the United States of 'the Convention of the Republican Party', denoting the occasion of its meeting): that is the second act. Lastly, the word 'convention' denotes in legal terminology an engagement taken in common and the legal tie which thereafter binds the contracting parties.

The pact or convention embodies the original purpose and forms a permanent alliance for the service of this purpose. A human aggregate for a defined object has now been founded, whose members will pursue together the common objective. The assumption is made that the convergence of wills, which is taken under this theory to be the prime mover, will persist throughout the life of the association and that the purpose of the associates who have given it birth will remain the same. Associates may retire from a civil association of a lesser kind, but in the case of the state the highest authorities have taken the view that the wish of the moment must give way to the original wish which gave the state life. The event of capital importance is the original wish.

The theory allows the expediency of specially charging certain members of the association with serving its common purpose, of dressing them in the association's authority as representatives less of the associates themselves than of their original wish. These members hold rights as against the associates—rights which they derive from the convention; in other words, the relations between those who rule and those who obey in a state are of the nature of rights exercised by the former. They are, however, looked on as being merely the most active agents in the service of a common purpose, which is the same for all.

This conception of society's formation can be illustrated by a circular diagram: the future associates may be shown dispersed at first along the circumference and then joining up at the centre, to which his own will urges each man among them. There they all meet and plant a tree—the association, in other words—whose roots will be nourished and whose fruits will be distributed at the circumference to which, once the convention has been passed, the founding fathers return.

A purpose pursued by each and all, spontaneous convergence, assembly, pact, designation of representatives, persistence of the original purpose among the associates, faithfulness to their trust on the part of the representatives who have rights derived from the mission confided to them, the creation, in short, of a coherent body animated by the purpose which stays alive in each—there we see the model of the voluntary association, which is continually turning up in modern thought. The modern state is looked on as a voluntary association of citizens, whose obedience is the result of a spontaneous grant of power made by them to their rulers. 'Pacts' again are thought to have produced other kinds of association for particular ends, such as profit (joint stock companies), protection of the craft (trade unions), games (chess circles), or any other activity. The view has even been taken that the whole of human life, material and moral, is included in the principle of association: that is the socialist conception.

Examination of modern law and of the ideology of several preceding generations yields everywhere the same pattern of thought: association coming about in the way just expounded. That pattern was deep in the foundations of the League of Nations (and its sickly successor, the United Nations), with the additional oddity that it was thought possible to treat states as if they were individual men.

This model attracts aesthetically, but has still to be shown according with reality. That it does not do, as appears at once from any close examination of actual associations such as spring up around us every day.

Let us begin at the beginning: there is in fact no such thing as spontaneous convergence of wishes which have arisen simultaneously in the breasts of all. What we see in fact is, not participants coming together, but one or several promoters making incessant approaches to potential participants with a view to bringing them together. The process of formation gets into gear through the initiative of a single man, who sows among others the seed of his purpose; some of them, in whom it rises, turn into a small group of apostles for the scheme, and these form the nucleus that preaches and recruits. Each of them influences others, whose interest they arouse, whose support is progressively won. At length the association comes into being, not by a mere coincidence of wishes, but as the fruit of one man working on another. The mistake of the classical theory is to overlook the role of the founder—the *auctor*—in the formation of the group.

THE MODEL OF DOMINATION IMPOSED FROM WITHOUT

Graver by far is the mistake of the cynics; there is nothing like cynicism for darkening counsel. For the cynics the birth of a society is due to the violence done to a population by a band of conquerors who subject them to a social discipline which is to the conquerors' advantage.

History abounds in instances of conquest. There have been those which have brought together in a single association societies which had been till then distinct: there have been none which have brought together in society men who were formerly leading independent lives. But the strongest proof of the theory's absurdity is that it offers no explanation of how the conquering band came to be formed. Those who today conquer and bring together others must in some way have been brought together themselves. In what way? Are they perhaps those whom their chiefs have conquered? If so, how did these latter come to win so improbable a victory? Even if, what is certainly untrue, the assemblage of men could gain in extent only by violence, the start of the process cannot in any case have owed anything to violence. And Voltaire blundered badly when he said that the first king was a successful soldier.

There is a heretical taint in this second theory which makes it attractive to some. Basically, however, it is untenable and its fallacious character is much more pronounced than is that of the first theory—because it ignores the element of consent.

We reject utterly both these theories—domination from without and voluntary association; our own theory is that of association brought about by the summons of a man.

DEFINITION OF AUTHORITY

By 'authority' I mean the faculty of gaining another man's assent. Or again it may be called, though it comes to the same thing, the efficient cause of voluntary associations. In any voluntary association that comes to my notice I see the work of a force: that force is authority.

No one doubts the right of an author to use a word in his chosen meaning so long as he gives fair notice of what that meaning is. That is not to say that confusion does not result if the meaning he gives it is too far removed from its usual meaning. I may seem at first sight to be offending in just that way since in current usage 'authoritarian government' signifies one which has large recourse to violence, both in act and threat, to get itself obeyed. Of such a government it would have to be said, according to my definition, that its authority is inadequate to the fulfilment of its plans: it must therefore make good by intimidation.

But this corruption of the word is of quite recent date, and I am doing no more than give it back its traditional significance. And how rich in meaning is the word *auctor*.

The *auctor* is, in ordinary speech, creator of a work, father or ancestor, founder of a family or a city, the Creator of the universe. This is the crudest meaning; more subtle meanings have become incorporated in it. The *auctor* is the man whose advice is followed, to whom the actions of others must in reality be traced back; he instigates, he promotes. He inspires others with the breath of his own purpose, which now becomes that of those others as well—the very principle of the actions which they freely do. In this way the notion of father and creator is illumined and amplified: he is the father of actions freely undertaken whose source is in him though their seat is in others.

But how can a man be the source of actions freely undertaken by others? By, in the first place, giving them the example—this is another meaning of the word *auctor*—but also by answering for the rightness of the action, for the certainty that it will yield good fruits to the man who undertakes it. The *auctor* is the guarantor, the man who vouches for the success of the enterprise; and this, it seems, is the most primitive meaning. The root of the word denotes the idea of augmentation: the guarantor increases the confidence of whoever embarks on action at his instigation or backed by his security, and the action undertaken thanks to this increased confidence will prove in the end a means of advancement for the man who does it. It would hardly be possible to express more clearly both the condition needed for and the result accruing from human co-operation.

VIRTUES OF AUTHORITY

Everywhere and at all levels social life offers us the daily spectacle of authority fulfilling its primary function—of man leading man on, of the ascendancy of a settled will which summons and orients uncertain wills. Man is, under Providence, apt to receive the impulsions of other men: but for this gift we should be ineducable and unadaptable. The counterpart of this receptivity is an activity. The complementary gift is the impulsive power—authority. No one is entirely without this power, but it takes very different forms, and we have it in very different degrees.

This impulsive power never ceases its work of mobilising human energies. To it we owe every advance we make; it may fairly be called providential. It can, like every other gift, be used badly.

Disposing looks to be a superior activity to proposing. Does not the proverb say: 'Man proposes, God disposes'? But in human relations this classification is wrong, for everyone all the time is, by the mere fact of living, disposing of his actions and of whatever lies in his power. And if everyone did nothing but dispose, there would be no such thing as Society. Society in fact exists only because man is capable of proposing and of affecting by his proposals another's dispositions; it is by the acceptance of proposals that contracts are clinched, disputes settled and alliances formed between individuals. The faculty of proposing is part of every man's natural equipment, but in this respect we are very unequal when it comes to taking an initiative. We are more unequal still in the faculty of getting our proposals accepted. It often happens that a proposal which, when Primus makes it, is disregarded meets with support when Secundus takes it over.

What I mean by 'authority' is the ability of a man to get his own proposals accepted. Authority of this kind shows itself strongly in any gathering of children, one of whom will get his companions to join him in games suggested by himself or have his settlement of a quarrel accepted by the others. Authority of this kind is essential to the forward march of every society, for collective actions and stoppage of disputes cannot be dispensed with. It is certain that, were men deaf to all authority, they would have among them neither co-operation nor security—in short, no Society.

ORIGIN OF SOVEREIGNS

It is an idle question whether the formation of associations was due to violence or deliberate choice. All that was needed for their formation was that some one man should feel within him a natural ascendancy and should then inspire others with trust in himself. Occam's razor is here very much in point: when we can see every day associations forming all around us, why should we imagine them forming in the distant past in some different way? What makes leaders, now as always, is natural ascendancy—authority as such. We see them arising under our very eyes whenever there is a rescue to organise or a fire to put out.

Command was at first an observable fact. It became institutionalised by a complicity below the level of consciousness between leaders and led, who combined to stabilise a state of things, in itself unstable, which had proved beneficial. Though it was a natural ascendancy which founded the beneficial organisation, attachment to the latter has itself aroused a new regard for those who are its centre and symbol. They are now allowed an induced ascendancy as well which will henceforward sustain the natural ascendancy or make good its lack. It was the prestige of the founder which won acceptance of the organisation; it is the prestige of the organisation which will support his successors in leadership.

We see this happening every day in associations founded by a strong personality: when he disappears, his successor is able to continue the work because he enjoys an induced authority—he maintains and develops what he could not have begun. Perhaps sceptics will say that there is superstition in the halo which is bestowed on the sovereign-successor and is the prop of his weakness. But it is this reflected prestige which keeps associations of men from dissolving on the disappearance of their founders; and the advantages of associations cannot be had if they do not last.

Loyalty to the organisation is the fruit of loyalty to its original promoter and is reflected in loyalty to those who are for the time being running it. From this comes their power, which is nothing more than the capacity to make themselves obeyed. Power, however, is something very different from authority. The distinguishing mark of the latter is that it is exercised only over those who voluntarily accept it: if the rulers have authority over only a part of their subjects, they may receive from that part a strength sufficient to subject the others to their power. Thus it appears that means of constraint are an appanage of power in virtue of the partial authority which remains with rulers, and do not survive that partial authority's collapse. Of all states that is the worst whose rulers no longer enjoy an authority sufficiently extensive for everyone to obey them with good grace, but in which their authority over a part of their subjects is sufficiently large to enable them to constrain others. This state of things—power over all by means of authority over a part—is the mark of the authoritarian State.

This line of thought makes clear what a mistake it is to oppose authority to liberty. Authority is the faculty of inducing assent. To follow an authority is a voluntary act. Authority ends where voluntary assent ends. There is in every state a margin of obedience which is won only by the use of force or the threat of force: it is this margin which breaches liberty and demonstrates the failure of authority. Among free peoples it is a very small margin, because there authority is very great.

The decline of authority in a state is a great misfortune. It may happen either through the inadequacy of the rulers or through their excessive pretences, but also for a third possible reason—the destruction of the halo which upholds authority. Instinctively and unwittingly, men everywhere find new prestiges which add to the stature of their rulers. When scepticism attacks these prestiges and denounces them as bogus, it undermines in the citizens their willingness to obey and in that way weakens voluntary co-operation. One of two things then follows: either friction and anarchy grow in the nation's functioning, or else constraint must play a larger part in it. It was the prevision of these twentieth-century evils which inspired in Royer-Collard his great lament: 'Authority is shattered.'

Since the dissolution of human aggregates is the worst of all evils, police regimes come in when prestiges go out.

THE VARIOUS KINDS OF ASSOCIATIONS

Let us return to the infancy of human aggregates. We have already seen that personal ascendancy is their efficient cause. Conversely, the final cause of the authority brought about is to assure the continuance of the aggregate and make co-operation certain. It leaps to the eye that the characteristics observable in this binding force vary from one form of necessary co-operation to another.

Take the case of a crew racing on a river: the oarsmen make each movement at the bidding of the cox, whose voice synchronises their strokes exactly. Obedience of this kind is the condition of success in the case of a joint action of a simple kind. Or look at the case of men whose task it is to lift a very heavy rail: they will achieve success only by grasping it at the same moment, which is indicated to them by the blast of a whistle. These are two unadulterated instances of what we will call 'action-groups'. Let us observe that, though the authority of the cox or the man with the whistle is very great at the time of the action, it may at other times be non-existent as regards the same persons.

Now let us take a look at a group of fishermen, each in his boat, fishing the same stretch of water. There is no need in their case for a fishing commodore: all of them operate as independent individuals. Yet there will be times when their nets foul each other, when there is dispute as to the ownership of particular fish, when quarrels arise. At such times an arbitrator will be needed who can by his appeasing influence restore peace. And it is a condition of success in the part that the arbitrator enjoys an habitual respect.

Two species of authority emerge from these mental pictures: the one commanding, the other placatory; the one intermittent, the other habitual. Dumézil, drawing on a phrase of Tacitus, has felicitously denoted these two species in two words: *dux*, the leader, and *rex*, the rectifier.

A *dux* there must be to lead a collective action with a precise end in view: such would be a warlike foray, the chances of success in which are in proportion to the chief's success in planning it, in arousing enthusiasm among those taking part, in allotting the various roles judiciously, and in getting his orders obeyed promptly and exactly. But action of a military kind, or action of a kind which, though not military, requires a quasi-military discipline, is intermittent and, in primitive societies, rare.

There is, on the other hand, nothing intermittent about living as neighbours. That is a condition of life which leads men on to serve each other and to make easier the existence of all by a process of reciprocal adaptation—always provided that they live in an atmosphere of confidence. Simultaneously, too, neighbourhood makes for quarrels, and the quarrels call for remedies. For that reason the species of authority called *rex* can never be dispensed with if confidence is to be assured and quarrels overcome: it is in our view the original source of sovereignty.

The *rex* lays down rules of conduct, enforces contracts, arbitrates disputes.

THE SURETY

Nothing could be finer than the reasoning which says: 'No doubt obedience is a nuisance: but it is still more of a nuisance to be on your guard against your every neighbour, to fear his depredations, to be unable to trust his word. Let us therefore give ourselves an arbiter in common who can act as each man's surety for the conduct of all the others.' But had it been necessary for the constitution of political authority and settled society for everyone taking part to reason on those lines, the moment would perhaps never have come, for this clear and passionless conception, which is that of Hobbes, itself belongs to an advanced condition of society.

The assent given to authority was emotional at first, not rational. And in the same way, though the benefits conferred by authority, agglomerator and co-ordinator, were always keenly appreciated, the process by which it fetched them was not at first analysed in the positivist terms familiar to us. Thus men have been known to ascribe to authority indiscriminately not only the advantages, such as internal security, for which it is really responsible, but others as well, such as abundant harvests.

For perhaps tens of thousands of years men have been aware of a correspondence between the functioning of political authorities and the well-being of the group. This correspondence found expression in a language little understood by us—the mythological; we even look down on it for being so very different from our own clear and distinct vision of effects following causes.

A plethora of hymns, which anthropologists have collected or archaeologists have discovered, attest the fact that men once believed in the procreative virtues of good government, as regards both men and crops and livestock. Call this belief, if you like, an absurd superstition; but there is also to be found in it an intuition which observation has buttressed. It is beyond question that the establishment of security and the growth of co-operation are conducive to the growth of families, the advance of cultivation and the increase of livestock. The primitive way of putting it was elliptical but not absurd. It was the obverse side of these beliefs that the sovereigns were held responsible for times of want; and even in our own days have we not seen governments held responsible for economic crises, even though no direct causal relation can be established between their acts and these public misfortunes?

The ancient notion of the *fas* ascribed every sort of social prosperity to a mysterious excellence in the government; conversely, public misfortunes were ascribed to a mysterious vice—the *nefas*—in it. A man reasoning along modern lines by long chains of causes and effects—not that all the men of our time do it—will ascribe to governments the consequences of nothing but what they have done or left undone. Yet it may well be that this is to underestimate their influence. For social prosperity in all its forms depends largely on the dispositions of the citizens; the connections between these and the dispositions of the rulers, though they do not admit of exact formulation, exist for all that.

What we find incongruous in the beliefs of old is the conception of the action of rulers having a direct effect on natural or supernatural forces, bending them to the service of the public prosperity; in our view, on the other hand, its effect is only on the good ordering of human energies. In our view the dams and canals which the Pharaohs had built and maintained brought about the Nile floods and their fertilising effects, whereas the Egyptians said that the floods came about through the merit of the Pharaoh and the obedience of his people, as shown in their labour on the dams and the canals. The two approaches come to the same thing so far as the two important words are concerned: good Pharaoh, good floods. Rather, it is the subjective background to the reasoning which is different. The one approach is positivist, the other poetical.

AUTHORITY AND METAPHOR

Treatises on rhetoric picture metaphor to us as an ornament added to a thought with a view to making its expression more beautiful and striking. But this is to fall into complete error as to the way the mind works. Man thinks by pictures, and style without metaphors is not a natural style before ornamentation, but rather one which has been systematically robbed of the pictures necessary to the progress of the mind. This act of denudation is a laborious and late refinement of which Stendhal gives an example. So natural to man is thinking by pictures that even scientists have had great difficulty in constructing the modern theory of light because their observations did not allow them to choose between two patterns: as a succession of waves or as a discharge of corpuscles, and they had to combine the two pictures.

For this reason poetry is the earliest form of philosophy—a poetry rich in truths which cannot as yet be formulated in any other way, and myths should rightly be regarded as the primitive form of political philosophy among societies of men—one which has morally buttressed the structure of co-operation.

No systematic study has yet been made of the myths collected or discovered by anthropologists or archaeologists. They are as different from each other as were the peoples over whom they held sway. But it can safely be said of all of them without exception that they represent authority as bearing gifts. The sense of this feature of it has been lost in our own day because the public authorities have by stages assumed so many functions as to raise the natural question whether this or that one assumed compensates the community for the corresponding burdens imposed on it. Suppose, however, that, in successive cuts, we took away from the public authorities their responsibility for a host of services the advantage of which to the citizens did not seem so striking as to be commensurate with their cost. A point would come when the residue of functions left to them would be seen by even the most prejudiced mind imaginable to be of a worth incomparably greater than the cost.

This experiment, which can be tried in argument on anyone, drives home the point that, confined to their essential functions, the public authorities give far more to the body social than they take from it. And that is truer still of bare authority, which takes nothing and has no function but to give. Men have found it hard to believe that the immense benefits conferred by the exercise of authority derived from small modifications introduced under its aegis into their own behaviours; they have not viewed the social benefits conferred as the fruit of their own adjustments, but supposed that these benefits rained down from on high thanks to the mediation of the ruler.

The enrichment of life due to organisation has been conceived as a boon provided by invisible powers who were friendly to the ruler. The man who had caught in his net the energies of men was thought initially to have caught divine energies. It was not enough to think of him as clever—he must be blessed as well. That is a point of view, of course, which no modern man could admit—at any rate no comfortably civilised modern man.

But anyone who has seen active service well knows that men demand of their leader not merely cleverness in disposing the forces entrusted to him, prudence and sagacity. To feel assurance they must believe as well (perhaps they need believe nothing else) that he is a lucky man who ordinarily has good fortune on his side. When they are risking their lives, men do not stay within the positivist modes of thought of which they are ordinarily so proud; rather they return to primitive forms—which they will laugh at when the danger is over—and then they look on their leader as surety for their own safety, much less by reason of his skill than because of the mystical 'protection' which he enjoys himself and passes on to them. Sufficient experience of a certain kind will cause every observer to admit the reality of this attitude of mind, which shows itself without regard to either place in society or convictions normally displayed. We must recognise in it the momentary emergence of deep-seated beliefs, ordinarily suppressed by pride.

What men today banish from their beliefs was naïvely accepted by them in the past: that certain leaders are chosen of heaven. This feature of the leader, if he has it, is the simplest explanation of the benefits of life in society; and it is a most salutary one as well, for, in buttressing the authority which is the binding force, it strengthens the social tie and makes co-operation smoother and more fruitful.

THE LIGHTNING CONDUCTOR

Let us note that an authority of the type *rex*, which is thought to function by divine prescription, must of its nature be one of the least exigent forms of rule imaginable. Pursuing no defined end, it has thus no need to mobilise the energies of the citizens for one purpose or another. It has, moreover, no demands to make on its subjects, since it dispenses its benefits without having to call on the help of others. And it is indeed by its mere presence, the confidence which it inspires and the guarantee which it furnishes, that co-operation is set in motion—co-operation being the direct cause of the benefits of which the authority is the indirect and antecedent cause.

We have only to think along these lines to realise that the entire political vocabulary to which we are accustomed falls to the ground as inadequate. People ask why men allow to another the position of *rex* and from whence he draws his title to command them. But it is not a question of a right of command vesting in him; rather, his subjects are convinced that it is greatly to their advantage to share in the benefits brought them by the *rex*. He is over them, he is their sovereign, for precisely the same reasons that cause us to place a lightning conductor on our roofs. As a lightning conductor he saves them from danger; as a well of prosperity he ensures them the ample supply of their creature needs.

But this capacity of bringer of good things makes a prisoner of him. Many instances can be given in which the *rex* finds himself almost kept in confinement. Without going back to primitive times we cannot fail to be struck as we read French history by the anger of the people of Paris when the Fronde robbed them of the infant Louis XIV and when Louis XVI tried to escape. Worse still, peoples have been known who, if they meet with a succession of bad harvests, punish the *rex* for it.

AUTHORITY AND THE SOCIAL TIE

Authority is, we have seen, the creator of the social tie, and its position is consolidated by the benefits which spring from the social tie. It makes few demands and has no defined rights, but it is under the necessity of justifying by the event the reputation for divine prescription which upholds it. That is how the thing which would later become political power looked in its early years.

CHAPTER 3

THE OFFICE OF LEADERSHIP AND THE OFFICE OF ADJUSTMENT

The ascendancy of one man over others has for its purpose sometimes the assemblage of a group of individuals called to some action
in common and sometimes the remedying of the antagonisms which
spring naturally from the intersection of human wills. There are,
then, two species of authority, often combined in a single person;
the function of the one is essentially that of stirring and that of the
other essentially that of calming. Light can be thrown on the
contrast between them if we think of the Bridge of Arcola and of
the Oak of Vincennes.

THE BRIDGE OF ARCOLA AND THE OAK OF VINCENNES

The engraving which shows us Bonaparte hurling himself at the
enemy and thus inspiring his soldiers to follow represents in an
instant the man's entire effect on them from the day he assumed
command. The troops when he came to them were morally dis-
heartened and lacked all offensive spirit. He breathed into them his
own fire; the effect of his famous proclamation was to fill them with
his own ambition, so that they became the joint executors of his
purpose. In his famous proclamation he transmuted his need of
glory into his followers' need of shoes, he made them feel their
tattered state, and so his vast dreams took in their eyes material
forms—'the fertile plains of Lombardy'.

Out of a collection of passive factors Bonaparte constructed an
active whole; he himself, the leader, is pictured to us always as
upright and in headlong rush. Our picture of St Louis, on the other
hand, is that of a man seated under an oak. Chance has accentuated
the contrast between the two pictures, for the scene of the Bridge of
Arcola has been popularised in crudely violent colours and that of
the Oak of Vincennes in lithograph. St Louis, like Bonaparte,
affects, but in the opposite direction, the general appearance of those
around him: the suitors arrive in haste, urged on by the heat of the

quarrel; they come away calm. The active prince acts as a source of heat and agitates the social particles that he may fill them with a capacity for collective expansion; the pacific prince acts as a source of cold and slows down these particles that he may attenuate their mutual clashes.

This source of heat, which is the principle of movement, and this source of cold, which is the principle of order, constitute the two poles of life in society. The changes brought about by the one get re-incorporated in a new equilibrium by the action of the other.

THE FIXITY OF THE FRAME

The first social activity taught to a child is how to name things. The things which he learns to name are the phenomena which make up his universe, and the right names become more numerous as this universe of his grows larger. The child is already quite big by the time that he becomes aware that his mother has a name other than 'Mama', and bigger still when a particular river becomes for him 'the Seine'.

Vocabulary is, if ever there was one, a social thing; in acquiring it, members of the group are assured of landmarks in common. The Avenue Joseph Stalin may arouse among inhabitants of St Denis varying emotional reactions, but it is the same fact for all of them and all can look to it for guidance in finding their way. A man who goes wrong about a word in common use, as by taking Piraeus for the name of a man, proclaims himself stranger to the group. Social position may show itself by vocabulary. A Canadian may have the same stock of common nouns as a Frenchman but not the same stock of proper nouns. A man to whom a learned word conveys nothing does not belong to a certain cultural group, just as a man for whom a first name does not denote a certain person does not belong to a particular fashionable set.

A social whole, be it large or small, is thus seen to be characterised by continual reference to a host of common landmarks. They give it a general feeling of security; they are its bases on which relations and interchange of every kind can be built up. But it is only the fixity allotted to them which enables the landmarks to play their part, and fixity requires the unceasing correction of individual factual judgment by the judgment of others: it is natural to think of the river which is the continuation of the Saône as Saône, but, unless I call it 'Rhône' and allow it to be the Rhône, my conversation will give rise to trouble. Fixed determination to call Louis XVIII, when king, 'Capet' is both a sign and a cause of disturbance. But this accommodation of factual judgment to social perspective is only one of the conditions for the successful use of landmarks. It is above all else necessary that the familiar objects keep their essence and do not continually change.

If I have promised my neighbour a spade, and in his hands it turns into a serpent, whether the transformation is apparent to everyone or only to him, social life becomes in any case impossible. Indeed, it would be to live in an atmosphere of nightmare if apparently solid objects were continually changing substance, unpredictably and in obedience to no ascertainable law; the anxiety caused thereby would make human life intolerable. We may say then that outward solidity in things around us is necessary to our existence. And it is significant that human thought took wing in the contemplation of the stars and in the observation of the celestial orbits, being the things which, of all that men can see, are the most constant and change most slowly. Doubtless it is true that man could have neither thought nor lived in a world whose every rhythm, his own excepted, had been speeded up suddenly. Or set him down, with the duration proper to himself, in the world of molecular movement in which all fixed shapes are lost beneath continuous and unpredictable shocks: intelligent action would be impossible.

Man has always been aware that fixity in environment was necessary to him; it is indeed the very condition of his efforts to change this environment. Routine in things makes possible innovation by man. But human environment is the product, not of solid objects, but of phenomena in which the parts respectively taken by the human or social and the non-human or natural are not easily discernible. And in fact a man, if he is to work on another, must be able to count on the latter's stationary propensities. This inertia is the former's Archimedean point: the revolutionary himself banks on it even in those whom he is stirring up. He reckons that, once they have received his impulse, they will continue to evolve along the lines laid down for them by himself. This extreme example brings home the part played by the inertia of the object in all human calculations.

This is the explanation of the importance in human societies of the concept of 'stationariness'. The man of today banks on the stationariness of everything which he places in the category of the natural order and discounts it in human behaviours which are the product of manners and are buttressed by the law. Attention has often been called to the great difference between these two kinds of regularities. And it is clear that so-called primitive societies have utterly failed to distinguish the natural factor from the human factor in the surprises inflicted on them by environment. Their tendency has been to look for the one safeguard with which to counter every sort of surprise. The systematic study of mythologies, whether relating to the distant past of civilised peoples or to the quite recent past of peoples who are still the subject of ethnological studies, brings almost everywhere to light cults directed to keeping things in place and men answerable for keeping them there.

THE CROWN

The whole of our present knowledge about societies which are by our standards backward seems undoubted proof of the extreme diversity of the various human ensembles; but this diversity is in the course of time steadily reduced. The idea of 'primitive society' shaped in a single mould has today been quite abandoned. Features which in societies examined by us seem particularly common were, it is very possible, entirely absent from societies which have disappeared; perhaps they disappeared for lack of them. In societies which have, in good or bad shape, survived into our own time, government makes its appearance under the most different aspects, and seems sometimes to be entirely absent; but there is one factor which is met with almost everywhere, except among peoples, such as the Eskimos, whose destiny is particularly wretched. That factor is the presence of an authority acting as preservative, which is also the sanction for regularities of conduct. Of what is it preservative? Very often not only of the social order but of the cosmic order which has not been distinguished from the social order. A friendly world, without drawbacks such as drought and famine and epizootic diseases and disappearance of game—that is what is asked for, and the disorders which occur in the social group are often put on the same footing as troubles in the natural order. The genie who sends the rain also guides the arrow to its target, the criminal action is just as likely to provoke the elements as the anger of neighbours, and ceremonies and rites are insurances taken out against risks whose variousness is not analysed.

It is one of humanity's basic ideas that structures are images of one another—hence the enthusiasm with which the late-nineteenth-century physicists pounced on the notion that the atom reproduced the planetary system. These reproductions can become almost unrecognisable through transformation (in the mathematical sense), but the relationship between the original and the copy is taught by esoteric knowledge. The explanation of every magical action is this: it is exercised on a representation with a view to influencing the thing represented, as when a pantomimic representation of fertilisation induces fertility.

Older far than discursive thought, the symbol was guide long before it was illustration. A circumference suggests irresistibly the idea of order, equilibrium, perfect arrangement. It is a form into which no distortion could be introduced without the eye wishing to reconstitute its roundness, as many experiments attest.[1] So it is that the crown, that simple circlet, is the image of a desired good; for this reason in all ages crowns have been offered to the gods in gratitude for the order which they maintain and as an inducement to them to continue to maintain it. In the same way the burial crowns which accompany the dead to the grave, where they are displayed to view, express the prayer that the higher powers may be friendly to them. Sappho and many others tell us that sacrifice to the gods was effective only if the man making sacrifice was crowned. So it is too today with the priest, whose tonsure is the definite representation on him of the crown, without which he could not celebrate the sacrifice of the mass, by which he is marked as dedicated to this sacrifice. The priests in Greece were long called 'crown-wearers'.[2]

The ceremony of coronation is a consecration to the office of stabiliser; it acts as a rein which keeps the wearer to his destiny and end, and equips him for the supplications he must make to the divine powers. All that is well established; it would be daring perhaps, but tempting, to ascribe the garland of the conqueror to the same notion, to see in it a means of exorcism, a consecration to order of the force which has been deployed, a charm preventing the

[1] Our tendency to see perfect shapes in the imperfect shapes submitted to our vision has been well expounded by Koffka. Kurt Koffka, *Principles of Gestalt Psychology* (New York, 1935).

[2] Cf. R. B. Onians, *The Origins of European Thought about the Body, the Mind, the Soul, the World, Time and Fate* (Cambridge, 1951), pp. 454–62.

use for destructive purposes of the 'fury of wrath' employed against the enemy.[1]

The crown, in a word, marks essentially a consecration to the maintenance of order, and not in the least, as is often supposed, power over men; the sign of that power is the sceptre or baton, embryo of the weapon and the tool. Note how in our own days the crown and the sceptre have been separated; the crown is on the head of the priest, the baton is in the hand of the marshal who commands and leads men. The reunion of the two, with one above the other, belongs to a way of thinking already tinged with positivism, in which an executive power is regarded as indispensable to restrain disorders of human origin. In reality, it is another kind of baton which is more truly akin to the crown—the rod of divination on which Oedipus leaned when he answered the riddles propounded by the Sphinx, the rod which is also the staff of the pilgrim (the traveller in search of God), and is in all likelihood the original of the bishop's crozier.

'REX' AND 'AUGUR'

These considerations lead us to regard as the focal point of a society an authority which guarantees to it stability of environment. That end it achieves mainly by interceding with the gods, for which purpose the special virtue of the *rex* is essential; also by proclaiming, through consulting the omens, what is pleasing or displeasing to the gods, what behaviours and actions will meet with blessing or the reverse. This is the justification of the association of *rex* and *augur*, met with in Virgil.[2] It is clear also that, in proclaiming what is pleasing or displeasing, the king exercises a force of opinion over actions; and that, even in a society in which the harm done by one man to another does not call for public punishment (there are many examples of such societies), the individual act which may disturb the universal order and call down misfortunes on the city must,

[1] Victory in the field demands of the warrior a violence which must afterwards be made to disappear, lest it injuriously affect internal order. This idea has been admirably worked out in *Horace et les Curiaces* (Paris, 1942) by George Dumézil. Particularly noticeable is the way in which the necessary cooling-off is pictured by the three vats into which, one after the other, the Irish hero Cuchulain is plunged after his victory: his state of excessive heat cools in their water. Furthermore Roman historical records all tell us how careful the Romans were about reintegrating the warriors in civil society: the example of Cincinnatus was deliberately stressed.

[2] *Aeneid* IX, 327, quoted and commented on by Dumézil in *L'Héritage Indo-Européen à Rome* (Paris, 1949), pp. 205-6.

when recognised by the *rex* for what it is, demand the punishment of the impious wretch by the whole people.

In this respect a passage of Aristotle throws a vivid light on the essential character of an authority aimed at keeping things in place. Writing of the Constitution of Athens, as he knew it, he treats of the still-continuing role of the 'king': 'He holds the court that tries charges of impiety and disputed claims to hereditary priesthoods. He adjudicates between clans and between priests in all disputed claims to privileges. Before him also are brought all murder cases, and proclamations of exclusion from customary rites are made by him.... The king and tribal kings try also prosecutions of inanimate objects and animals for homicide.'[1]

The king, it is clear, intervenes whenever the question is one of religious cults or impious acts. At this very secular stage in Athenian civilisation, matters of this kind were less important than in earlier times; it is significant, however, that they are still the province of the king, and the conclusion is that they were already his essential province in the earliest times. Another instructive passage in Aristotle's text is that in which he sets out the duties of the Archon, who emerges in very early times as the double of the king: 'Immediately on coming into office the Archon first makes proclamation that all men shall hold until the end of his office those possessions and powers that they held before his entry into office.'[2] How can we fail to see here the reflection, in the specifically social sphere, of the guarantee of solidity and cosmic stability given by the king? Students of the declarations on accession made by kings in historical times very often find in them an analogous formula by which acquired rights are consolidated.

Doubtless the functions of mediator and *augur* which the *rex* exercised enabled him to pass off as pleasing to the gods whatever happened to please himself, and to metamorphose, if he wished, a stabilising authority into an arbitrary power. Africa and Asia both offer instances of this metamorphosis; the Greeks and the Romans, on the other hand, confined the *rex* at quite an early date within an office of stabilisation of a very abstract kind. The later peoples of Europe found an intermediate solution, recognising their kings' right to the concrete powers necessary to the maintenance of the established social order, of what was conceived as unchangeable

---

[1] Aristotle, *Athenian Constitution*, LVII, 2.
[2] *Ibid*. LVI, 2.

custom. Moreover, the power of change by way of legislation did not historically belong to the sovereign; it was a victory, achieved in the sixteenth and seventeenth centuries, which paved the way for the fall of the monarchy.

The mission of the *rex*, which was essentially to preserve and consolidate the order in being, was at first accomplished much more by the mysterious operation of his special 'virtue' than by any concrete methods; this explains the mystery of the hereditary transmission of the crown. It is a matter of capital importance to society that every bundle of rights and powers should, on losing its incumbent (especially by his death), immediately receive another about whose designation hesitation or dispute is impossible, so that it may not become a prey to every casual appetite: it was of the greatest positive advantage to France that, on the death of the king, everybody knew at once who his successor was. But this advantage can be had only if there is no possibility of hesitation, as there is none where primogeniture in the male line is the rule, brought in though it was slowly and with difficulty. Of positive disadvantage, on the other hand, is any vague system of family heredity, under which any member of the dead king's family may be his successor. The choice of successor being limited to the one family, capable outsiders are excluded without any certainty that quarrels will thereby be avoided. As a system, it seems the worst of all; yet it seems to have been practised almost universally and to have proved an inexhaustible source of civil wars. The explanation of its wide extent is to be found in the fact that the benefits conferred by the *rex* were linked essentially to a favour from on high; this favour was common to the whole royal family, but it was not known in advance in which of its members the faculty of conservation was most highly concentrated.

Among the Franks, all the princes of the blood, who were demarcated by their long and decorated heads of hair, had an equal vocation for the throne; often they were called collectively *reges criniti*, and the vocation was lost only if the head of hair was shaved off—a Merovingian queen is said to have preferred the deaths of her grandsons rather than that they should suffer this humiliation. The princes born while their father was on the throne (born in the purple) were considered to have a better right than those born before he came to the throne, but the bastards had as good a right as the legitimate sons. Perhaps, however, the reference here should

47

not be to 'right' but rather to the probability of one having more of heaven's favour than another; whichever of them it was that the subjects thought had most, had to be chosen as the most likely to bring good fortune.[1]

Here there is a striking parallel with what Roscoe tells us of the Baganda; among them too the princes born to a king while he was on the throne, 'drum princes' so called, are preferred to the others, who are called 'peasant princes'. On the death of the king the mayor of the palace (*Katikoro*) arranges for the mobilisation of the princes by their chief tutor (*Kasuju*), and these two dignitaries pass the princes in review in front of an enormous crowd. Finally, after seeming to hesitate, they draw out one of them from his place in the line; in his name a challenge is thrown down to the others who, if it is not taken up, are told: 'You are all peasants.' They are then led off to a gargantuan meal while the chosen one is conducted to the body of his father which he piously covers with bark.[2]

Notwithstanding the various precautions taken by different peoples to avoid competition for the throne, the notion that members of the royal house are carriers of special favour leaves them still a danger—and this is the explanation of the massacres of persons of royal blood so often met with in history.

The examples given bring home the fact that we should not speak of a 'right of command', which is an invention of very late date and one that democracy has taken over from absolute monarchy, but rather of the interest which a people has in providing itself with the best lightning-conductor, the most favoured of heaven of all those favoured, the best able by the use of mysterious faculties to consolidate the framework of life and maintain the regular burgeoning of the forces of fertility.

THE LESSON OF BATHSHEBA

Every people has its 'foundation-legend', in which a forceful hero appears and the forces of chaos are tamed. This legend, be it noted, seldom lacks its crime. Theseus, for instance, the founder of Athens, betrays Ariadne and causes the death of his father, Aegeus; Romulus, the founder of Rome, murders his brother. By a happy inspiration Rousseau recognised the significance of the contrast between

---

[1] Fritz Kern, *Kingship and Law in the Middle Ages* (Oxford, 1948).
[2] John Roscoe, *The Baganda* (London, 1911).

Romulus and Numa, between the unresting creator and the peaceable stabiliser,[1] and this contrast has been powerfully worked out in Dumézil's fruitful labours.[2]

But the Bible itself offers the same diptych: David-Solomon. David, the warrior born, who beat Goliath for a start, who killed 'his ten thousand', is the true founder of the Kingdom of Israel. He is a leader, as was said to him by those who came to find him on the death of Saul: 'And moreover in time past, even when Saul was king, thou wast he that leddest out and broughtest in Israel.' He is called 'ruler over the people of Israel'. Support had already started to come to him when he was fleeing before the wrath of the king; once sovereign himself, he mobilises the people and numbers them, though this last was accounted a sin on his part, and assembles foreigners and materials of all sorts to build the house of the Lord God.[3]

Yet, though he collected all the materials for building the temple, David does not build it. He calls for his son, Solomon, and addresses him as follows:

My son, it was in my mind to build an house unto the name of the Lord my God. But the word of the Lord came to me, saying, Thou hast shed blood abundantly, and hast made great wars: thou shalt not build an house unto my name, because thou hast shed much blood upon the earth in my sight. Behold, a son shall be born to thee, who shall be a man of rest; and I will give him rest from all his enemies round about: for his name shall be Solomon, and I will give peace and quietness unto Israel in his days. He shall build an house for my name; and he shall be my son, and I will be his father; and I will establish the throne of his kingdom over Israel for ever.

Now, my son, the Lord be with thee; and prosper thou, and build the house of the Lord thy God, as he hath said of thee. Only the Lord give thee wisdom and understanding, and give thee charge concerning Israel, that thou mayest keep the law of the Lord thy God. Then shalt thou prosper, if thou takest heed to fulfil the statutes and judgments which the Lord charged Moses with concerning Israel.[4]

Every word is significant. Solomon, man of peace, will give rest to Israel, he will be wise, he will guard the law and his throne will be strengthened; he is, in short, the stabiliser. He will have neither

---

[1] *Du Contrat Social*, Book IV, ch. IV (my edition, Geneva, 1947), p. 331.

[2] Notably in *Mitra-Varuna, Essai sur deux représentations indo-européennes de la Souveraineté* (Paris, 1940), a work of capital importance for political science.

[3] I Chronicles xxii, 1–4.   [4] I Chronicles xxii.

to improvise nor to struggle. It is noticeable that, when Solomon numbers the people, there is no question of the census being imputed to him as sin.

The distribution of parts between David and Solomon is as clear as it could be. The choice of Solomon out of all David's sons to dispense to the people of Israel peace and happiness must seem remarkable when it is remembered that he was Bathsheba's son. David had sinned in taking possession of Bathsheba, the wife of Uriah the Hittite, and had made it much worse by having this particularly faithful servant[1] put in the forefront of the battle, where his companions by order of the king had to abandon him 'that he may be smitten and die'. The first-born of the union thus brought about died young, but later Bathsheba bore him Solomon. It is worth noting that the same Nathan the prophet who reproached David with his crime and prophesied to him the death of the first-born of Bathsheba, was the man who, confronted with Adonijah's presumption, demanded of David that he should designate who should reign after him and sit upon his throne, and that he made no protest when David designated Solomon, son of Bathsheba, but was on the contrary one of those who mounted Solomon on the king's mule, brought him to Gihon and anointed him king of Israel.[2]

Reflection on the various episodes which centre on Bathsheba makes us inevitably ask whether their lesson is not that violence and defilement are natural to the enterprise of founding worldly dominion. There was no uglier action in the life of David than his setting the trap in which Uriah died; yet but for it there would have been no Solomon. Solomon puts the coping-stone on the work, but David set it going. The natural rhythm of things does not conform to our simple classifications.

THE STABILISER

Let us now give attention to the function of stabiliser and peacemaker. We have advanced the opinion that the crown symbolised the vocation and end of preservative authority, the point of equilibrium in all the various social and world structures. A symbol may be found for the means whereby this equilibrium is maintained in

[1] See II Samuel xi: recalled from the army, he did not go down to his own house but slept at the door of the king's house.
[2] I Kings i.

the shield which, according to Roman tradition, fell from heaven in the reign of Numa, the *rex* who was priest and consolidator. The shield protects; it is by means of the protection fallen from heaven that the intercessory *rex* shields his people from misfortunes, and it is to be noted that the shields given by the gods often carry human activities, as did the shield given by Zeus to Achilles. Worldly order is guaranteed to him who is beloved of the gods; he is the guarantor of it.

According to the particular people and its temper, and according also to the period, the buffets of fortune will seem due more or less exclusively to the actions of the gods, or in growing measure to the actions of men. If the action of the gods does everything, the only succour is in changing the *rex*, who has been unable to win their favour; but once it is admitted that impiety on the part of a member of the people or of the whole people can draw down misfortune, a causative part gets attributed to human action. Thence is logically deduced, if not a repressive power in the *rex* in regard to impious actions (for the arrival on the scene of specialised repressive agents seems to occur at a very late historical stage), at least his role of condemner of those who foster impiety; in this way the people themselves are brought to punish them as the cause of any collective misfortune.

It was, however, impossible for men not to perceive that their misfortunes were often caused directly by human agents. Without pretence of laying down any general rule, it seems that these injuries were at first avenged by the injured man or his relations, and not by society or its representative. Nevertheless it was clearly necessary to damp down these vendettas, which were a source of disturbance. In this way the maintenance of the equilibrium has made necessary the intervention of authority in the capacity less of judge than of mediator.

A society keeps in being only in so far as each man does not encroach on what belongs to another, keeps his sworn oath (*Dius Fidius*), acts contractually (*do ut des* or reciprocal justice) and generally answers to another's expectation. Disappointed expectations are the death of life in society. For that reason authority answering to the name 'that which increases confidence' must necessarily counter nonconformist behaviours with a view to getting things back into their normal bed. This temporal role may be exercised either by the king himself or by his alter ego. The study of the development of power gives the impression of its developing by a process of duplication; very often the man who is surety for the gods has as his double the man who checks the disturbances of order brought about by men. In time, however, the influencing of the gods becomes the business of a *sacerdos* and the *rex* gives himself exclusively to mortal affairs.

Whoever plays the part, the result is in any case to safeguard respect for usages. For a usage disturbed breeds successive waves of trouble. Let us take an example: in a people among whom heredity is by way of the maternal uncle to the nephew, as is often found, a father wants to pass on his property to his son. But, if he so leaves it, the dispossessed nephew has a grievance; he may either react with violence against the son or may in his turn demand to inherit the estate of his own father, thereby dispossessing the nephew of the latter. So trouble spreads. Let us take another example: in a people divided into two exogamous groups (again no uncommon thing) the women are bought, say with cows. But then some Romeo carries off his Juliet. The family of Juliet is thereby deprived of additional cows which were necessary to enable the men of Juliet's group to acquire in their turn girls of the family of Romeo. Juliet's group may react either by repressing Romeo's act or by imitating it. If they imitate it, a different practice becomes generalised. It is tempting to ask whether the story of the rape of the Sabine women does not fix the memory of some such change.

We realise from the two reactions to a change which are possible that there are two ways in which the stabilising authority may act. It may repress every change by means of an increasing vigilance, or, once a change has come about and tends to become generalised, it may formally approve it and make of it a new usage. But, whichever it does, its part is always to ensure the repetition of the same thing. For the certitudes which it provides are impossible without regular behaviour.

It leaps to the eye that in a very advanced and complicated society, such as our own, the role of the preservative authority is at once as essential as it is delicate. It is essential because the more that men depend on one another the more indispensable to them is regular behaviour on the part of others. The entire day of a civilised man rests entirely on others being at their social posts. Though ours seems to us a very mobile society, it is in reality far more conditioned by routines than are other societies which we call inferior. The maintenance in place of the numberless driven piles which are the foundation of our existence is not of course primarily the work of authority, which merely acts as surety for it and is bound to intervene to strengthen the piles which show signs of shifting. But it is also true that the progress of a civilised society turns on the action of leaders who, at different points of the body social, propagate novelty. It is in admitting these novelties, or some of them, while continually adjusting the general equilibrium (or at least supervising its adjustment), that the delicacy of the task consists. Authority is no longer merely preservative; it has, as well, the office of adjustment.

But in stressing this aspect of its functions, we must never forget that the essence of authority's task is still conservation. In any society the part of change needs to be small and the part of regular behaviours very large. In other words the individual can digest change only in small morsels. It does not matter that the Avenue Henri Martin is renamed the Avenue Georges Mandel, but if all the Paris streets were given new names once a week the result would be chaotic. What does not change conditions what does change: if the Avenue Georges Mandel is the street which begins at the Trocadero and ends at La Muette all is well—but all is not well if the Trocadero and La Muette also get new names. What is true of names is much truer still of behaviours.

We see then that authority which preserves is the social authority *par excellence*. Without it everything collapses. But we realise too that it may have the effect of immobilising a society. And that is not difficult, for initiatives are uncommon and promoters are few and far between. For that reason too great a vigilance as regards innovators, whether the vigilance is served by the deepest convictions or merely by the will to repression, will extinguish every innovating light. Just as initiative is cumulative, so is inertia, and thus it may happen that the stream of initiative and leadership may dry up in a people. Different causes may produce the same effect: sometimes the absence of initiatives, and sometimes the disorderly rout of peripheral initiatives which the central power can neither stifle nor adjust, may equally call to the seat of power an authority which leads, shakes up (in that case it will often come from outside) or co-ordinates. In that way the leader (the *dux*) comes back into his own. It looks, however, as if human societies cannot support having for very long a central power which is continuously of the *dux* species. A preservative authority is normally at the head of a society and the authorities which make for change are at work under its aegis. Only at intervals is an authority of the latter species at the head.

A PRINCIPLE OF CLASSIFICATION?

The foregoing considerations make it perhaps easier to classify the various attitudes open to the public authority (to, in other words, those who exercise it). If it is completely absorbed by its office of guarantor of regular behaviours, of surety as regards each several behaviour of another's and of preserver of an order which is known with certainty, then it will view with disfavour anything which introduces derangement, and it will wish to restrain not only every deviation from the norm in individual behaviour, but also every summons to novelty from whatever source it issues. For this reason it will aim at suppressing anyone with a capacity for leadership along new paths who raises his head in the body of society. And it will be the protector of routines, the enemy of initiatives and conservative to the point of social immobilisation.

It will, on the other hand, be called liberal if it views with a favourable eye the various innovating forces which arise here and there in the Whole it is at the head of. But there can be no hiding the fact that the appearance of every new behaviour allowed by it disturbs another's certainties; and the public authority will not be fulfilling its office of social guarantor if it does not continually apply itself to remedying the injury done to the certainties of some by the innovations of others. If it fails in this office of adjuster, the innovations will cause an ever-growing disturbance, and the members of the society in question will, almost instinctively, call for a public authority capable of giving them back certainties of some kind.

Yet a third attitude on the part of the public authority is also possible. Instead of granting a general licence to the various innovating forces which appear in a society, it can give itself the monopoly of innovation; instead of preserving a society in its present state, as in the first case, and instead of letting it evolve, as in the second, it may lay claim itself to cause its evolution and determine the course of it. Those in authority may reason as follows: change is good but the adjustment of a large number of independent changes is difficult, whereas harmonisation of these changes will be much easier if all are decided on by one and the same mind. Experience may or may not justify this reasoning,[1] but its logic seems impeccable. It will be noted that a public authority which thus decides to assume the entire office of leadership itself must necessarily show as stern and repressive a front to private innovators making their appearance here and there in society as a public authority of the most narrowly conservative type. Just as a conservative authority cannot tolerate whatever disarranges the existing order, so an authority in which all leadership is concentrated cannot tolerate whatever disarranges the dynamic order whose progress it directs. Consequently the authority which fears all change and the authority which directs all change will have features in common; both stand in opposition to the authority which permits changes to happen. Only this last presents problems which are of real interest. Necessarily it acts as a more or less discriminating filter to innovations in behaviour and diversions from the norm; necessarily, too, it is on guard to remedy the resulting uncertainty. It is in this process of filtering and remedying, in this unceasing work of repair to an equilibrium, that the question of the Political Good is most often posed.

[1] See its powerful refutation by Michael Polanyi, 'The Span of Central Direction' in *The Logic of Liberty* (London, 1951). Now is our chance to acknowledge our debt to this lofty intelligence.

CHAPTER 4

THE GROUP

The 'isolated' man is not a natural phenomenon but a product of intellectual abstraction. That which is natural (in the sense of both primary and necessary) is the group. Without the group man is an impossibility. We issued from the womb in so helpless a state that, but for the protective and supporting cover furnished us by the group, we must have died. The group also imprints on us the human characteristics which at birth are only potential.

The very century in which the natural independence of man was a postulate of philosophers saw a fashion among painters of depicting births, marriages and death-beds—all occasions when a man is surrounded by his own group; he is, that is to say, in his true natural state. He cannot exist except among his own, as each of us instinctively knows. Hence the belief, met in every age and place, that the dead man still has need of his kin and continues to serve them.

That each of us is unique and has his own distinctive essence is a valuable belief, and is easily squared with the observable fact that none of us can live alone. From this it follows that to consider groups as secondary phenomena resulting from a synthesis of individuals is a wrong approach; they should be regarded as primary phenomena of human existence.

Obviously this is not true of every group whatsoever; even less than the individual, is the type of 'society' with which we in our time are acquainted the right starting-point for the study of society. It is a highly indefinite type (where, for instance, does 'western society' end?) and lacks the hall-mark of necessity (for, until very recent times, a man lived in incomparably narrower societies); it is the product of actual unions and coalescences which have happened in our own time. And what has been said of 'the society' in this sense is equally true of 'the nation'; this is a quite recent formation and the process which brought it into being is in our memories. If it is neither natural nor possible for man to live in isolation, neither is it necessary for him to be embodied in groups of the size and complexity that we now see; and when, as is the fashion, we speak of 'the relations of the individual with society', we are using terms which in either direction go too far, for the individual cannot exist by himself and the existence of society in its present form is not inevitable. The result is a disastrous under-valuation of the truly basic communities.

What we shall consider here are the primary social formations, those which may be found in all ages and places and which, though not completely identical in detail, always present the same general features; it will be seen that each tends to spread its constituent principles into wider social edifices.

We find these formations to be three in number: the domestic unit, the milieu of existence, the team of action. Under the most widely differing social conditions, a man breaks his bread alongside others; he lives surrounded by a circle of his fellows who spring no surprises on him, for he knows what he may expect of them and what they may expect of him; lastly, he acts, regularly or on occasion only, with those who form with him the members of a team. Man seems always to have formed part of these three species of association, each of which has given rise to very deeply rooted ideas in us. Such are the notion of community, proper to the domestic group; the notion of rational discipline, proper to the team of action; the notions of rights, just return, common safeguard and general interest, proper to the milieu of existence.

THE HEARTH

A man, on being born, calls for help. His first obscure cries will be the expression of demands. Always he is expressing demands, and one would think most of the great political authors were childless not to have been struck by this fundamental characteristic. For that reason our most indispensable institution is the one which answers these demands. The species could not have continued without the domestic community in which the adults share their means of livelihood with the children; it is the nursing milieu of the species, its hub of growth. If, like ourselves, the animals share food and shelter with their young, the slowness of human development requires that the home endure much longer—and there is another feature of difference as well: as far as is known, man is the only species in which the adults share not only with their offspring but also with their old, which not only protects the future but also preserves the past (herein, perhaps, is the seed of man's historical memory). His is the only species which gives proof of piety as well as instinctive foresight; and the piety reaches to long dead ancestors who have libations poured to them.

The meal taken in common is the most tangible expression of the domestic unit; it nourishes not only the bodies of those partaking but their union as well. The gathering of family members round the fire, or, later, round the table, suggests a circular cell; the *paterfamilias*, king and priest of the group, may rule, but the true centre of the circle is the *materfamilias*. In this meal in common men have always seen the symbol of limitless solidarity; so great was the importance attached to it by the Romans that, with them, the marriage rite of the patricians, *confarreatio*, took its name from the sharing by the bride and bridegroom of a cake of meal, *panis farreus*.[1] This domestic group has continued down the ages through various changes in composition and extent; in our own society it is seen at its narrowest. It has always kept the same basic characteristics.

The French word for guests at a meal, *convives*, is revealing, for its literal meaning is 'those who live together', and so the *convivator*, the host, conveys to his guests that he is including them within the feeling of solidarity proper to his immediate family, just as the acceptance by the guests of their role is a sign that they accept this participation in the family ring. That is why, when a joy or a sorrow of the little group—a baptism or a marriage or a funeral—calls for a family gathering, the universal custom is that the members should sit down to a meal together. It is also why the refusal of such an invitation is an insult, as is seen in the parable of those bidden to the wedding who would not come (St Matthew xxii). It explains too why a crime on the part of a member of the group makes it necessary to refuse him participation in the bread and salt, and, lastly, why the re-incorporation in the group of one who has left it is made the occasion of a feast (the fatted calf). The tie of affection takes both recognition and life from participation in the common repast; the more sacred the character which is ascribed to the repast, the greater is the effect.

It seems that the human intelligence has not always clearly distinguished kinship from guestship. It has never been doubted that the family repast strengthened ties of kinship, and perhaps it

[1] Fustel de Coulanges, *La Cité Antique* (ed. Hachette), p. 46.

was thought too that habitual participation created such ties. Otherwise it is hard to explain the fact that those peoples who set most store by kinship were also the most convinced that adoption produced all its results. However that may be, the part played by the meal in common in forming ties is something which is met with everywhere.

From this stems the idea that the feelings of intense solidarity found in the domestic group can be generalised by habitual attendance at the same board. In the spiritual order, where participation is in a food which is the free gift of God, this is possible; but in the material order it does not so work (or it works badly), as the common repasts of the Spartans remind us. The children, whose weakness it is which justifies and necessitates life in common, were not present. A community of unequals who are necessary to each other's existence is natural, a community of equals is artificial. So soon as those sitting at table are autonomous contributors to the feast, comparisons may be drawn between their contributions; the feast is then a cause, not of unity, but of division. The consequences are so unfortunate that the Church found it necessary to strip the communion of the character of solid repast in common, which at first it had.

Let us sum up. We have noted the existence, as universal as it is necessary, of the domestic group, the seat of community of feeling, the place of growth and nourishment, the only group to which a man belongs in his earliest years. It may be seen gathered about the mother and protected by the father,[1] *dominus* or master of the house, its protector and representative as regards both visible and invisible powers, its priest and its judge. In former times he was himself a child in a house, and from having been one and seeing himself as such, he now lives, and his own with him, beneath the shelter of the 'mother-house of the *gens*'.

THE MILIEU OF EXISTENCE

Every man moves and has his being in a milieu of existence. This milieu does not necessarily form a coherent and definite whole; indeed, in our own state of society it has become less coherent and definite. The best definition which we can give of it is the following:

---

[1] Ihering recalls the Sanscrit root, *pâ*, which denotes to nourish, to protect, to maintain. *Histoire du Développement du Droit Romain* (ed. Meulenaere), p. 46.

the milieu of existence of Primus is the whole body of individuals in a position to know him. These individuals may in our own day be widely scattered, but until very recent times they all knew one another. Watch a man on his entry into a public place; if each person greets him by his name, then he is in his milieu of existence. Equally he is there if another whispers to a man who does not know who he is: 'But he is so-and-so's son.'

When today we assure someone to whom we are writing of our 'distinguished consideration' for him, we are in effect saying that we are aware of his personal and distinct existence and of his personality, that we distinguish them and are paying attention to them. 'To be the bearer of a name' and 'to cut a figure' are also phrases which denote the same phenomenon, even though they are generally kept for those whose personalities have especially impressed themselves. But there is no man who does not bear a name for certain others, for whom, hearing it, it will call to mind his face and features.

For and among those who know who he is, Primus has his own position, his own status and his own rights; they may differ from person to person, but each knows his own with equal certainty. Until quite modern times everyone lived in a milieu of existence which was coherent and limited, where each man was known, where each knew well what he was worth, what belonged to him, what was due to him. A milieu of that kind formed naturally a jury of fact, competent to pronounce that Primus is the son of so-and-so, has made delivery to Secundus of something for which Secundus is accountable to him, and so on.

In a milieu of existence which is traditional and coherent Primus has no need to justify his presence. He is, so to speak, 'on the foundation' by reason of his ancestry; only quite rarely need he give formal proof of anything, for his name and fame are already common property. Nor is there occasion for recourse to abstract principles, for it has never occurred to members of the group to reduce to formulae the rules of conduct at which they have arrived empirically. They have learnt to read, to feel and to interpret their natural and social environment by a process of unceasing co-operation below the level of consciousness. Their 'community of views' is the more complete the more irrational it is.

Within a milieu of existence so conceived, the individual man enjoys a dignity which he will never be able to recover elsewhere.

However well he may be treated when he is but a nameless bearer of human characteristics, the consideration shown him will never be of the same quality as that addressed to him in right of the personality which distinguishes him from everyone else. When he is unknown, he will have to give documentary proof of his rights—a thing which every noble nature feels as a humiliation.

How equivocal the word 'society' is! Used by the anthropologist, it brings to mind what we have called a coherent milieu of existence. Those who know Primus know one another, and everyone knows Primus, if not directly, at any rate through an intermediary; the place of Primus is in a congregation. The whole course of social evolution for several generations has tended to the destruction of congregations of this kind. It is true that a cosmopolitan civilisation makes a few names known to an unprecedented number of men, but it is certainly no less true that the ordinary individual is known to people who are not only fewer in number but form a less coherent milieu than was that of so-called primitive societies.

Perhaps it is the narrow circle now called 'good society' which presents to us the most significant picture of the social state of tradition. Known as he is to people who all know one another and whose ancestors knew his, recommended by this coherent circle of relationships to those who have not met him personally, only 'the man of the world' is now left to enjoy what was in past states of society the position of everyone without exception; when such a man speaks of 'society' he means that circle of people who know him or to whom he has easy access, and he is bearing unconscious witness to an age-long truth, namely, that men did once live in societies which were hardly larger than this one and in which all were, or could be, known to everyone else.

But in the society of today it happens frequently that Primus, having lost touch with those who knew his family, is personally known to people most of whom do not know each other, compose no congregation, and do not act as a coherent circle around him. From this arises the sense of isolation which steers men towards political congregations, less perhaps to further the aims of those congregations than with a view to recovering there a milieu of existence, an organic whole of relationships along with the symbols which are its cement.

THE TEAM OF ACTION

The team of action is the social formation by means of which human existence has been and still is being transformed. No doubt the human race is not the only one in which individuals seem able to form teams with a view to modifying their environment to their advantage. But in all the other co-operative species, so far as our knowledge goes, all team action is directed to reconstituting a mould which has been given once and for all. The animals with social inclinations seem to us, subject to what may hereafter be discovered, to be directing their action to an end which is always the same, has been equally perceived in one way or another by all the members of the group, acts as a spur to them all and causes them to serve it in formations which are always the same.

The distinguishing feature of man is the diversity of the plans which he is capable of evolving, the freedom to choose his ends; it is also the liberty of choice or indifference possessed by others as regards the ends set before them. A man conceives an end: the end presents itself to his mind in the form of a picture—in, it might be said, an image in relief. Upon the image of an experienced reality, given and present, is superimposed the image of a future reality, planned but still to be made. The word 'project' denotes a projection of the mind on the plane of the visible universe, the imprint of a will. This image can be communicated to others. Such is the disparity between a man's imagination and his powers that every project of any size requires for its realisation the powers of several or many others, possibly for a very long time. And the minds of other men are accessible to his proposals, are capable of assenting to the project and of devoting themselves to its realisation. Thus are brought into being the teams of action moving toward their ends, which compose at any given moment of history what is rightly called the onward march of society.

The team of action, being a group which propels and draws, is the perfect opposite of the domestic group. It is now a case, not of living together but of acting together, not of consuming but of getting and winning. The domestic group can be pictured as a round cell at the centre of which is the mother rather than the father. The team of action, being a group in movement, tends to be streamlined and should be pictured as a spindle-shaped cell; it is the leader or the promoter who activates this group.

Of all the social formations, the team of action is most readily understood, because it has been assembled for an explicit end. That being so, its structure is explained by subordination to the end, and can be approved or censured as being more or less proportioned to this end—which is the true meaning of the word 'rational'. Let us suppose two trails of footsteps: the one has been made by the daily to-and-fro of the inhabitants of a village, the other by a team of beaters and sportsmen. The second is, relative to the first, clear and coherent, for all the movements derive from a single principle.

An infinite variety of opinions is possible on groups in general, as regards both their worth and their improvement; for there are many aspects or qualities by which their excellence may be reckoned and many dimensions by which they may be measured. Different men will weight their several aspects or qualities differently and will thus arrive at different totals, and they will find any change proposed more or less desirable by reference to this intricate but unconscious process of assessment. But the merits of an action group are, on the contrary, easy to assess; having been formed to attain a given end or to perform a given task, it exists only for the purpose, and there is thus a definite criterion by which to measure its worth and improvement. The criterion is success in fulfilling the task or speed in attaining the goal. The end of a combat group is victory, the end of a team of sportsmen is to return with the largest possible bag. Thus there is a single axis of reference along which measurements must be made.

Because the team of action has a final cause known to all and is addressed to a precise objective, success or failure are ascertainable facts; the degree of success can be related to the volume or intensity of the factors used and it can be said that these have been more or less effectively employed. This, therefore, is the formation amenable by its very nature to rational thought, and indeed experimentation with this type of formation leads to the development of rational thought. For what else is rational thought but a working back from an end willed to the means whereby it can best be achieved?

The object of the action group being to win a specified result or to go as fast as possible in a given direction, the best shape for it is that which will facilitate or speed up this progress; the best members are those whose contribution to the result has been the greatest, and the best leader is he under whose leadership the widest measure of success has been attained.

Every other sort of social formation confronts the mind with a complexity which baffles it, and, when we try to relate all its characteristics to some supposed end in it, we are aware that what we are doing is arbitrary. Only the action group does not baffle the mind, the reason being that it has been constructed with a view to realising a precisely declared idea; for this reason action groups constitute those parts of the social edifice which, being amenable to measurement, are directly subject to our understanding. It is this feature of them which caused Hobbes (and many others) to seek to make the action group the model of the political society, and to postulate in the origin of political society the same vision of the advantages to be had from it and the same acceptance of necessary conditions as go to the formation and organisation of a team of sportsmen; but therein is manifest error and fiction. The laws of effective action, which must logically preside over the formation of teams of action, do not necessarily preside over the organisation of social structures of a complex kind.

The mind of man will never tire of generalising too far from principles which are, within their limits, well-founded. It is absolutely true that the human race must seek preservation only in the community; but the natural domain of the community is the domestic group at the centre of which is the mother. It is absolutely true that the human race advances by way of combined actions which require the impulsion of a promoter and the discipline conferred by a *dux*; but the natural domain of this discipline is the team or the enterprise. The 'natural law' immanent in and specific to each of these forms of association influences, it is true, the whole social complex, but neither of them can regulate it exclusively. It is as futile and dangerous to aim at making of society one large family, as sentimental socialism seeks to do, as to aim at making of it one large team, as positivist socialism seeks to do.

We will now expatiate further on the action group, as the great cause of the changes, tensions, conflicts, advances and disorders which occur in societies of men.

THE MAN OF THE PROJECT

Doubtless the project issues from the man, but the man, once he has espoused it, becomes the man of the project, determined to make it succeed and disposed to judge everything that crosses his path in life from the angle of the project: 'good' is what helps the project, 'evil' is what hinders it. Even the most modest project—that, for instance, of a clerk wanting to put on a theatrical performance by his colleagues—calls forth in the promoter unsuspected qualities of inventiveness, energy and perseverance. He pleads, presses, convinces, calculates means, rounds awkward corners, chides those taking part, flares up at accidents. The 'irascible power of the soul', spoken of by the Schoolmen, is deployed to bring success; this power, if it is sometimes used laughably, is the expression of a valuable quality of constancy in the pursuit of ends which have once been taken up. The project becomes an imperative which obsesses the whole man, which he serves with all his might, which renders him almost impervious to the lure or threat of adventitious motives. 'He follows his idea', runs common speech, thereby expressing well the pull exercised by the idea on the man.

All real understanding of social movement is denied to those who think of an achievement as the fruit of an intention simultaneously conceived with equal force by all the participants; equally untrue is it that the effect of an achievement is merely to add another floor to what was there before. For the intention spreads outwards from one man, the one who had it in the first place; it is sustained and revivified by those who hold it most strongly, and the achievement disarranges what was there before, by destroying its order and equilibrium.

The man of the project summons and recruits among those who are receptive of it; he waves it like a flag and rallies forces to it. He leads these forces in the task of his conception, spurs on the laggards, breaks through the opposing forces of inertia, whom he harries, attacks and routs. There is no project, however beneficent, but does harm as well as good. There cannot be a realisation of a conceivable possibility without the destruction or exclusion of another conceivable possibility. For this reason there is never a project against which objections cannot be raised from one point of view. Hence it is that those who leave nothing unweighed do not make promoters; for 'promoting' there is needed, rather, a rude vigour of convictions or desires. The man of the project is a lover.

THE MASTER BUILDER

In every living being, taking action is linked with paying attention; with animals attention is fleeting but with men it lasts longer. But it is not natural even in a man to apply himself without any break to the pursuit of an end, even of one which is most important for himself. In unforgettable pages, Balzac tells us in his *Adieu* how the remnant of the Grande Armée, when they had arrived at the bank of the Beresina, 'forgot' to cross the river, necessary as crossing was for their safety, and he shows us some of the officers struggling to arouse this rabble and make it go forward.

Therefore every difficult and long-term enterprise requires, for success, men whom it obsesses and who will exercise continuous psychological pressure on the inertia or inattention of their associates; we have only to think of the language used to their followers by Alexander or Columbus or Cortes. This pressure is a cause of conflict.

The man who has dedicated himself to the success of the project, the master builder, no longer has any freedom: his conduct is now determined altogether by the constraining force of the end. Logically, therefore, he is bound to require at every moment from his companions whatever will best serve that end, and he demands of them imperiously whatever he thinks is of that nature. This imperiousness, though to immediate view that of the master, springs ultimately from the project itself, for it is the project which is in command. In the eyes of those under him, however, it is the master who hustles them, and they think him inhuman by reason of his disregard of their moods and personalities and his inability to see them other than as servants of the project (like himself).

This irritation on the part of those working on the project will be all the livelier the less they are in its grip and the less zealous they are on its behalf; this will the less dispose them to hear in the voice which harries them the voice of the project, and will dispose them the more to take it for the voice of a master.

Moreover, resistance to the exhortations which are really directed at slackness or lack of moral enthusiasm finds a convenient pretext and justification in the criticisms which can always be made of the effectiveness of the action required. Anyone telling me that the particular action required of me in the name of the end is by no means well-conceived or well-thought-out provides me with a reason for declining this action—not because of any rational judgment I had passed on it but merely because I found it disagreeable.

Conversely, the master builder, irritated by collaborators who do not subordinate themselves to the project as totally as he does himself, is always inclined to regard the most legitimate criticisms of his orders as a blind for inertia.

THE PSYCHOLOGICAL ANGLE

The law of all modern states takes account of associations, whose members, in theory, pursue the common end with equal zeal. The experience of all associations proves, however, that this is not the case,[1] and that a lively, constant and vigorous awareness of the end is found only in a minority of the associates; an association is really rather like a comet—a large tail of docile followers dragged along by a small dynamic head.

The duality of leaders and led recurs in every association and action group. But the more novel and difficult the action is, the more certain is it that one man will be found leading the leaders, the master builder, the *dux*; whereas the management of the whole can be more diffused the more routine are the actions required of the whole. Indeed, if actions become so systematised as to resemble a complex of invariable rites, habit makes leadership needless, and the oligarchical structure, though it tends to prolong itself, loses its point.

These considerations make it clear that a very progressive society, in which new projects are brought to birth and undertaken without ceasing, will be characterised by the numbers and energy of its promoters—the master builders, the chiefs of teams of action. Leaders there must be; without them there would be no initiative or novelty in a society. The onward march of society is by means of

---

[1] See for example the remarkable study by Joseph Goldstein, *The Government of the British Trade Unions. A Study of Apathy and the Democratic Process in the Transport and General Workers Union* (London, 1952). Mr Goldstein embarked on the study of a local branch where direct democracy prevailed. He showed how small was the number of those attending meetings, which was hardly affected by total numbers (24 on the average, whether the branch had 300 or 1000 members), and that a still smaller core of active members, who were always the same, took for practical purposes all initiatives. He leads us to picture this association as a huge, unstable protoplasm, whose elements are in rapid change, at the centre of which is a narrower and more stable circle of effective participants; at the heart of this circle is an active core which is very small and very stable.

projects realised under the impulsion of leaders and the management of master builders. Modern sensibility would like to dispense with higher command. Let there be no doubt as to the price to be paid and the conditions which would make it possible. They are either that no task is ever undertaken which one man could not do by himself—a condition which makes civilisation impossible—or that every undertaking which requires the collaboration of numerous agents makes an equally strong and clear appeal to the mind of each single one—a state of things never seen except in the systematised and monotonous actions which their collective instinct bids social animals take. The more routine that systematised activities are, the more nearly they are of the monotonous character seen in the habits of social animals and the less necessary are master builders; the more novel actions are, the more necessary are master builders. Dislike of the leader and the promoter, though linked emotionally to progressivism, is linked logically to total conservatism. Conversely, an authoritarian approach, natural enough in the instigator of new activities, is unjustified in the mere overseer of routines.

'MILITIAE' AND 'DOMI'

A progressive society is characterised by a great proliferation of action groups of all sizes and natures; they die and are born. Teams of action are seen now working together and now in conflict; it is a process of unceasing movement in the course of which no state of things is stable, and the adjustments continually in process call for frequent intervention by authority. It is in the nature of things that the multiplication of initiatives should multiply frictions and tensions; but the human spirit, in love with contradictories, yearns after the stability of primitive societies, and some think to get there by uniting everyone in the service of some global project which will end at last in the establishment of a future routine.

Of all the simplifications to which the human spirit naturally inclines, unable to reconcile itself to the complexity of the real, there is none more dangerous than the attempt to integrate the whole of society in one vast, permanent action group.

The disciplinary relationships imposed by an action in common and necessarily prevailing in an action group are acceptable only under one of two conditions: if the entire man is governed by them, then they must prevail only for a very short time, or, if they have to last for a long time, they must take up only a part of his daily life. Thus, a man may be entirely subjected to the regime of an action group for the duration of a campaign or a war, or he may be partially subjected to it on a long-term basis, while doing something which does not take up his entire time.

As every action in common involves a discipline, every man in the capacity of member of an action group is subject to its discipline. But the whole man is not a member of an action group for the whole time; he is not completely and permanently subject to the discipline of the team. He undergoes it during that part of his daily activity which is given to teamwork; he escapes from it in every other capacity, and he has besides, in a society of multiple action groups, a choice of the organisation whose discipline he will accept—and disciplines are not all the same. Obviously these liberties disappear if society is reduced to a single action group; the individual is then subjected completely and permanently to its discipline. And this discipline of the team is something quite different from and much stricter than the good behaviour which a man finds himself bound to observe as member of a society.

The contrast can be illustrated by Roman usage. When war occurred, the citizens left the city under the lead of the Consul who waited to pass the *pomerium* (the open space outside the walls) before putting on the *paludamentum*—the scarlet cloak signifying military authority—which acted as notice to the citizens that they must no longer behave as such or expect to be treated as such, but were thenceforward legionaries subject to the military discipline necessary to victory. This discipline lapsed at once on return from the campaign, from the moment when the Consul, before re-entering the precincts of the city, put off the insignia of an occasional authority. The entire stock of relationships which suited in war— *militiae*—was regarded as inadmissible and improper in peace—*domi*. We have the measure of how right the Romans were in this respect in the experience of the intellectual and moral impoverishment brought about by total mobilisation.

The contrast between *militiae* and *domi* is essential to the social order. Allow men to behave in an army or in a foundry as in their own homes, *domi*, and your army will be beaten and your undertaking collapse. If, on the other hand, you stretch them for every moment of their lives on the discipline of action, what you will have then created is nothing other than totalitarianism.

The discipline of action is rough. There is no violation of liberty in submitting to it: indeed, it accords well with human dignity to accept it for some desired end. When he chooses an action group to whose rules he accommodates a part of his personality, man remains in some way superior to its discipline. But man is swamped when the plurality of action groups in a society is exchanged for one all-comprising action group which swallows up the whole of social existence and imposes on the whole of life a discipline only tolerable within limits.

It may further be noted that, when this happens, the hierarchy of the large action group provides the social hierarchy. But life in society is altogether sweeter and richer when social positions of eminence can be reached from various starting places than when they reflect a single hierarchy.

CHAPTER 5

OF THE RELATIONS BETWEEN AUTHORITIES

I speak of there being a 'hub of authority' when I note that propositions emanating from a certain source exercise a positive influence on the actions of certain men, who are, I would say, for that reason within the 'area of authority' of that hub. This hub may be pictured by anyone liking graphic images as the seat of a potential, which is able to affect the movements of the moving bodies in its area. Strictly speaking, each single man is a hub of authority, for there is no one who has never been the cause of another's actions. But it will be natural to confine the expression to a source which habitually causes the actions of others.

The social field is strewn with hubs of authority, and, as a general rule, a man is conscious of being affected by the action of several hubs. The only exceptions to this rule are the child, who is actually aware only of maternal authority, and the slave, who knows in principle no other authority than that of his master. Incidentally, this remark reminds us that the condition in which a man sees and feels one human authority only is the condition furthest removed from liberty. Far different is the condition of a man who chooses among propositions emanating from different sources.

Before we broach the great question of the relations between hubs of authority, we will classify authorities according to their constituent principle and the source of their potential.

NATURAL, INSTITUTIONAL, AND CONSTRAINING AUTHORITY

We have said earlier that human association was not to be thought of as issuing originally either from constraint exercised by the stronger, or from a spontaneous juncture of purposes, but from the ascendancy of one man over another—in short, that it was a natural fact. It is natural to man to dispose of his actions; the propositions and suggestions of others affect the dispositions which he makes.

It is an exercise of authority, in our meaning of the word, when Primus uses an ascendancy over Secundus to make him act and behave as Primus has proposed or suggested. There we see bare authority, naked and natural, the principle of formative attraction in all primitive groups. Secundus finds himself drawn into an enterprise conceived by Primus, or joins himself to the planetary system whose regular movements are maintained by Primus. The deference shown to this ascendancy is entirely voluntary, or, if the word 'voluntary' connotes an exercise of the reason which is most often absent, this deference is spontaneous.

But natural authority is precarious and its holder is mortal. Always and everywhere the human race has felt obscurely the value to itself of the social molecules formed by authority; the sense of being 'we' which a whole engenders works against dissolution, exalts the image of the founder, requires that the part which he has created shall still be played, and carries to the credit of whoever takes his place the prestige of his memory. The successor will call the founder to witness and will invoke or take his name; he will have recourse to the fiction that it is still the founder who is there. The founder has instituted an office; the successor derives his prestige from the institution. Authority is institutionalised; artifice prolongs the effects of nature, just as a weak voice is strengthened by such helpful devices as the rostrum and the loud speaker. And that is necessary; without consolidation of that kind, social formations would be much too fluid to provide society with the foundations necessary to its development. On the other hand, consolidation may create rigidities obstructing the formation of new molecules by new natural authorities. We begin to suspect at this point that we have found the principle of a tension which is immanent in every society whatsoever—between the advantage of preserving by a sort of mummification the work accomplished by past natural authorities and the advantage of allowing new natural authorities arriving on the scene to do their work. It is certainly untrue that institutionalism can be dispensed with; the passing of the head of a family or of an enterprise makes instantaneous replacement necessary—the quick are summoned by the dead—and the successor has need of institutional prestige. But it must also be admitted that this institutional authority is inferior in quality to a natural authority.

Constituted public authority is the crown of the social edifice. As in its case continuity is particularly important, it is the recipient *par excellence* of borrowed prestiges. It sits on a throne, it wears a crown;[1] the danger that its proposals will not be unanimously accepted has been met by their conversion into commands, to which the subject learns the duty of obedience; lastly it has had put at its disposal means of constraint, whose intimidatory power supplies defect of natural authority. These means of constraint have had to increase with every detraction from the prestige of the person of the sovereign: when majesty goes out, the police come in.[2]

The public authority stands high above all others; also, however, it is the lowest in quality, as standing most in need, especially in the societies of our own day, of the support of intimidation.

VARIOUS FORMS OF THE IMPERATIVE

The link with authority plays an essential and never-ending part in social life. It is, therefore, reasonable, before going further, to analyse its somewhat complex nature. The imperative is the mood used by every authority, but that is not to say that the imperative is always of one kind; it takes, on the contrary, the most widely varied forms.

How widely varied they are appears at once in contrasting the imperatives at either extreme of the gamut, that of prayer and that of threat. The imperative 'Come!' may have the character of a supplication addressed by the weak man to the strong, and, especially, by the worshipper to God: 'Veni creator spiritus.' There is nothing unseemly in the continual appearance of the imperative in prayers: 'Salve—Exaudi—Parce (save, hear, spare)', for the distinguishing mark of the imperative is that it tends to set in movement the person to whom it is addressed; in the case which we are now considering, the compassion of the Supreme Being is being sought by the speaker on his behalf. This is a useful example, showing that the imperative is not necessarily linked to a speaker in a dominant position; here the imperative ascends from low to high.

Examples of this imperative of supplication may be found even in the sphere of human relations, as in the appeal for help of the drowning man to someone he sees on the bank, the appeal of the

---

[1] In a museum at Istanbul the dresses of the Sultans are on show. The eye is at once struck by the vastness of the turban, its purpose being to render the person and the head of the sovereign more impressive.

[2] The transition from the ancient regime to the modern regime is marked by a growth in the numbers of the police.

abandoned lover to the loved one, or, more simply, the appeal of the debtor on the brink of bankruptcy to the rich relation. These are imperatives which could all be put much as follows: 'Come: otherwise I die, I languish, I go bankrupt.' It is, in all these cases, in consideration of misfortune afflicting the man who speaks imperatively that the man addressed is expected to take action.

At the other extreme is the 'descending' imperative, which connotes the intimidation of the man addressed. In common parlance it runs: 'Come, otherwise I shall punish you.' It implies a power held by the man speaking over the man spoken to. It is relations of this kind that the word 'imperative' evokes in most minds; yet, oddly enough, it is certain that the most frequent use of the imperative in social life does not correspond to this extreme any more than it does to the previous one.

Men habitually make use of the imperative to others on a footing of equality with themselves, as a means of giving them pressing advice. 'Join up behind my white cockade' is imperative in form, and this imperative is explained by what follows: 'You will find it always following the path of honour.' Here there is also something implied: assuming that men such as you are, or want to be, are determined to take the path of honour, and that I for my part am embarked on it, then my cockade is the sign that teaches you the path which you should logically follow. 'Forward!' is an elliptical expression which implies the same train of reasoning. The speeches put by classical authors in the mouths of historical heroes reproduce with a remarkable regularity the launching of an imperative followed by the development of arguments to prove that what has been imperatively put forward really is what needs doing, whether as honourable or as expedient or as both. In what we may call the 'egalitarian' imperative, such as is addressed to men who are not in the power of the speaker, persuasion is the logical instrument to give support to prescription. The association of the imperative and the persuasive is, it may be noted, equally observable whether the speaker is a military leader or a judge, but the sequence of the two will be different in the two cases; the leader throws in the imperative like a charge and supports it later by reinforcements which to some extent consolidate the result of the first shock, whereas the judge first weighs the arguments and then concludes imperatively.

In either case, however, the effectiveness of the imperative does not entirely, or even mainly, come from the reasons adduced; it comes from the prestige, personal or institutional, of the man speaking—a prestige linked to the guarantee furnished by the exalted character recognised in him, whether it is his or that of his office.

What we are here discussing can be tested by experience, most easily, indeed, by experience of the commonest kind. Every man in modern society is exposed to publicity; how does it proceed? Exactly in the way we have described in the case of the leader who gets himself followed; it launches an imperative 'Buy X', supports it with reasons (in smaller letters), and the surety for the imperative is either an already well-known trademark or else some public figure who is shown praising the commodity. Effective publicity presents an instance of authority in our present meaning of the word; it makes an imperative statement which affects the actions of others.

THE LINK WITH AUTHORITY

Men are said to hate authority, but experience belies it. It is true that intimidatory imperatives arouse resentment in them, but it is true no less that they are ever seeking imperatives to guide them. To start with, man is at heart essentially imitative, and this tendency brings it about that the various advances made get stabilised;[1] and imitation implies an authority, though the imitator is often unconscious of it.

When a young man rejects paternal authority, it is, sometimes, in order that he may himself take effective command of his own actions; but in how many cases is it not rather that he may follow in the footsteps of some companion whose company he seeks and by whom he loves to let himself be led? If the new leadership brings him to a critical situation, will he not be inclined, not himself to choose the solution of the problem posed, but to seek counsel and guidance elsewhere which will cut the knot for him? Thus his progress will have been from one authority to another.

It would be a gross psychological blunder not to recognise that there is a demand for authorities, which is the obverse side of the willingness to be authorities of men who like decision and do not fear responsibility. The centres of authority are, therefore, the natural result of anxieties finding their reassurance. Indecision

---

[1] The importance of Tarde's thought on this subject should be emphasised.

being intermittent, an authority waiting for calls upon it from those needing its help could not assure to them the benefits of stable order. Thus it is driven logically to seek continuity of action. It is also driven to it psychologically, for love of command, either for itself or for certain ends, is natural to those whose talents lie in this direction, and, in those in whom these faculties are lacking, vanity or appetite excite it.

Now natural ascendancy presupposes contact between the man who exercises it and the man who undergoes it. Drawn by the ascendancy of Primus, Secundus has been moved to join him spontaneously; Primus retains him, and so Secundus enters the circle or band of Primus. This phenomenon may be seen among street-urchins.[1] The relations between Primus and Secundus will be real and daily, and the imperatives issued by Primus as regards Secundus will spring from their intercourse, and for that reason be adapted to the nature and the characteristics of Secundus. It is to mistake the very essence of the phenomenon to suppose that the orders issued by Primus to his band consisting of Secundus, Tertius, Quartus and Quintus will be precisely the same as for four quite different followers taking their place. His actual followers and companions are factors in the decision which Primus takes; it is the fruit of a process of interaction. Political theory has no category for denoting the regime prevailing in his band; it is not democracy because of the uncontested primacy of Primus, it is not aristocracy because the decision of Primus is not independent of his followers and does not seem alien to them. However overbearing Primus may show himself, his orders are beyond question less alien to Secundus than the edicts of some distant office, even in the case in which the office is in law subject to the pleasure of the banded followers.

THE LINK WITH AUTHORITY IS NOT A LEGAL TIE

Primus, in our example, has no legal right to the obedience of Secundus and his other followers; he gains their obedience by his ascendancy, and also because his orders are adapted to their characters and inclinations. Let us now suppose that, after a long

---

[1] On this should be read the remarkable work of G. C. Homans, *The Human Group* (London, 1951), and especially ch. VII, 'The Norton Street Gang', which gives a close picture of a band of adolescents on the foundation of Whyte's study, *Street Corner Society* (Chicago, 1943).

exercise of this natural seigniory, Primus leaves his companions and goes far away; before his departure, they promise him, either spontaneously or at his demand, that they will conform to the instructions which he will lay on them. That is the moment at which an authority *de facto* becomes an authority *de jure*, when a convention intervenes to supply the loss of personal loyalty. It is a safe prediction that sooner or later the abandoned followers will no longer conform to the instructions of the seignior *de jure* now that his personal ascendancy is no longer felt among them; either they will join another circle, or else, if the whole which they form has been solidly based, they will transform themselves into a headless committee. This is an evolution which it will only be possible to check if a system of beliefs vastly enhances the prestige of Primus and, more important still, if means of constraint come to the support of his instructions.

The more distant that an authority is, the more it needs a halo, or, if no halo is available, the more policemen it will need. For this there are two reasons: one is that its remoteness no longer makes possible the play of natural ascendancy, the other that this same remoteness renders the authority's orders less appropriate to those who receive them. When Primus lived surrounded by his followers, the orders he gave were conditioned by the interaction of the members of the group; they had in relation to the group a quality of immanence, now replaced by a quality of transcendence. Clearly the first requirement in an authority is to be a manifest and immediate presence.

ARE MEN INCONSTANT AS REGARDS AUTHORITIES?

Men are thought, wrongly, to hate authority. No less wrongly, they are thought to be inconstant as regards authorities which they have once accepted. As proof of this, it will be enough to examine the case of trade unions; these are bodies which are particularly rich in lessons for the political scientist, because it is possible within the memory of a single man to note their birth and follow their development. The history of a trade union partakes usually of biography; its pre-history is the narrative of individual initiatives which have failed, its history begins with a leader who progressively strengthens and extends his authority. The trade union is his work. Born in the democratic age, trade unions have all received an internal constitution which enables the members to elect their chiefs; it is worth remarking that, during the period of a trade union's growth, this right has hardly ever been used to replace the leader by someone else. The unionists have stayed faithful to the chief who brought them together, and nothing is more natural.

Because the same man is always found at the head of a trade union which is growing, would it be right to call its government monarchical? It would be. Because this authority is sustained by a loyal warmth and is exercised in accordance with the needs of its adherents, would it be right to call it democratic? It would be. The reality falls outside juridical categories.

Another point to note is the malady which overtakes the trade union if it cannot find an adequate successor to the first leader when he has gone. Its authority then becomes impersonal and bureau-cratic, the oligarchs in control of the apparatus of command defend themselves against criticism by muzzling its expression, the members withdraw themselves from its authority by disregarding its instruc-tions and taking others from men within their immediate circle. The entire crisis of British trade unionism, now in progress as we write, testifies to this crisis of authority. But the crisis is not itself proof of the inconstancy of men. All it shows is that their constancy toward individuals whose authority they have recognised is not transferred easily to impersonal institutions. And that is reasonable enough, for the individuals had something which the institutions lack.

THE WEAKNESS OF THE SOVEREIGN

These reflections have given us an idea of where the weaknesses of the sovereign lie. The supreme head of a large whole necessarily finds himself, merely because of its size, far removed from the individuals he commands. For them, therefore, his decisions are foreign and cold. They will be anonymous as well if the sovereign is a legal creature. If I live with Primus as his companion, if I know that I am in his mind and if he tells me himself of any decision affecting me, then, however small my part in that decision, it will be for me neither foreign, nor cold, nor anonymous. But, if it is taken far away by men who are unaware of my existence and whose very names I do not know, then it will be all these three things. And I do not believe it when I am told that those who decide for me take their instructions from me.

For that reason it is to the sovereign's advantage, whenever he has to get himself obeyed, to have his decision endorsed by some more immediate authority; an instance of this was the action of the British Government, anxious for the wage-earners to moderate their wage-claims, in asking the trade unions to adopt and put their hands to moderation as a policy. Consideration of such an example helps to dissipate the illusions in vogue about parliamentary assemblies; the belief dies hard that they were instituted to restrain the absolute power enjoyed by the king in former days. The very different truth is that the king, fearing for his authority if he addressed himself directly to his far-away subjects, called together, very sensibly, a body of men who, each in his own part of the country, were in a position to make themselves heard; and these he asked to oblige him by becoming the echoes of his demands. By thus adding their authorities to his own, he enlarged the sovereign power.

For this enlargement to happen it was, of course, necessary that those whom he asked to do a sort of speaking tour on his behalf should themselves have some authority. Naturally this would not be the case if Parliament was composed of men of no consideration. Originally, therefore, it was a meeting-place of people of importance; in the same way the Chairman of the Stock Exchange, if there is a Stock Exchange crisis, calls together the large financial houses that they may by their combined action and joint guarantees combat the panic.

'THE PEERS'

Let us now place ourselves in imagination on the highest level of command. The spectacle offered us by society below is of a fascinating complexity. Currents set in motion by the activating authorities cleave their way through the placid lagoons formed by the milieux of existence in their path. All movement and arrangement revolve around the men who bring both about; at every moment their authority, one man's rising and another's falling, is seen at work. How many are the decisions taken while we are watching! Each has required care and effort in the making of a difficult choice, and each presupposes the labours of others in the field of execution. How vast is the work accomplished by these social ferments! Viewing them as the sovereign views them, may we not say that this incessant toil of the social authorities takes the burden off him?

The sovereign authority, it was said in former days, decides only in the last resort; it is always there in reserve. It is available to decide what it has proved impossible to decide by other men or by other means, or to review bad decisions. It is the residuary legatee of all problems. This statement of its functions, which seems reasonable enough, presupposes that the sovereign authority to some extent recognises as its 'peers' the other authorities at work in society. By 'peers' I mean here not those who are equal but those who are alike, as being committed to tasks of an identical kind.

I call this point of view reasonable since every decision requires much of a man's attention and no man has an unlimited supply of attention to give. Whatever it is that he aims at doing or deciding well, he must give it an adequate amount of his attention; and he will be unable to give sufficient attention to any single problem, if he has too many problems to cope with. For this reason it is a wise economy only to use sovereign authority when there is no other available or when it is necessary to repair the harm done by another.

This attitude on the part of the sovereign authority will, it may be noted, have very different consequences according to whether the social authorities on which it rests are established authorities which it will buttress by its acknowledgment of them, or authorities on the upgrade whose credit it will enhance by its favour to them. Few laws are needed to swing the balance in one direction or the other, to encourage, that is to say, either the factors making for stability or those making for change.

THOSE GOING UP AND THOSE GOING DOWN

Let us pause to note how different the results for a society are according to whether the favour of the sovereign authority is shown to the old social authorities or to those in process of formation. For instance, the fall of the French monarchy at the end of the eighteenth century was certainly not caused by despotism on its part. A weaker government has rarely been seen and its financial difficulties were the sign of its weakness. The king did not feel himself strong enough either to raise enough money in new taxation or to cut down the scale of his liberalities by a like amount. Moreover, the easy successes gained by every movement of revolt was proof of the feebleness of the government's financial administration, which was weakened still further by the extreme reluctance of the king to make use of the few sources of strength effectively left to him.

Indeed it was not against the monarchy that the feelings which were to issue in the Revolution were directed, but rather against the old social authorities which blocked the rise of the dynamic elements in society. Writing at the time of the Restoration a résumé of the spirit of the Revolution for the instruction of the Duke of Orleans, Roederer brought out unequivocally that what had made the Revolution was the will to rise of the dynamic elements who met with obstacles in the old society—obstacles which had risen higher throughout the eighteenth century, by reason of the weakening of royal authority which occurred at the death of Louis XIV and was never repaired afterwards. The French had been accustomed to find their kings clearing the way of ascent for the *homines novi*, the 'upstarts', and dismantling the defences which established interests are forever putting up; but for various reasons the Regent and the two kings of the eighteenth century proved incapable of keeping the older notables on the move and thus favouring the advance of the new men. Weak rulers were ceaselessly giving in to the pressures of those who had arrived and confirming or extending their privileges to the detriment of the rising. And that was as true in the case of the corporations (closed professional circles) as in that of the nobility. The whole of the eighteenth century in France should be read with the understanding that the cry of despotism was raised by the privileged elements, whenever a minister touched their acquired rights, even though these rights obstructed the natural flux of society. And the situation was, no doubt, complicated by the fact that not all these attacks on acquired rights were made in the name of social progress—as that of Turgot certainly was—but were often inspired by motives of a less disinterested kind. Taken all in all, however, what was despotic in the eighteenth century was not the sovereign authority but the fossilised social authorities, which were the real objective of the revolutionary wave; that wave should, logically, have found an ally in the king, but he, good-natured and stupid as ever, stood by those who had hitherto flouted his authority, and in the end perished with them.

This is admittedly only a very crude outline of events; I developed these views in *Power* and will one day develop them again. What matters here, however, is not their historical exactitude but the outline itself. I use it here to emphasise the very different results occurring when the sovereign authority supports hated and fossilised social authorities which are no longer on the upgrade, and when dynamic social forces which are rising support it.

The battle which raged at this decisive period of French history was not the struggle of the people against their oppressors. It had the more positive aim of freeing ambitions from the obstacles opposed to them by those in place and power, who had been enabled by the favour and feebleness of the sovereign to dig themselves in as never before. I have emphasised this because it enables us to see more clearly the danger inherent when the sovereign authority does not make its presence felt. If a retiring spirit on its part is accompanied by the feeling that the authorities to favour are the old authorities, *laissez-faire* of this kind will be conservative in character, not progressive. (It is important to note that there are these two kinds of *laissez-faire*, each with its own spirit.) Then the thwarted ambitions will bring the whole edifice down, except in the event, unlikely in such cases, of the sovereign authority disposing of repressive strength on a considerable scale. Whereas quite the contrary will happen if the social authorities to whom the sovereign gives his confidence are those who are rising in the scale; in that case there will be no revolutionary pressure.

We see, then, that the relations of the sovereign authority with the authorities existing or forming in society are matters of the greatest importance.

THE GREAT SERGEANT-MAJOR

To whichever of these two groups of authorities, the old or the young, the descending or the ascending, the sovereign authority gives its head, it is in either case acting in a way quite contrary to the ideas now in vogue. The present fashion in thought is that the sovereign is directly responsible for society as a whole; the latter is admittedly conceived only within the limited framework of an existing political authority, the framework being, in the case of western society as we know it, a national state.

Whatever limits are set on society, it remains true that it is a human edifice of vast complexity. The mind of man finds this complexity repellent; his liking is for what is clear and symmetrical, for orderliness and simple relationships. To whatever subject he applies himself for the first time, he resigns himself only gradually to the absence of the simplicity for which he looks in it. We have carried this taste for simple arrangement into astronomy and physics, where it has long served us well, and into chemical science, where it has affected our progress adversely; organic chemistry, biology and sociology disconcert us by the complexity of the structures which we find in them. But in sociology at any rate we can reconstruct to our taste the formations which we do not like, even when it ought to be clear to us that our new structures are unstable.

We have spoken of a fashion of thought, when what is really in question is more truly an aesthetic feeling. For this fashion is something irrational, being in conflict not only with the work of nature but with the causative activity of man himself. Yet it is our perverse habit to call rational a structure which answers to our fashion of thought.

This conflict between the demands of the intelligence and the actual structures it finds in being is a large subject and very pertinent to our times. But we are not now concerned with it, and I have mentioned it here only to indicate how, as government is increasingly required to answer intellectual calls and satisfy an intellectual critique, it cannot but play the part of 'Sergeant-Major'. The strict alignment actually achieved on military parade grounds is nearly akin to the dreams of idealist reformers, and numerical systems, based on tenths or twelfths, have attracted some of the greatest philosophers, such as Plato or Confucius. Nor is this kinship accidental, for both are children of the same habit of mind.

The word 'theory' derives from the Greek 'theoria'; it may denote either some simple pattern into which men fall during a religious ceremony or the pattern which the intelligence seeks to impose on things. It is likely enough, though discussion of this hypothesis would take us too far afield, that from the array of men in simple patterns for religious ceremonies has sprung the whole gamut of processions, ballets and military spectacles. (Louis XIV, one of whose major passions was military spectacles, was reproached with making his soldiers into ballet-dancers.) If all these formal arrays of men descend from the 'theoria' of religion, that 'theoria' itself conforms with the widely held idea that men must pay the gods the compliment of appearing before them properly patterned; and the regimentation of society is directed to the arrangement of men in some proper pattern, such as the dullest mind can instantly appreciate.

If such is the aim, it is obvious that every autonomous centre of authority will disarrange the geometrical pattern sought: therefore there must be no such centres. But their emergence can only be prevented by doing violence to nature. Only the powerful solvent of repressive measures can dissolve them when they are fully formed, and the better course is to detect them in infancy. Inquisitorial powers flow from this need. The watchword of such policies is 'No authority except the sovereign authority'.

A watchword of this kind is directed against both authorities of long standing and authorities in process of formation; as regards the former, it is revolutionary, as regards the latter, despotic.

THE SOVEREIGN AND LEGAL PERSONS

In practice, the constructive role of inferior authorities has, under different forms in different periods, been recognised by the law; the form they have taken in our own time is that of the legal or fictive person. Authorities today are impersonal, bloodless entities. Jurists have much concerned themselves with the question of the treatment of these legal persons by the sovereign authority. Political science, on the other hand, has paid hardly any attention to them; it has failed to see that in the law governing legal persons are involved the entire question of the division of authority between the sovereign authority and particular authorities, and the whole range of questions raised by the rise of new authorities, the consolidation of old ones into institutions and the actions taken by vested interests on the defensive. Incidentally, it will be noted that the France of today and the France at the end of the *ancien régime* are alike in this, that in both the particular authorities which win the ear of the government are those asking for the consolidation of privileges, and not those asking for a clear field for action.

This concrete example testifies to the fact that what has here been presented in abstract form has a bearing on political problems which are very much alive.

PART II

THE POLITICAL GOOD

CHAPTER 6

OF BENEVOLENCE IN THE SOVEREIGN WILL

A feeling of obligation to obey the commands of the established public authority is found, varying in liveliness and effectiveness from one individual to another, among the members of any political society. Those in whom this feeling is focused on the same centre are thereby members of one political society.

The natural disposition of a man to draw inspiration from another for his own actions is one thing; the conviction that it is his duty to act in accordance with the proclaimed will of that other is something else.

No feeling of obligation enters into *natural* obedience: I act as Primus wants me to act because he has infused his will into mine, and for just as long as this endures. Whereas in the case of *civil* obedience I act as Primus wants me to act because I acknowledge the duty of submitting my action to his will and act as though his will were also mine. Natural authority has for me the pull of a lover; it is an attraction bound up with my liking for Primus. Constituted authority has for me the pull of a rope to which I have first been tied; it draws me on even though Primus has no sort of personal attraction for me. What tie the members of a political society to the public authority are invisible ropes. Or, to put the contrast in more popular language, a man is, as regards a natural society, a subscriber, and, as regards a constituted society, a debtor.

Does constituted authority issue from natural society? Is the creditor for obedience the child of the creator of obedience? And, if so, how does this come about? We have already broached this question and will not here raise it again. Neither will we examine whether, as was thought in the Middle Ages, the obligation felt towards constituted authority is the same in kind and degree as the other obligations felt by man in society, or whether it is superior to those other obligations; the latter is the view of modern juris-prudence, which holds that social obligations are mandatory only because public authority has proclaimed them. This vast question is treated in another section. Lastly, in considering the creditor-debtor relationship in the matter of civil obedience, we shall approach it not, as is usually done, from the point of view of the debtor but from the point of view of the creditor.

A seventeenth-century author would express our intention more formally by saying: 'My purpose in writing is to instruct, not subjects in their rights, but sovereigns in their duties.' The sentence exactly expresses our thought, which is in that respect far removed from the current preoccupations of political science; not for a long time have the obligations of sovereigns been its theme. As we have already noted, political theory in our time is concerned mainly with the question of who is to be the creditor for obedience, and, secondarily, with the laying down of limits to obedience: never does the use made of obedience get discussed.

The problem of benevolence in the sovereign Will must not be confused with that of the sovereign Will's validity. A comparison will bring this out. Imagine a country in which there is full and complete liberty of testamentary disposition. To prove a will there and make it executable it will only be necessary to show that it is the act and deed of the deceased and that all formalities have been observed. If these conditions are satisfied, the executors have to carry out what is in it, whatever it is.

In this hypothetical state of things, the judge does not pronounce on the content of wills; all the same, he may privately consider the content good or bad, and say to himself that, if he had been able to advise the testator in time, he would have tried to get him to make a better will. Here, as is obvious, are two quite distinct positions: that of the judge only concerned with the validity of the will, and that of the adviser anxious that the will should contain good provisions. Political science has for long played the role of the judge; our ambition is to drive it into the role of adviser.

The example is apt, for the analogy between full and complete liberty of testamentary disposition, which we have postulated, and full and complete liberty to give orders, which characterises public authority in our own time, is a powerful one.

THE ABSOLUTISM OF THE SOVEREIGN WILL

Every man is, naturally, sovereign of his own energies and can use them as suits him. But the law (*Jus*) of the society of which he is a member forbids him certain uses of them and enjoins on him certain other uses. The *Jus* confronts him with both bans and obligations; in the case of some of an individual's obligations, such as the contracts into which he has entered, it imposes sanctions. In this way the citizen finds his liberty of action much restricted, and in general nobody doubts that it must be so. At first sight it would seem natural to find that anything which is stronger than the individual has been tied down more strictly than himself, and it is an oddity of modern law that, by their acquisition of bloodless personalities (*personae fictae*), powerful groups can get themselves a liberty equal to that of the individual—sometimes a larger one.

How do matters stand in that respect with the sovereign himself? It was long believed that he, no less than his subjects, was under the law, which was then conceived as something fixed so that the sovereign, like the subject, was compelled to move within a defined framework. (Let us note in passing that, no less than the private person, the monarch who stayed within bounds might make either good or bad use of his restricted liberty.)

In course of time intellectuals came to be heard protesting with increasing vehemence against the prison made by this framework: their protest was based on two powerful arguments, the one logical and the other empirical.

On the logical plane, it was argued that, while it accorded with the majesty of the prince to recognise that the laws were over him,[1] yet his deference to them was a matter for him alone, because in his case no one could be entitled to adjudge whether he had infringed them. For who could be his judge? Was it to be each separate person? That would give rise to hideous disorder, were each man to consider himself bound to obey only those orders which seemed to him conformable with the law. Or was it to be a body of persons? But this body, called on to act as judge of the sovereign, would provide a superior to one who, by definition, should not have a superior, and would attract to itself the sovereign authority; the same problem would then arise as regards the body.

On the empirical plane the gradual recognition that some rules did in fact alter over time and according to situations led to the notion that rules are not good everywhere and always. But, in that case, who should change them? Who but the ruler? Hence the assertion of Hobbes which scandalised his own time: 'There is annexed to the sovereignty the whole power of prescribing the rules

[1] Bossuet, *Politique tirée de l'Ecriture Sainte*, Book IV, fourth proposition.

whereby every man may know what goods he may enjoy and what actions he may do, without being molested by any of his fellow-subjects.'[1]

An absolute power was, in the eyes of Bossuet, only a power on which there was no compulsion to obey the laws, but which should regard itself notwithstanding as subject to them;[2] Hobbes looks on it as the creator of every rule of life and as possessing in consequence what has been called in our time 'the competence of its competence' (Jellinek).

The adjective 'absolute', generally used today as a vague term of abuse, has in reality a well-defined meaning: it translates the phrase '*legibus solutus*'—freed from the laws. Now who is the more uninhibited by the rules? The man who is morally bound to observe the rules, though not subject to sanctions, or the man who is in a position to change them at any moment? Clearly the latter. For that reason the movement in time toward a sovereignty with unrestricted legislative power has been a movement toward absolutism, and the period which we call the absolutist period was in fact only that of the gestation of absolutism.

The movement of intellectual protest, when it reached the seventeenth and eighteenth centuries, was directed first at particular acts of power when it went outside the limits set by the existing law, and next at general acts (or legislation) changing those limits. It resulted, paradoxically enough, in the establishment of a legislative sovereignty—a thing as absolute as anything could be.

The first phenomenon, that of particular acts transgressing the existing law, no longer has a *raison d'être*, by reason of the unceasing activity of the sovereign as legislator: seeing that he can at any moment adapt by laws the existing law to what he means to do, it is never necessary for him to infringe it. Whoever is able to vary at will the rules of action need never infringe them. The modern absolutism, which we find the most natural thing in the world, would have been quite beyond the dreams of the most absolute of kings.

No doubt we shall be told that the absolutism of the sovereign

---

[1] Hobbes, *Leviathan*, part 2, ch. 18.

[2] 'Like others, therefore, kings are subjected to the equity of the laws, both because it is their duty to be just, and because they owe an example to their people in the observance of justice; but they are not subjected to the penalties of the laws: or, as theologians might put it, they are subjected to the laws not as regards the power of the laws to coerce but as regards their power to guide.' Bossuet, *Politique tirée de L'Ecriture Sainte*, Book IV, fourth proposition.

Will grew only as the incumbent changed, and loses much of its danger from the moment that 'he who wills' is, not a man, but 'the People', or, for practical purposes, an elected body. We do not deny for a moment the importance of this change; all we are denying is that it solves by itself the problems of political theory. Whoever may be the 'he who wills', whether he is a simple or a composite person, the content of his will may still be either more or less 'good'; and the less his will is bounded by an external framework, the more important it is that it should be subjected to an internal check—or, in classical terminology, the more absolute it is, the less arbitrary should it be.

THAT THE CHANGE OF INCUMBENT DOES NOT AFFECT THE PROBLEM OF BENEVOLENCE IN THE GOVERNING WILL[1]

There is a considerable literature on the duties of sovereigns;[1] it comes to an abrupt end with the close of the *ancien régime*. It is as though only kings had stood in need of exhortation and guidance— never the citizens, whose hold on the sovereignty is but theoretical, nor the representatives either, who are a sort of 'seigneurie' and wield the effective power.

Is that really so? The line of reasoning is, of course, as follows: concern for my interest is not entirely natural to my master, who must be exhorted to think of it and made to feel and know that here is a duty incumbent on him; but, when I am my own master, it is natural for me to think of my own interest: therefore exhortation is needless.

In this line of reasoning there is a mistake of substance and an omission. It is a mistake of substance to regard the People as just a person, at once ruled and ruling; and to ascribe to myself, being a subject, the will of a majority of the legislative body or of one of its ministers is just as much a juridical fiction as to ascribe to myself the will of the monarch or of one of his ministers. I may say to myself in both cases that what is involved is the sovereign Will to which I must submit myself, but it would be equally untrue in both cases were I to say to myself: 'The will at work has been yours.' The most I can say is: 'You ought to act as if the will at work had been yours.'

---

[1] The best-known specimen of it is the 'Directions pour la conscience d'un Roi', composed by Fénelon for the benefit of the Duke of Burgundy (ed. The Hague, 1748).

The ruler-subject duality is not, in fact, resolved by the democratic state, and, for that reason, the ruler, whoever he is, must continue to be a respecter of duties. But that is not all. Even if we admitted the truth of the vision we have just rejected, and regarded 'the People' as just a person unable to will anything but his own good—unlike the monarch for whom it was a duty to will his people's good— it still remains as true of the People as of the monarch that the discernment needed to identify the good and to win it may be lacking.

Popular and monarchical governments are alike in that under both it is necessary to good order that the validity of the decisions taken by the competent authority should be accepted by the subjects; but in neither are the decisions taken necessarily good decisions, and in both those who take them stand in the same need of exhortation and enlightenment. The best chance of good decisions being taken is in that regime, it may be said, in which there is most preliminary discussion and the widest measure of popular consultation; yet all still turns on the morals and intelligence of those called into consultation, be it narrow or wide, private or public.

AS TO THE QUALITIES REQUIRED IN THE GOVERNING WILL

The qualities required in the governing Will may be classified as 'external' and 'internal'.

External qualities are those, such as firmness and vigour, which make a Will heard by its outward aspect. The ruler, be he leader or adjuster, compromises the respect due to his will, if it seems hesitant. Hesitation, irresolution and inconstancy are fatal to authority. Here we will say no more of the external or formal qualities.

We will give our whole attention to what we have called the internal (perhaps the substantial) qualities. They can all be boiled down to two, combined in the general formula: 'the sovereign Will must tend to the public good.' In this formula two conditions are implicit: desiring the public good and knowing what it is—a right aim and a right judgment.

Rousseau in his *Contrat Social* has developed admirably the first condition. None has seen better nor spoken more clearly that it is with a citizen as with a king: goodness is only possible to either on condition that both subdue their private passions and have no other thought than the good of the whole. At the moment of voicing an opinion as citizen on public affairs a man must forget his private interests entirely (including those of any group in the state), and direct his will exclusively to the public good. Rousseau's terminology has much misled his readers: what makes his 'General Will' general is not the number of those in whom it forms but the object at which it aims.[1] It is the Will which is related to the collective or general ego, as distinct from the private ego; it is the Will which should prevail in so far as a man thinks of himself not as an individual but as a loyal member of one body.

Rousseau's famous treatise is essentially that of a moralist concerned to hymn the advantages to be had from a certain moral attitude and to demonstrate the disastrous results of its opposite; it is in addition the work of a sociologist with a pessimistic slant, concerned to point out that this moral attitude grows necessarily weaker with every step away from the model of a small, rustic and traditionalist society.

Our modern democracies would have appeared to Rousseau as the very type of the corrupted State,[2] since clashes in the legislative

---

[1] He did hold, however, that agreement on the object was certain to bring in its train convergence of opinions: 'When several men met together regard themselves as a single body, they have but one will, which is related to the preservation of all and the general well-being. Under those conditions all the machinery of the State works vigorously and simply, and its maxims are clear and luminous. There are no tangled and contradictory interests, the common good is visible everywhere and, to be seen, demands good sense only.' *Du Contrat Social*, Book IV, ch. I, pp. 319–20 in our edition (Geneva, 1947).

The postulates that unity in opinions follows unity in intention and that immediate discernment of the good follows desire for it will not be discussed here. It is enough for our purpose to bring out the condition laid down by Rousseau: the man voicing an opinion must be thinking only of the body of which he forms part—he must have separated himself in some way from his own ego at the time of giving his views as citizen.

[2] 'But when the social tie begins to loosen and the State to grow feeble; when particular interests begin to make their presence felt and small societies to influence the big one, then the general interest is affected and finds opponents; unanimity no longer reigns in opinions, the general will is no longer the will of all, debates and contradictions arise, and the best opinion does not get by without dispute. Lastly, when the State, near its final collapse, no longer keeps going except in a vain and illusory form, when the social tie lies broken in all hearts and the lowest interest impudently decks itself out in the sacred name of the public good, then the general will becomes dumb; all, guided by undisclosed motives, no longer voice opinions as citizens, no more than if the State had never existed; and unjust decrees whose only aim is some particular interest are allowed to masquerade under the name of Laws.' *Du Contrat Social*, Book IV, ch. I, p. 321 in our edition (Geneva, 1947).

It will be remembered that for Rousseau the 'little societies' which influence the big arena are now much less between differing opinions as to the common good than between differing particular interests (tenants against landlords, wage-earners against employers, etc.).

Thus, with Rousseau's help, we have marked out the first condition necessary for the sovereign Will to be good: the condition is a moral one—the Will forms, that is to say, only in minds inspired with a feeling for the whole to the exclusion of all else.

Assuredly, it is no easy thing for man to forget himself. And it is the harder now in that it is demanded of him in regard to a vastly larger whole. For that reason every community has sought to bring about in those to whom the commanding will is committed a moral transformation, ridding them of the individual 'ego' and implanting in them the collective 'ego', or the 'we'.

That is what we are now going to examine.

THE SOVEREIGN WILL GENERALISED

Every man possessed of power is disposed to make use of it for his particular ends. Nothing could be more natural. Taken up as he is with his own ends, a man applies to them his own resources and strives to mobilise in their favour the resources of others. (Therein consists, as we have seen, political action of a rudimentary kind.) He normally regards every compulsive force available to him as a possible instrument for his designs and is, in consequence, inclined to regard under this aspect the public compulsive force which has been entrusted to him. I am not, of course, denying that he may resist the temptation to make egoistical use of the public compulsive force: all I am saying is that this temptation exists and is, so far from being a monstrosity, something natural.

For this reason it is dangerous to entrust power of any kind to a single individual, it being only too possible that he will use it, not for the common good, but to further his private desires. But the same danger is present when the power is entrusted to all: if each sees in it his chance of using the public authority to serve his own ends, it is true, no doubt, that by reason of the conflict of wills no one person will be completely successful in getting his way, but

one are all of them groupings which have an interest of their own and press it against the general interest; and this is true for any syndicated interest whatever. Remember also that here the word 'State' denotes the political society: it is that which grows feeble when the social tie loosens.

the tuggings hither and thither of authority by scuffling egoisms are liable to be much more harmful to society than the handing over of the public authority to a single egoism. Rejoicing in his absolute authority, the single egoist will exploit it methodically, whereas a mêlée of egoists will bring about a ruinous disorder and a disastrous cleavage, because the contrariety of the appetites to be satisfied will prevent the satisfaction of any single one. Clearly, then, the effect of the pursuit of private ends under cover of the public good will be worse if there are many with a hand in power than if there is only one.

There is no remedy in the form of government for the evil caused by the instinct for despotism. By 'instinct for despotism' we mean the tendency of a man to use power for his personal ends.

Political institutions of the most archaic kind and the usages of the peoples we call primitive attest the fact that the problem of 'generalisation' of the will was recognised in times before written history. There has always been a more or less confused notion that those who will for all must kill 'the old Adam' who pursued selfish ends and be born again as men who have made their own ends those of the whole.

The analogies often drawn between a coronation and an ordination stem from a related logic: in both ceremonies the central figure formally abandons one way of life and pledges himself to a new one. In ordination he gives himself to God's service, in coronation to the care of the realm. He becomes other than what he was by reason of a new spirit which descends on him. He has, in the language of the Baganda, 'eaten the drums'—their summons to arms will, in other words, issue from him—and he has 'eaten Uganda', in the sense that he is now identified with the realm.[1]

From failure to understand the magical significance of the act of coronation, rationalist authors have gone completely wrong on the meaning of the formula 'The king can do no wrong', which is found in some form or other almost everywhere. Well before it was addressed to the people, with a view to imposing on them respect for the declared will of the sovereign—a respect making for order—it was addressed to the sovereign himself, its force of suggestion serving to impose on him respect for the character which he had assumed and loyalty to the new man which he had become.

---

[1] John Roscoe, *The Baganda* (London, 1911), p. 188. This work is exceptionally important for political science.

In thus having recourse to the thought, naturally expressed in poetic form, of the men of long ago, we are in danger of giving an exaggerated picture of their credulity. From what is known of their demeanour toward crowned kings they did not hold the belief that the king, once he had been crowned, was necessarily and automatically changed from what he had been before—as is a body which has undergone a chemical change. Spiritual changes are more precarious and more volatile than that. All they must have believed was that the man who had been crowned was now capable of conducting himself 'royally'—a difficult thing to do—without ceasing to be liable to conduct himself naturally.

A man who has taken vows and received the help of grace has both the duty and the opportunity of proving himself changed, but he is always liable to backslide. These primitives of ours, who thought less in terms of mechanics and much more in terms of psychology than is usually supposed, certainly had the feeling of the precariousness of human resolutions.

The ruler's entire environment tended to buttress him in the moral outlook which the coronation must have impressed on him. If the ample satisfaction of his material needs did not succeed by sheer force of satiety in purging him of desire for the common objects of envy, his people's expectation kept him to his role of benefactor. For there is no sort of doubt as to the very real pressure on the mind exercised by the expectations of others. In popular belief it is possible to cause another's action by wishing him to take it, to induce its performance by a sufficient degree of concentration. If this belief is not justified by experience, we are at least entitled to say that proclaimed expectations weigh heavily on the man from whom much is expected, and particularly so when what is expected of him has been the subject-matter of a formal undertaking. Everybody is reluctant not to keep an appointment which he has made; the reluctance is enhanced not only by the degree of importance of the circumstances which gave rise to the promise, but also and much more by the degree of intensity which is known or supposed in the expectation of the friend. The intensity of the expectation of another acts on us as a sort of bond: we are here in the sphere of what is more than and earlier than legal obligation— here perhaps are the sources of obligation themselves. Obligation is the child of expectation.

The ancient usages of the western peoples, no less than those of the peoples we call primitive, offer innumerable proofs of the proposition we are advancing. We will not, however, set them out, for it will, we think, be more convincing to appeal to the experience of the reader himself. Will he not find, if he examines his thoughts on the subject of those who rule, that he considers their proper mode of life to be an indispensable condition of the public weal; and, in making this reflection, must he not take the view that both the trappings and the climate of feeling amid which rulers pass their lives must be such as to recall them to their highest conception of themselves—the selfless servants of the public good?

THE PAIR OF SOVEREIGNS

We have said earlier that vigour was an external characteristic essential to the sovereign Will. States have been known to come to grief under the rule of a 'benevolent Will' which lacked force: an example is the *regnum Francorum* under Louis I of France, called 'the good-natured'. It can even be said that, whatever may be the intentions of the rulers, the worst of all states is that in which they lack authority: for, if the task of the sovereign is to make men act (and refrain from acting) in the interests of the common good, the necessary condition of his efficacy is the capacity to induce action.

Now though there are men whose hearts are particularly open to the inspiration of the common good and who reach the point of desiring the good of the whole rather than their own, it by no means follows that they have any special faculty for getting themselves followed. Indeed it almost seems as if the two things are but rarely found together in the same person. They cannot but be found together—it is logical necessity—in the founder of any sort of political organism, be it state or another. It is he who conceives and desires this organism, and it is his will which, with all the strength conferred by egoism, enables the organism to reach its rudimentary good, which is to exist. There are good reasons for the fact that every community has been inspired to make the members of the founder's family succeed him, for in them the love of the organism is a natural thing, like the attachment of a peasant to his father's domain; in his descendants, education forms and the cult of the ancestor necessitates the love of the organism, so that Lares and Penates merge in the love of the fatherland itself.

But it has still to be seen whether these descendants' natures will fit them for rule. And if, though this is rare, the rulers are chosen by some other method, but still with reference to the likelihood of their serving the public good, in this case too they are no less likely to lack the gift of leadership.

The possibility of divorce between devotion to the public good and ability to make it followed and obeyed explains what is often met with—the duality of sovereignty.

In the island of Tonga, for instance, a monarch called the Tuitonga was revered.[1] On his appearance all prostrated themselves and kissed his feet. If he took part in a gathering, which he did not do very often, no one dared to sit beside him. If he spoke, all listened attentively and, when he had finished, cried out as one man: 'How true!' For all that, he did not rule. His life was lived apart, in meditation, prayer and ritual. The man in whose hands were the reins of government bore another name, that of the Tuihaatakatana or the Tuikanobalu. These titles being hard to cope with, let us speak of the 'passive king' and the 'active king'. In the Fiji Islands the two rulers bore most revealing names: 'the respectable king' and 'the root of war'—a contrast which suggests strongly the *rex-dux* duality.

They reached their positions by very different roads. The *rex* was always taken from the same family and in Tonga the succession had come down in that family forty-four times. The *dux*, on the other hand, was the winner in a contest for this office.

Here is an account of how things were done on Mangaïa, one of the Hervey Islands. Whether the *dux* had passed away naturally or because of the amount of discontent which he had caused, the entire island took up arms on his death and the leading chiefs plunged into combat. One of these chiefs carried the day, and thereby gave proof both of his own strength and of the attachment felt for him by his companions. He had after that to seek out the *rex* and to be invested by him. Fresh from victory though he was, he had to approach him on all fours and listen with the greatest submission to the instructions which were given—instructions by which he would have to govern himself. Let him fail to satisfy the *rex* completely, and the latter would refuse to have the sacred drum beaten and to offer the customary sacrifice. And this mattered, for only the beating of the drum put an end to the state of war and

[1] Robert W. Williamson, *The Social and Political Systems of Central Polynesia*, 3 vols. (Cambridge University Press, 1934).

made the carriage of arms, and even the gathering of the wood from which arms were made, a criminal offence. Nothing but the sacrifice restored fertility to the soil and made the earth cultivable anew. So, under pain of insecurity and famine, the *dux* had to promise to govern righteously—just as any one of his rivals in the competition would have had to promise if he had been successful.

Anyone can see that this constitution, if that is the name for it, had the effect of placing in the seat of government a most vigorous occupant, while confining his zeal within the limits of a law not of his making.

In other islands in the same area the active leader was chosen by a less warlike method. When the month of September came, the candidates and their respective supporters went in a body to the highest mountains on the island, where a poll of a most peculiar kind was held. Victory went to the candidate who, either himself or by his henchmen, was the first to find a nest of certain very rare birds. The *rex* gave the starting signal and awarded the victory; naturally the odds favoured the largest and most determined party.

This custom prevailed on Easter Island, but here the enfeebled authority of the *rex* no longer allowed him to dictate policy to the active leader, so that, according to some authorities, victory was followed by the banishment of the unsuccessful competitors. In Samoa, lastly, where the authority of the *rex* had completely disappeared, civil war, sometimes open and sometimes latent, was endemic. Power was seized by the strongest party, which bore the name of *malo*. The *malo* assembled in the *fono*, or parliament, and there worked its will, oppressing or despoiling the rest of the population, called the *vaivai*. This continued until rising discontent turned the minority into a majority, which rebelled, seized power in its turn and used it in the same arbitrary spirit.

These examples embody important lessons. Rulers must feel mystically certain natural obligations to which Power is subject. The capacity to feel them is not necessarily associated with the gift of effective leadership. It is not irrational to regard the sense of these obligations as subsisting in a single family, from among whom that member can then be chosen who seems most alive to them. No more irrational is it to regard the choice of a good man of action as requiring a somewhat violent contest, victory in which will demonstrate the faculty to rule. Those chosen by these two methods can then be joined together, the first acting as mentor to the second.

They will form between them the sovereign pair, such as there was in the example we have just given. The alternative course is to strive for the combination of the two capacities in a single man by first choosing a man of action and then imbuing him with the spirit of *pietas*; inducement will be used to harness him to the service of the good. The procedure of the Baganda seems to illustrate this idea in practice.

There is among them only one king, who is chosen from a very large field of possible choices. This choice is valid only if the man chosen shows himself capable of rule, and it is followed by a magical dedication of the prince to his vocation. The heirs-apparent or 'princes of the drums' are very numerous by reason both of polygamy and of the equal status of every male in masculine line of ascent to a reigning king.

On the death of the king these heirs, each of whom has been brought up in isolation by a private tutor, are assembled on the summons of the prime minister, who is called Katikoro. An exalted dignitary, the Kasuju, who is in general charge of their upbringing and to whom each private tutor makes periodical reports, fetches them and lines them up in front of the royal enclosure before the assembled people. They are passed in review by three men, the Katikoro who understands the requirements of the State, the Kasuju who is acquainted with the characters of the princes, and, lastly, the Kimbugwa who is the authority on fetishes and signs. The minister says formally to the tutor: 'Give us a prince for a king.' The tutor passes slowly down the line of heirs-apparent, stops at last, takes one of the princes by the hand, leads him forward and says: 'Here is the king.' He has now been designated, but it remains to be seen whether he inspires respect and fear. Addressing those who have been passed over, the minister shouts to them: 'Let those who want to fight, fight now.' And the result is often a scrimmage. If no one stirs, they are told: 'You are peasants.[1] Fight if you like and we will put you to death.' They are then conducted to a banquet, while the selected prince is led to his father's corpse, to which he pays all filial respect.

It now remains to imbue him with his duties. He is led out to the sacred hill, which is strictly guarded. To the king-designate, however, the resistance offered by the priest and his escort, armed

---

[1] 'Peasant princes'—the ineligible—are the descendants of kings who had not yet come to the throne when they were born.

with sugar canes and plantain leaves, at the foot of the hill, is only simulated. At dawn on the second day the king is conducted to the top of the hill, where there is a small enclosure in which Semenobé, the priest, is standing. The king kneels and crawls in. The priest then strikes the ground with a stick and raises the prince, who says for the first time: 'I am the King of Uganda.' He then plants in the ground a big branch in token of the fertility which he promises, receives the royal spear, has his mourning clothes taken off him and is clad in a stole.

But that is not the end of the process of striking his imagination. With his queen, he is conducted back by the priest to the foot of the hill. This time publicly, the priest cuts down a tree from whose wood spear-shafts are made and offers it to the king, saying: 'With this, triumph over your enemies.' A little further on, Semenobé gathers some reeds of a kind with which baskets are made, and says: 'May your life be like a basket which, when it falls, is not broken like an earthen vessel.' Lastly, they visit a place where wild plantains are intertwined: the priest offers some to the king with the words: 'May you excel your subjects in wisdom and understanding.'

The king is said after that to have 'eaten Uganda', and savages, it is known, identify the eater with the thing eaten. 'I have eaten Uganda' is, in the mouth of a black king, equivalent to saying: 'I and my people are one.'

The new king must pass another six months of mourning in a camp erected beside the sacred hill before the old king is buried and the drums stop beating. These six months are spent in conversation with the sages. Only after that does the king appear before the assembly of the people. The dead kings issue their orders to him by the mouth of Mugema, Minister of the Dead, and it is he who presides over the ceremony. 'You are king,' he proclaims, 'govern your people well.' 'I will.' 'Make all your judgments just', continues the Mugema. 'I will.' The Mugema then hands him two javelins which the king takes, being careful to turn their points not at his people but at himself. 'I will never fear to govern Uganda, my country', he says. After each answer he tosses at the people coffee-berries which are eagerly picked up. Turning towards the crowd, the Mugema demands of it: 'In times of war and troubles, never abandon your king in his difficulties.' And the people make answer in unison, after which the king and queen are raised on the shield.

THE MORAL HOLD

The effect of such ceremonies (there was much more of them than we have set down here) on an unsophisticated man can be imagined. He must, after all these rites, have felt himself to be different from what he was before—to be now clothed in majesty and dedicated to a certain role. The subjective will which guided him as a private individual has been, as it were, emptied out of him, and he is filled with the objective Will which should henceforward dwell in him as the man who has 'eaten Uganda'. A new nature has been grafted on to his own; a strong man armed has received a moral armament.

The private will in the seat of power is dangerous both to the people and to itself. This truth is illustrated by the superstition surrounding royalty among all primitive peoples. Frazer gives several instances of how touching and handling the royal insignia is thought to call down terrible misfortunes on the man who is guilty of it, as well as on the tribe itself. And that holds true even if the rash hand is that of the designated king himself, before his consecration—before, in fact, he has been exorcised and purged of his private will, before he has been clothed in his new objectivity.

Superstitions do not affront the reason as much as is thought. What is erroneous in them is, generally, that they confound the sign with the thing signified, and assume that what affects the one affects the other—as when pins are driven into a doll which represents an enemy; for that reason 'burning in effigy' is now the playful residue of what was once conceived as a punishment of terrible effectiveness. If this confusion is borne in mind, superstitions no longer seem absurd, those, especially, which have a bearing on Power. Power is as dangerous as it is salutary, and it brings forth its fruits of beneficence only to the extent that it is wielded by a purified will from which the subjective taint has gone out.

All that has gone before has been written with reference to monarchical authority, but it applies no less to popular authority. The personal sovereign needs to receive the imprint of a certain moral attitude; the assembly in the part of sovereign needs to receive it no less. The problem of the purgation of private wills is the same in both and was, in the ancient republics, grappled with by the same methods: the religious rites with which these assemblies opened—rites which had become mere formalities by the time of decadence—were regarded in the great days as of high effect. The problem differed from that of the royal consecration only because it was now a question of changing the attitude of many more men for a much shorter time (the day of the assembly). The same new birth was aimed at for the magistrates by means of ceremonies of investiture. Investiture, as the word implies, consists in clothing a man anew in robes which are at once pure and majestic.

In this connection we may call to mind a precaution taken by the Roman candidate for office—called the 'ambitious', one in other words who makes the round (*ambitus*) of the electors, just as in our own time, too, candidates visit markets and fair-grounds (the fair-ground in this respect is the equivalent of the *forum*). This candidate would whiten his toga with chalk[1] before the contest, and in this may be seen the symbol of the purification to which he aspired—the preface to the ceremonies of purification which accompanied his installation. The last survival of customs met under a hundred different forms may be found in the obligation, by which some men entering on public life consider themselves bound, to sell any shares in companies which link them to particular interests. Generally speaking, however, the mystical feeling of transformation within, which should accompany the change from a private to a public station, has been lost. Possibly, too, the need to symbolise the transformation is less strongly felt, because the effectiveness of symbols in this respect is ranked lower.

THE WILL FOR GOOD AND THE INTELLIGENCE

In politics the 'Will for Good' is the Will that has made the Whole (the organised 'us') the centre of its affections rather than the 'me' (or, let us note with Rousseau, a fraction of the body politic, a fraction preferred to the whole).

Must we go on to say that to will the good is all that is needed to understand what good is? It is certain, for instance, that Louis XIV thought he was doing what was good in revoking the Edict of Nantes: he acted not as a man in an uncontrollable passion but as one who thought he was doing his duty.

Does the craving for the good necessarily result in happy issues? Or can conscience itself go astray? If the first question is answered affirmatively and the second negatively, that man who wishes to rule the Whole for the best will be infallible as regards what profits

---

[1] The word 'candidate' is derived from this.

it. If the opposite is true, then intelligence will be needed to throw light on the common good.

As we shall see in the next chapter, the common good is not at once revealed to the 'Will for Good', and has to be sought intelligently.

However, there is a preliminary question which we can broach even at this stage: it is not always necessary to have an exact understanding of an end in view to know where one's immediate duty lies.

THE SOVEREIGN AND HIS MODEL

If we envisage an order established once for all which it is the office of the sovereign to maintain, if we picture this sovereign as the successor of a long line of predecessors who supply him not only with general models of conduct but with exact precedents for every situation which may confront him, then, certainly, he should need no other guide for his actions than the 'Will for Good'.

There will be a host of precepts to guide him in detail, precepts which are illustrated by exact precedents and are all imbued with the general imperative to maintain by hook or by crook whatever is established where institutions are concerned and whatever is acquired where rights are concerned.

The role of the sovereign has, it seems, often been conceived in this way. And, under these conditions, he has no need to know in what the good of the Whole consists: all he has to know is what actions of his own are good.

He is not composer but executant of a score which is ready-written.

But the less stationary a society is, the less its good is held to consist in this stationary condition and the more inadequate this view of the sovereign function will come to seem. And we must note the continual retreat of conservative ideas in regard to the social order, so that no-one nowadays, not even those styled Conservatives, regards this order as a *datum* to maintain, but rather as an artifact which is never in final form. Now it may be possible for one whose duty it is merely to maintain an existing order to have no ideas as to wherein the beauty, the goodness and the excellence of this order consist; but one who must be continually adapting to change cannot be in this state of darkness. He must know at the least which are the goods to be preserved and enhanced.

CHAPTER 7

THE PROBLEM OF THE COMMON GOOD

There are a hundred different ways of saying that men in authority should use it in the general interest and for the common good; that the interest of the people should be the rule of their decisions and the public good the end of their actions. Exhortation of this kind never comes amiss. Traditionally it has been directed at the sole and absolute ruler, but it is no less necessary when authority is diffused, when the regime is one in which responsibility for decisions is widely spread. There is, in regimes of this kind, a temptation for individuals to regard their tiny ration of public authority as a piece of private property which they can use for their personal advantage. For that reason it is desirable to remind them that, as participants in the public authority (even if only as voters), they hold a public office and are morally bound to seek the common good in their decisions.

Salutary as the reminder is, it is not the last word in political ethics: it is only the first. To the philosopher who bids him seek and promote the general interest, the magistrate may reply: 'Tell me how I may know it. Give me a clear idea of it, or supply me with criteria which may help me to select from the various open courses the one which best serves the public good.' So presented, the problem is full of difficulties. But political science cannot escape the problem without renouncing its own purpose and end; let political science shirk its duty, and all it has left to do is to compile procedural manuals and commentators' monographs.

Before embarking on this problem, our first question is whether it is necessary to handle it at all, as clearly it will not be if the solution is always staring us in the face; our second question is whether there is not always an infinite number of solutions.

FIRST QUESTION: IS THE COMMON GOOD SELF-EVIDENT?

People often talk as if men in positions of authority had only to wish to use it in the general interest for the problem of the common good to be solved. This assumes implicitly that public-spirited intention necessarily brings instant understanding both of the substance of the public good and of the means by which it may be realised.

If this assumption were well founded, politics would be an extremely simple affair. All the men in a state who cared for the public interest—the good citizens, in short—would also be in perfect agreement as to the best decision to take and the right course to adopt. The same spirit in each would bring the same illumination to each, with the result that all these 'good wills' would, by being good, compose a single will: the 'general will', which is necessarily righteous. It would not, certainly, be the will of all, because all are not public-spirited in intention. But those who have no public spirit, or have so little that it does not prevail over care for their private advantage and does not reveal to them the common good—the bad citizens, in short—would find themselves powerless in the presence of the good. Each of them would be thinking only of himself, and this very selfishness of their preoccupations would disperse their wills; by reason of this dispersal, their wills would on every occasion be found weak against the single will of the good citizens, which is compact and coherent and wears the impressive livery of virtue.

It might, of course, happen that the particular interest in question was that of persons so powerful or of a class so numerous that it would be able to block the 'general will', the will of the patriots. But in that event the patriots would feel entitled to destroy the peccant social authorities and to forbid the private associations which obstructed in this way the pursuit of the common good. And anyone agreeing that the flame of their virtue had merited the revelation to them of the common good would have to allow them the right to pull up by the roots these parasitic and obstructive weeds.

Thus, the postulate of the self-evidence of the common good to patriots takes us straight to the views of Robespierre—views which have found favour with many others since. The republic will necessarily be well governed by the solid phalanx of the public-spirited, who will necessarily be in agreement among themselves and will form the only legitimate party—themselves. The only obstacle to be found is the inevitable conspiracy of the wicked: this must be broken.

Those opposing cannot but be wicked. They are not men who

are only mistaken; they must have evil intentions as well. Allow to any one of them the smallest spark of patriotism and the doctrine collapses. The moment that someone who does not see the public good where we see it is given credit for public-spirited intention, the admission has been made that patriotism may go astray in its judgments; and if I admit, as regards this someone, that the patriotic conscience is not infallible, then it is not a whit more infallible in us.

This infallibility of the patriotic conscience can only be safe-guarded by denying that the man in question is a mistaken patriot, for, if he was a patriot, his judgment would necessarily accord with ours. Since it is different from ours, he is a rascal whose patriotism is only a cloak, and he must be reprobated the more, the more of a patriot he seems to be. Give credence to his patriotism, and his opposition to us leads to one of two conclusions: either patriotism is not infallible—which destroys our doctrine, or we are not patriots —which destroys our reputation. For that reason, Robespierre and his like are bound to represent the dissident patriot as shamming patriotism for ulterior ends.

This has not been the predominant point of view in the countries of the West. In them it is admitted that the same care for the public good may inspire very different opinions and that equally good intentions may be found in different parties, acting though they do as respectable façades for the sectional or egotistical interests which find shelter in each of them. Once admit that good intentions are not all on one side and it becomes impossible to hold that good intention brings in its train sure and immediate knowledge of the common good. A regime in which debate is free and to whose institutions debate is fundamental implies the assumption that the men who seek the public good do not find it easily and help one another in the search by making it an object of public debate. Evidently, therefore, this is a quest in which the philosophers must take a hand.

SECOND QUESTION: IS THE COMMON GOOD ENTIRELY SUBJECTIVE?

But this quest is perhaps a vain one; perhaps the common good (or the general interest) is only a name which each of us gives to his own ideas or imaginings. This is a formidable difficulty. The idea that I have of the common good is something definite; the idea that someone else has of it is also something definite. But are these different ideas reflections of something which has an absolute existence, the real common good, or is there no such thing and is the common good only the generic name for a bundle of individual conceptions differing among themselves? Here once more is the old dispute between 'realists' and 'nominalists' about 'universals'. If we adopt the nominalist thesis, no two people speaking of the common good are speaking of one and the same thing and neither of them can be wrong, for, when each of them says 'This is what the common good is', he is merely declaring 'For my part, what I call the common good is this.'

In the large family of private notions to which the name of 'common good' is given by individual minds, no single one is false for the man who professes it or true for other people. It follows from this that the obligation laid on rulers, 'Act for the common good', loses much of its force, for now it only means, 'Act for what you call good.' It cannot be said that a recommendation of this kind is altogether futile, for it instigates rulers to act with reference to their judgments of value, to consult their principles and put some coherence into what they do; but it does no more than that.

Yet, if we rejected the nominalist thesis and looked for the 'real' common good, a nominalist would have good cause to reproach us with only formulating our subjective preference. For that reason we can only build solidly if we make the nominalist position our starting point.

I do not deny that the idea of the common good that I can make for myself is only my subjective preference, valid for myself only. But it is a preference in relation to something. That something I call 'France', and my compatriots and I, when we speak of 'France', have the feeling that we are talking at least of one and the same thing. France brings to my mind a great collection of men who have, as individuals, certain satisfactions, certain aspirations, certain discontents, certain attitudes of mind; I also envisage their relations between one another, their daily intercourse. In the complex of which I am thinking, there is more than individuals and their unceasing interaction; there are also emotions felt in common (as in a time of national disaster) and actions taken either simultaneously (as when we go to vote or pay our taxes) or in combination (as when we go to war side by side). And it is the possibility of these collective movements which makes the difference between a collection of individuals and 'a people'. Finally, we note that foreigners pass judgments on this whole which are collective; they speak well or ill of France and the French.

If I now declare that the virtue and prosperity of Frenchmen, the excellence of their mutual relations, their capacity to feel and act in common and their reputation in the outside world are my great preoccupations, will any Frenchman be found to tell me that these preoccupations have nothing in common with what he has in mind when he thinks of the public good? On the contrary, will he not agree that so far, at any rate, we are talking of one and the same thing, or of one and the same complex of things? That agreed, I am safe in concluding that in differing notions of the common good there is in fact a common substance.

But, I shall be told, this agreement is obtained only because of the vagueness of the statement. The reputation desired for France may vary widely from man to man; the virtue and prosperity of a great collection of individuals may be conceived in an infinite number of different ways. Though that is true, what I have said is not that there is no room for subjective preferences, but only that, in speaking of the common good, we are talking of something with a definite meaning. I would point out, moreover, that there is one phrase in the statement which is almost entirely free from subjectivity: the capacity to act simultaneously or in combination is a concrete fact, which takes us into the domain of the objective. We can now embark on our examination of the problem.

THIRD QUESTION: IS THE COMMON GOOD COMPRISED IN THE GOOD OF INDIVIDUALS?

'Did you ever expect a corporation to have a conscience', asked the first Lord Thurlow, 'when it has no soul to be damned, and no body to be kicked?' The radical inferiority of legal persons to men could not be more forcefully expressed. God became incarnate for the salvation not of the Jewish State or the Roman Empire but of men. It can, therefore, be maintained very plausibly that the duty of rulers is exclusively to individuals and that the good of a social whole is entirely comprised in the personal good of each of the individuals who compose it. Let us adopt this opinion provisionally with a view to seeing where it leads us.

If our rulers have been notified that the common good which it is their duty to serve consists in the particular goods of the subjects, it leaps to the eye that their difficulty will be to reconcile all the particular goods. That difficulty vanishes only if the particular good is made to consist in the acquisition of virtue, and this will not readily be conceded. Conversely the difficulty will get worse the more that the particular good is made to consist in the acquisition of scarce things, such as wealth and honours. Thus we find our attention drawn to the necessity of defining personal goods, and a road-fork comes into view.

What meaning should be given to the personal good of each? Is it what the rulers conceive to be his good, or is it what each conceives his good to be?[1]

Let us first go down the second road, which seems to show most affinities with our basic thesis. When we have exalted the individual by making him the end of governmental action, would it not be contradictory to lower him by refusing to let him be judge of his own good? So we will here treat as his good what it seems to him to be, his perceived interest. But a man ordinarily sees his good in the satisfaction of his desires, which are in conflict with those of others. The result of our instructing the public authority that its duty is to serve personal interests as perceived, and of our telling the citizens in the same breath that it is their right to set authority in motion for their own ends, is that the rulers are inevitably beset by contradictory petitions. Each man asks of them a decision which hurts others. It has often been said that the duty of the public authority was to limit and deaden the natural clash of interests; but the assertion that it is the servant of those interests is bound to stimulate the latter to assert themselves in clamorous fashion and to encumber the forum with their scuffles.

What is the public authority to do then? It has the choice either of trying all the suits or of declaring itself incompetent and dismissing the suitors.

To try the suits is no easy task, for it has received, as the criterion of the common good which it must serve, the personal good of individuals as they themselves conceive it to be. How can it choose between two personal goods? Crudely, by reference to the volume

---

[1] It is clear that, in the case of individuals, the question of a 'real good', different at once both from the good they imagine for themselves and from the good as it is conceived for them by the rulers, does not arise, for the ruler cannot possibly work towards what is for him an indeterminate end, which neither his own intelligence nor the declarations of those concerned have disclosed to him.

of noise each makes, or by the subtler method of weighing the two goods? One method suggested is to weigh the respective satisfactions which the two camps at issue may gain or lose by any given decision and to return the verdict which ensures that the winners gain more satisfactions than the losers lose. As the estimates on which a calculation of this kind has to be based are very debatable and the basis itself is open to challenge, a verdict so arrived at would never be received with respect; it would serve as mask for a compromise rather than as a criterion. The long and short of it is that the public authority is merely tossed about between opposing pressures.

Will it, then, dismiss the suitors? What reason will it give? That it holds itself bound to the service of the interests of individuals only so far as they are common to all? This leads to definition of the general interest as that part of the particular interests which is held in common. But in setting off along the road of our choice we conceded that the interests in question were the interests perceived. It is possible to think that, taking the citizens' individual interests as a whole, the essential and major part is made up of interests which they have in common; but that is certainly not true when the interests to be considered are those of which they are aware. The interests which unite them are felt but feebly, whereas those which divide them are felt strongly.[1] The result is that a public authority which confined itself to serving only those particular interests which the citizens were at one in thinking important for all would condemn itself to virtual inactivity.

It thus appears that the road of our choice leads us either to handing over authority to the disorderly scrimmage of particular interests or else to a drastic curtailment of the competence of government. Let us therefore make our way back to the road-fork and take the other road which was open to us: the public authority is still conceived as there to serve individual goods, but now we shall establish it as judge of what those goods are.

We are repelled at the outset. To know each man's good better than he knows it himself is something within the competence of God alone. It is the duty of a father, ruler in his tiny realm, to perceive wherein the good of each of his sons consists and to set the feet of each in his proper path while making the others help him in the task; yet with how many blunders does even a father exercise

[1] Hume, *A Treatise of Human Nature*, Book III, part II, sec. VII.

this function! Clearly it cannot be exercised over a large population, for the indispensable adjuncts of a jurisdiction of this kind are personal knowledge of each single subject and unceasing vigilance in his regard. For this reason it may cause confusion to say 'Authority is paternal', when in fact it can have neither the knowledge of the personal good of each nor the care for these personal goods such as are proper to a father.

The infirmity of human intelligence makes it impossible for the ruler to consider individual goods particularly; he can only conceive of them in general terms. Therefore he will make himself a diagram of the good and contented citizen, and he will reduce living people to the measure of this diagram. He will, in other words, stigmatise as misconduct all conduct deviating from that which, according to him, the citizen should practise for his good, and he will consider unjust all spontaneous relations which will not establish the citizen in the condition in which he wishes to see him. An authority of this kind will be equally detestable whether it is exercised by one man or by an oligarchic group; nor will it be less so for being borne along on a current of opinion, for it must of its nature always be persecuting nonconformist elements. If the model of particular good is taken from the past, a regime of this kind will have a suffocating effect and will act as a barrier to any sort of novelty; if the model is conceived as a dream of future bliss, it will justify sanguinary upheavals.

Thus, to put the public authority at the service of particular goods has equally deplorable results whether the goods have been conceived by individuals or by the authority. It is an idea which leads to disorder in the first case and to tyranny in the second. Our conclusion is, therefore, that it is not the office of the public authority to procure the personal goods of individuals.

FOURTH QUESTION: DOES THE COMMON GOOD CONSIST IN THE SOCIAL TIE ITSELF?

The natural effort of each to procure himself his personal good is made within a society. And the notion which he forms of this good is itself conditioned by the spectacle of society; the various goods, spiritual and material, which he sees in others, inspire in him both his noblest and his grossest objects of desire. Imitation is so powerful a principle of behaviour that God himself has made use of it, by setting before us through the Incarnation the living exemplar of our Sovereign Good.[1]

Society furnishes us with opportunities for conceiving what our good is to be; it furnishes us also with opportunities for realising it. It is in society that a man meets with the various co-operators and traders by means of whom he assures himself of a material comfort such as he could never acquire in a state of isolation. It is in society again that he finds occasions for romance, enthusiasm and devotion, in other words, his spiritual good. It is by means of social relations that moral and intellectual truths are propounded to him: the gospel was first preached in gatherings of people.

Therefore life in society is the condition of each man's individual good, indeed of his being a man at all. For life in society is natural to man in the sense of being necessary to the realisation of his true nature. Is it also natural in the sense of being primary, or is it in that sense artificial, as being the product of actions which have created it?

The greatest political thinkers, such as Hobbes and Rousseau, have called it artificial and have made us the spectators of its creation. For this they have been strongly attacked on the ground of the extreme improbability of man ever having lived in any other state; the argument comes down to saying that man was found in social formations of an elementary kind from the moment that he passed the threshold of humanity. But these great geniuses had very good reasons for compressing into a single day, 'the day of creation' of their imaginations, a process which took a thousand years; if it is untrue that society was made in a day, it is true that it is made and unmade every day. And the myth of instantaneous creation enabled them to bring out in sharpest relief the conditions on which social life is possible.

It matters little that society was not in fact founded on one bright morning by the deliberate and simultaneous assent of each of its members, if this hypothesis makes clear that a daily, if muddled, assent by each is necessary to social existence. It matters little that men did not in fact emerge from a state of war, in which their appetites clashed, into a state of peace, in which their desires are,

---

[1] Herein lies the seriousness of the monophysite heresy. If Jesus had not entirely assumed man's nature, if he was merely God in disguise, it would follow that human nature would be powerless to imitate him; and it is imitation of him which has been set before us.

so far as they clash, bridled, and are sublimated to tasks of co-operation; it is enough if this hypothesis demonstrates that the curbing of the ego and the awareness of the whole are essential to a viable society. Nor does it matter much more that men did not on any particular day give themselves a government and did not on another day receive a body of laws, if by means of this fable the reality of interdependence is brought out by the fiction of simultaneity.

Lastly and above all, it is better to picture society as artificial than to call it natural (in the sense of spontaneous), for only so can the point be made effectively that art is necessary to its support and development. The real purpose of those who postulated the formation of society as an act of will was to put us on guard against social dissolution; the victory which, in their account of it, was won in a single day by the forces of integration over those of disaggregation is the very victory which has to be won every day of life.

It will be noted that they have told us nothing as to the end or good which the rulers of the social edifice in being were to seek; may not the reason be that those rulers' entire task consisted in the consolidation and development of the social tie which had been formed? That, in short, the common good for which those in government were responsible, up to the limit of their powers, was the foundation in perpetuity of man's social condition?

We must never forget the admirable dictum of Rivarol: 'All executive power is in the hands of individuals'; it is never possible for it to be conveyed to the rulers, for there is never a moment in which, even under the most frightful tyranny, each man does not remain the master of his own actions.[1] Therefore the social state is merely one in which the executive powers of individuals are used not to hurt but to bring mutual advantage. As this state of things can never exist completely, the social state is a matter of degree; it is always in the making just as it is always in process of coming apart.

As a working hypothesis we will admit that the common good consists in the social state itself and in its successive advances. But what is meant by 'social state', and why do we speak of 'social good' and 'social tie'?

[1] There is a prevalent illusion that the power of constraint possessed by the authorities is great; at the worst they have only a power of intimidation, itself resting on assents on the part of the men who serve as their instruments. That, incidentally, is why a despotism always breaks down in the long run; it ceases to be served and with that it ceases to intimidate—two phenomena which are complementary to each other.

FIFTH QUESTION: IS LIFE IN SOCIETY THE
INSTITUTIONALISATION OF TRUST?

Human actions are, it is clear, based on confidence in others. The condition of a man would be miserable—it might be truer to say that he would never even have become a man—if at every moment he had to be on guard against the unforeseeable actions of every other man. Our progress in and towards the human condition presupposes that we live within a circle of peace and friendship, in which not only do we not anticipate attacks but we expect to be succoured at need.

There is in man, as in the animals, a power of affection, which inspires in him friendly behaviour. But he does not so behave to every other person without exception. It is unnatural for us to behave in friendly fashion indiscriminately; still less will those who do not give us their friendship receive ours. The very greatest saints, whose love knew no bounds and expected no return, thus acted only for the love of God. The affection which reaches directly only a small number of people is, therefore, extended to a much wider circle only by means of an intermediary—because strangers too are subject to the same loved whole. The friendly feelings inspired by the unknown family of a friend may also be inspired by the unknown members of a whole, the whole in the second case having as regards the unknown the effect of the friend in the first. In this way the fictitious person, the group, enlarges the circle of friendships, of those who will at their need receive our service and give their service at ours.

Awareness of a 'we' is aroused by real affections and is in the present indicative for persons known to us; it constrains our affections to the conditional future, or to the imperative, for unknown persons who are members of the 'we'. The 'we' breeds obligations which are really feelings of linkage. Awareness in each 'he' of these obligations constitutes for each 'me' a powerful safeguard. It enables 'me' to have confidence in 'him'. This confidence is the condition on which human activity can develop.

The activities of the fisherman in his boat and of the farmer in his field do not, it is true, directly involve any other person, except in so far as both of them need to have what they produce bought by others; but most activities of men in society are based very directly indeed on an anticipated intervention by other men.

The regular and foreseeable behaviour of these others and the possibility of anticipating their reactions with the smallest margin of error are the pillars on which every individual calculation rests. Hardly any plans could be made if the degree of uncertainty in the behaviour and attitude of other people was known to be very high. Therein is the miracle of society: my calculations, though calling for the intervention of a very large number of free agents, can yet be made as if there was no question of free agents at all. Mobile as they are, these agents yet furnish me with fixed points on which to hinge my action. Life in society can be denoted by the wide range of my certainties regarding others.

To say 'foreigner' is as much as to say 'enemy'—an agent whose conduct is not foreseeable. It cannot be foreseen because he is not a member of our league of friendship, because his folkways and probable reactions are unknown, and, lastly and most important, because I have no surety for his behaviour.

In effect the public authority of my group is surety, as regards me, for the obligations which its subjects owe me and on which I base myself. It cannot, obviously, ensure that whatever I undertake shall end prosperously, but it has a duty to provide me with sure foundations on which I can make my plans. These foundations are the obligations to me enforced on the other members of the group, obligations to which they are required to show themselves faithful.

Clearly it is in the personal interest of each individual to be able to trust others, and to trust them in two different ways. First, he needs to be able to count on the general complaisance of others, and that presupposes a social climate of friendship; next, he must know with reasonable certainty how others will conduct themselves towards him. This personal interest, which is particular for each and the same for all, constitutes a real common interest; it cannot be said of it *a priori* that it is an exhaustive description of the common good, but at least it emerges as its primary and essential constituent.

SIXTH QUESTION: CAN THE POLITICAL AUTHORITY PROMOTE SOCIAL FRIENDSHIP?

Anthropologists have taught us to regard the small family, typical of our times and western society, as the residue of the large family, which is characteristic of more primitive peoples. That the family of today is smaller in scale than the family of olden days has been sufficiently demonstrated by the fact that funerals brought together then a much more extensive 'family' than they do now. There is in existence a vast literature, brought into being, it may be said, by the researches of Lewis H. Morgan, on the various ways in which different peoples range degrees of relationships in importance, the descent in the female line often being considered more important than the descent in the male; but the thing in common found in all primitive peoples, as in our own distant past, is an awareness of kinship pushed to very great lengths. The old wives who concern themselves with establishing ties of kinship which strike us as distant and insignificant are in fact engaged on a task with an antiquity of many thousands of years; futile though we think it, it has beyond question played an exalted role in social progress. The upkeep by the old of a lively feeling for the most distant ties of kinship has been an historical mission of the highest importance, weaving a bond of comprehensive solidarity—a bond which is continually strengthened by the worship of common ancestors.

It sits well with logic that society was able to raise itself simply on a foundation of chains of kinships, by the web of personal friendships. If one friendship was sufficient to link two chains together by reason of family solidarity, a few friendships must have sufficed to weave a social web of one or two thousand people. This is the way in which both Aristotle and Vico conceived the course of events, and their view is a very probable one.

Friendships, in that case, are seen to be antecedent to political organisation properly so-called; they are an originating principle. Be that as it may, every people has proverbs which lay stress on the social importance of friendship. Friendship is a joy ('Friendship sugars water itself': Chinese); it is an encouragement ('The friend strengthens the heart': Sudanese); it is a force ('The friendless man has only one hand': Bosnian). And the wisdom of peoples has rated fidelity to friendships very highly ('To die with one's friends is a marriage feast': Persian; 'Is my life worth more than my friend?': Afghan). Pairs of friends such as Achilles and Patroclus, Nisus and Euryalus, Roland and Oliver, recur in all the western legends. It seems established that the 'troop of friends' really was a most important principle of social formation among the peoples who have made Europe.[1]

---

[1] Thus, among the Anglo-Saxons, the *gegyldan* or *friedborgh*, a small confederation for mutual guarantee, whose members brought each other help, jointly avenged the harm done to one of their number and assumed common responsibility for their individual acts.

But freely chosen friendship is, by very definition, an entirely subjective phenomenon; we cannot expect to find it forming naturally between all and sundry in a populous city or state. Our knowledge of the city-states of antiquity entitles us to think that kinships were linked together by freely chosen friendships, which became in time traditional, and buttressed, perhaps, the social edifice; if, however, that is our interpretation of 'phratrias' and 'curias', we must next observe that these buttresses disintegrated progressively and that their elements were broken down into the larger whole of the state.

Political struggles are illuminated if it is recognised that the aim of innovating parties is to break the primitive cadres, dissolve the 'troops of friends' and make their members directly subject to the state. This aim was naturally supported by those who, because they were new arrivals or for any other reason, had no place in these cadres—in short, the *plebs*.

But the destruction of old ties made necessary the formation of new ones. This is the origin of those civic rites which may be looked on as the method of establishing an artificial kinship. So, too, the institution of the adolescent training-group (*ephebia*) may be regarded as an attempt to promote friendship institutionally.

The ancient writers bear unanimous witness that the supreme good of a state and its greatest source of strength were looked on as residing in friendship between the citizens. Rousseau has honoured this preoccupation of classical times with one of his finest passages.[1]

The rulers are able to arouse this friendship between citizens by

---

[1] 'The Romans were distinguished above all other peoples on the face of the earth by the consideration of the Government for individuals and by its scrupulous care to respect the inviolable rights of all the members of the state. Nothing was more sacred than the life of the simple citizen; to condemn one of them, nothing less sufficed than the assembly of the entire people. Neither the Consuls in all their majesty nor the Senate itself had the right to do it; and in the most powerful people of the world, the crime and punishment of a citizen were a public grief. For this reason it seemed so harsh a thing to shed a citizen's blood for any crime whatsoever that, by the *lex Porcia*, the penalty of death was commuted into exile for any who wished to survive the loss of so dear a fatherland.

'Everything at Rome and in her armies breathed this love of fellow-citizens for one another and this respect for the name of "Roman", which raised the courage and animated the virtue of whoever had the honour to bear it.

'The hat of a citizen delivered from slavery, or the civic crown of someone who had saved another's life, were the sights which gave most pleasure in the triumphal processions; and it is worth noting that, of all the crowns awarded in war for noble actions, only the civic crown and that of the commanders whose triumph it was were made of grass and leaves; all the others were of mere gold. Such was Roman virtue and so did Rome become the mistress of the world.' Rousseau, article 'Economie Politique' in the *Encyclopédie*. Quoted in my edition of the *Contrat Social* (Geneva, 1947), pp. 391–2.

making them feel that they are all 'members one of another', by setting them an example of the consideration which they owe each other, and by forestalling the quarrels which are liable to disturb this harmony.

Setting the example of consideration is most important. If the man who is 'dressed in a little brief authority' treats private citizens rudely, contemptuously and even brutally, his conduct will be imitated by private citizens; they will see in it a way of showing themselves superior. If the ruler so behaves, they think that so behaving will get a man taken for a ruler. If, on the other hand, the least important private citizen is treated by the authorities with politeness, and if the ruler behaves with the greatest consideration, this attitude will be imitated in the relations between private citizens.[1]

As to forestalling quarrels, it is obvious that the way to succeed in it is to mark out clearly those *mea* and *tua*, uncertainty as to which is a cause of dispute, and to insist on the citizens honouring their given word.

UNCERTAINTY IS THE GREAT PRINCIPLE OF DISASSOCIATION

Some of the calculations made by man in society are speculative— that, for instance, of the merchant who hopes that there will be enough ships to carry the merchandise which he puts on offer. But most calculations are not in principle speculative; they are based on the behaviours obligatory in those dealt with. The workman, for instance, on his way to the factory reckons that his usual mode of transport will function without a hitch. Each single life in society is based on a whole host of certainties, which allow for the regularity of behaviour expected from others.

My fellows and I are in debt to each other for given behaviours. The clearest instance of such a debt is that which results from explicit promises made by me or as regards me; it is the given word, and scrupulous observance of the given word has been regarded by every people as a necessary virtue, and its opposite as an unpardonable vice.[2] It was for this reason that the Romans erected a temple

---

[1] For instance, the courtesy of the police in England is a formative element of the general behaviour.

[2] It is for this reason that inflation is the moral ruin of societies, for it authorises a debtor not to make effective repayment of the real sum which he and the creditor had in mind, but only of a smaller sum, which is the same only in name. It is a school of default on the substance of promises.

to Dius Fidius, surety for the given word and the pledged faith. Because of this supreme importance of the given word, contract has been called the foundation of societies.

But, though the citizen is entitled to expect the exact fulfilment of the promises which others have made to him, and though it is the duty of the public authorities to stand surety for their execution, the certainties founded on contracts form but a very small part of the certainties necessary for man in society. The greatest part of these certainties is based on the way in which he thinks others are sure to behave. He expects a man of a particular country to do and not to do certain things; and his expectations are even more definite as regards a man of a particular education, profession and status. Man in society is making bets, continuously and unconsciously, on the behaviours of others. Of these bets the public authority is the great underwriter. But here it must be observed that its task differs widely from one society to another.

The great majority of human societies have been ritualistic in outlook. A religious ethic, abounding in detailed precepts which have been instilled at first by parents and later by teachers and are for ever being recalled by the Doctors of the Law, exercises over minds a continuous power of suggestion and whispers on every occasion what should be done and not done, and even what should be said and not said.[1]

These precisely defined obligations can be specified in advance for every situation and for every condition, as in Brahminic India, and that without the classifications being necessarily too tightly drawn. Detailed and unchanging obligations, which are sustained by the force of unanimous opinion, assure a high degree of social certainty without requiring any extensive intervention by the public authorities; they must, however, clearly have an ossifying influence.

In a society of that kind, in which the moral sentiment of obligation is married to the precise formulation of the specific precept,

---

[1] 'In families where traditional customs and their power of cohesion still rule, the conscientious mussulman father who is concerned about the bringing up of his children will take great care to inculcate into them a whole body of rules as to what may be done and may not be done. He will attach more importance to this social conformity than to anything else. It will whisper at every turn what to say and what to think under pain of offending the common ethos. To speak his language correctly to an Arab it is necessary not only to know his words and syntax but also to possess, instinctively as it were, the turn of phrase and the arrangement of phrases which are appropriate for use in all the varying sets of circumstances.' L. Gardet, *La Cité Musulmane* (Vrin, 1954), pp. 252–3.

it is only too probable that flexibility in the precepts can be attained only at the price of an enfeeblement of the sentiment of obligation; a man who is faithless where the rituals of life are concerned will be faithless all round, as regards both God and his pledged word. For that reason a religion which stimulates the sentiment of obligation in general, while not associating it with a host of particular precepts, is, from the purely social angle, necessarily more favourable to progress.

THE PROBLEM OF OBLIGATIONS IN A MOBILE SOCIETY

Naturally, then, Christian societies have been very progressive ones, in which deeper and swifter transformations have occurred than in any other. The reason for this lies undoubtedly in the emancipation of the Christian, which was pronounced by Christ and amply expounded by St Paul. To say that the Christian is freed from the law is to say that his behaviour is no longer ordered in detail by a code of precepts appropriate to different circumstances, but is inspired by a new spirit. The specified obligations no longer act as a corset to his conduct; the sense of obligation must now become its very principle.

Still confining ourselves to the social standpoint, we can see here a major revolution; a precise and detailed code of behaviours to others, such as is found in the Old Testament and the Koran and was professed by the Pharisees, is contrary to the genius of Christianity. The obligation of the Christian is no longer limited to the observance of rules; to the unbeliever as well it no longer presents an orthodox code of behaviours to others. And in this last respect it leaves to temporal authorities a field which the codifying religions never abandoned to them.

As Christianity, in this respect sharply contrasting with Islam, is not social legislator, a Christian society, in which the new spirit animates different men differently, may show a very wide gamut of behaviours—a condition which necessarily makes the role of the temporal authorities a large one. That role is to define the obligations of positive law, obligations which, though they will form only a small part of obligation for the faithful, will keep in check those who know no other.

Specified obligations of this kind do not owe their validity to spiritual authority, and their substance may for that reason vary from time to time. So long as they are not immoral, the Christian faith underwrites them, though they are not of its making; it does not in consequence stabilise them once for all. Variability of obligations, though contrary to the spirit of the codifying religions, is not contrary to the spirit of Christianity. The specifications may change—though not, of course, just anyhow. But the proper determinants of change are a matter for philosophy guiding the practical reason much more than for theology.

It follows from this that Christian permeation has been favourable to transformations of law and society. But, propitious to social evolution though Christianity was, that evolution went its way without it in a society which was largely post-Christian. And thus arises the modern problem of uncertainty in obligations.

In so far as a man has not been morally renewed, it is natural for him to think of rights as his and of obligations as other people's. Social conflicts may be expressed in terms either of 'my rights' or 'other people's obligations'. New situations and new ideas create the feeling of new obligations due from others. If the idea which I form of another's obligations does not coincide with his own, I feel uncertainty as to his conduct; that leads to irritation on my part and determination to impose on him as obligation what I conceive it to be. Dissensions of this kind are a principle both of uncertainty and of rupture of social friendship; they are under both these headings opposed to the common good.

It is here that a mobile society confronts the authorities with their major problem, which has never been properly clarified, for all the leading discussions of the common good are based on the postulate of a stationary society. Even revolutionary thought has always been directed to an immobile society which has been renovated once for all.

Practically speaking, the problem is generally resolved by the positive consecration of new obligations with every strengthening of the sense of obligation among those bound. It might be said that the intensification of the gerund gives birth to the imperative. There is confirmation here of the remark that obligation is the daughter of expectation. But the formulation of every new obligation cannot but usher in a period of tension which is injurious to the common good.

Appearances to the contrary, we are still far from having cleared up the problem of the common good—indeed we have not even started on the difficulties. That we will do in the next chapter.

CHAPTER 8

OF SOCIAL FRIENDSHIP

IMMOBILITY AS A PRINCIPLE

The development of our argument has brought us to seeing the common good as residing in the strength of the social tie, the warmth of the friendship felt by one citizen for another and the assurance that each has of predictability in another's conduct—all of them conditions of the happiness which men can create for each other by life in society. And the essential function of public authorities has seemed to us to be to increase the mutual trust prevailing at the heart of the social whole.

So we have joined with the ruling preoccupation of Plato[1] and Rousseau: moral harmony within the City.[2] And with that we come up against the corollaries which these two high authorities drew from their thought—corollaries so displeasing to their modern admirers that they generally contrive to forget them. These corollaries, which are four in number, all stem from a single principle: so great a blessing is moral harmony that whatever tends to weaken it must be dangerous and bad. The first corollary is smallness: the City must not become too large, for otherwise, when the number of citizens is too great for intimacy between them to be possible, the harmony will be less intense.[3] The next is homogeneity: the introduction as citizens into the City of foreign elements (metics), whose upbringing has given them a different outlook from that of

[1] 'What greater good is there for the State than that which keeps its members linked together?... And is not that link the common sharing of joys and sorrows, when all the citizens rejoice or are afflicted together and in the same way on the same occasions?' *Republic*, v, 462.

[2] *Du Contrat Social* will always be misinterpreted so long as the reader, who has come by experience to think of political life as being always a state of conflict, tries to discover in it who in Rousseau's view should be able to make his will prevail; for what Rousseau was looking for were the conditions of harmony which would result in the conflict of wills failing to eventuate, and the union of hearts at which he aimed would be known as such in so far as the wills of various subjects operated as if they were one will: 'To the extent that several men met together look on themselves as a single body, they have only one will.' *Contrat*, Book IV, ch. 1.

[3] Thus Plato in *The Laws* limits his city to 5040 families. Rousseau, too, sees no possibility of perfection except in small republics.

the original inhabitants, would spell disaster to the psychological harmony of the whole.[1] The same anxiety is the reason for the third corollary: it is dangerous to allow the entry into the city of beliefs and customs from outside, for these create a motley variety of reactions and practices.[2] The fourth corollary is that of immutability, and condemns as a source of discord the spirit of innovation in all its forms,[3] as introducing disharmonies.

These four corollaries, in short, condemn the whole historical process, which is marked by just those four things—the enlargement of societies, the aggregation of disparate peoples, the contagion of cultures and the burgeoning of novelties. They meet for that reason with the inevitable disapproval of every contemporary mind, whose weakness it is, rather, to think that the march of history cannot but be good. Yet it would be presumptuous to reject as absurd corollaries which, in the view of minds of this calibre, flowed logically from the main proposition, with which we too agree. By treating these views as worthy of consideration, at least we shall learn a greater comprehensiveness and tolerance in regard to certain social attitudes; everywhere the social observer encounters refusal on the part of whole communities to receive and admit what they do not want to receive and admit. So it is with the case of societies, styled unprogressive, who reject the innovations offered them by a different culture. Should we dare to assert that the vigorous intrusion, even when in peaceful guise, of our western culture on the other four continents has destroyed nothing of value possessed by the peoples who have experienced that intrusion? When we reflect on the harm we must have done, do we not the better understand the instinct of Japan in closing her gates till Perry forced an entrance? But more than that, does the expanding state itself take no corruption and were those Roman Senators so foolish who saw in imperialism the graveyard of the republican virtues? The views of Plato and

[1] Plato in *The Laws* seems to rule out any naturalisation of aliens: the services rendered by them to the State cannot avail them more than an extension of their permitted stay, which can never exceed twenty years (*Laws*, VIII, 850). Rousseau praises the discrimination against freedmen practised in Rome in the days of the Republic (*Du Contrat Social*, IV, 4): 'Throughout the period of the Republic there is no instance of one of these freedmen, although a citizen, becoming a magistrate. This was a good rule.'

[2] Plato did not want his ideal City to be on the sea, for this exposure to the outside world would cause much diversity and perversity of manners (*Laws*, IV, 704). Moreover, he carried exclusion to extreme lengths.

[3] Even musical innovations were condemned by Plato (*Laws*, III, 700 and 701). The poets were subjected to a censorship.

Rousseau may assist us to moderate our indignation against groups who resist the entrance into their circle of alien elements, as in the case of those Welsh miners who, notwithstanding the exhortations of a Labour government and their own trade union, refused to admit Italians into their midst. The variety of cases is great, but what is present in all of them is the same instinct to protect an inner harmony which is already there.

Those who regard the City as a circle of friends must, in fact, admit that every extension of that circle or every introduction into it of heterogeneous elements is bound to disturb the existing union of hearts, and poses the problem of its reconstitution; even though the act of extension or integration gives promise of a future good by an enlargement of the area of common loyalty, it may still cause present harm by the rupture of existing ties—as happens when some take sides for admission and others protest against it. Their reasons for favouring admission should not render its partisans blind to the possibility that the climate of trust prevailing in the narrow group may never be felt again with the same intensity after the group's enlargement. Those who feel attachment to common joys and sorrows, as a means of demonstrating and reviving feelings of fellowship, must surely recognise that the intensity of the common emotion is in inverse ratio to the size of the society. For a very small society a funeral is an occasion in common; for a very large society deaths are a matter of statistics, and occasions of common joy or sorrow become ever more rare. For that reason only transcendental ties of affection could hold the human race together in a world-wide society; Easter might do what Independence Day cannot.

It is the fourth corollary that shocks our contemporaries the most. Happily, it is the easiest to refute. Trustfulness within the group is not only a moral good in itself; it is also the condition of the various advantages which the members can confer on each other. And the beneficence of this trustfulness is shown in nothing more than in the fact that it makes possible the birth of new relationships; trustfulness is a sterile thing if it can be maintained only at the cost of suppressing the individual initiatives making for new relationships. These new relationships, properly regarded, are the offspring of a state of trustfulness. The opposite attitude to them is that of Saturn devouring his own offspring, and can be justified only by the assumption that the actual stuff of men's relationships is, like themselves, already all that it should be, and that the advantages which the members at present confer on each other do not admit of addition. It is significant that western philosophers have applied this doctrine of unchangeableness only to mythical States which their imaginations have projected sometimes on to the past and sometimes into the future.

The enlargements of the circle of friendship can be justified by the same reasoning.

THE PRISON OF THE COROLLARIES

Let us retrace our steps. We had arrived at a reasonably clear idea of the common good. We then came across the corollaries which could logically be deduced from it. These we found unacceptable. So we fought against them and, perhaps, beat them. But we have to admit that it is a Pyrrhic victory.

Consider the case of the magistrate whom we have told that the common good consists in the union of hearts and in mutual trustfulness between the citizens. This conviction opposes him to anything which introduces disturbance, and what he does, being aimed at preserving the common good, will be in line with the fourth corollary which we have been examining. And then, having got so far, we call a halt to his work of preservation, and we justify our change of front by the vision of the future benefits which may, for later generations perhaps, be born of possible new relationships. At that point the magistrate is entitled to turn on us and say:

You have utterly destroyed the principle of action which you said you were giving me. I can take account of the moral relationships in being. Nor do I find that the problem of their improvement is hopeless; conditions of trustfulness and friendship grow perfect by fulfilment of expectations, to the extent that each man's behaviour accords with what his fellows expect of him within the established scheme of ideas and morals. It is there that I find what it is my duty to preserve against any disturbing element; and now you tell me that I must take account of possible future benefits which may result from new behaviours and beliefs, thus destroying my certain principle of action and substituting an uncertain and anyhow different one.

There is no denying that the criterion given to our magistrate by which to evaluate a particular change and govern his attitude in regard to it loses all certainty if he has to envisage the future benefits which may result from it. To start with, the mind of man cannot work out whole chains of consequences. Its imperfection makes it impossible even when he knows what the consequences of an act will be—but here there is much of the contingent. But, further, even supposing that the magistrate knew what state of things would result from the introduction of the new element which he had to evaluate, at what point in the future must he place himself in imagination to draw up a profit and loss account of the results? Nor is that all: can the magistrate evaluate the good and evil consequences resulting to future generations by reference to his own scale of values, when that of the future generations may be different? And what can his competence be to lay down for future generations what is good for them, when we have allowed him none as regards the men of his own day, with whom he is at least acquainted?

But then, too, the argument by which we refuted the corollary of unchangeableness carries with it the implicit disavowal of the main proposition which we had made our own. Already we had seen that the political authorities would find themselves in the greatest difficulty if what they had to aim at maximising was the personal 'goods' of individuals. We had, to get them out of this difficulty, identified the common good with the social climate. And now surely it is obvious that, in order to justify disturbance of this climate, we have resumed the criterion of individual 'goods' (which we had rejected earlier), making our present test the sum of individual 'goods' which the innovation may cause.

We had in fact been too quick in thinking that we had made our escape from the 'prison of the corollaries'. What we feel now is that the overthrow of these four walls is bound to bring down the whole building. If it is true that the common good consists in moral cohesion and if it is the duty of the political authorities to preserve and increase this common good, they must make it their business to see that individuals answer more closely the expectations of their neighbours[1] and must put a stop to anything which tends to introduce surprising variations of behaviour. These variations are brought about by two causes: examples and suggestions. Therefore, all examples or suggestions which may tend to cause variations will incur disapproval, more or less as they are more or less likely to be followed—disapproval, that is to say, will be the greater the more

---

[1] By this is meant that they must each answer more closely to the 'social type' for which they stand in the eyes of their neighbours.

highly thought of are the persons inciting change. At the end of this line of reasoning lies the justification of Herod and Caiaphas! Confining ourselves, however, to secular events, we must certainly see in it justification for the accusation and condemnation of Socrates.[1]

So dangerous indeed is the logic immanent in this system of thought that the dream-state which Plato conceived in his reaction against Athens, condemner of Socrates, could have endured the presence of Socrates even less than Athens could! At Athens the condemnation of Socrates might not have happened; in the Platonic republic it was bound to occur.[2]

THE COMMON GOOD AND THE COLLECTIVE SOCIAL INTEREST

What has gone before brings out the dangers of equating the common good with social friendship. These dangers are just as great when reformers aim at imposing on society changes which will in their opinion promote the cause of social friendship as when conservatives aim at preventing changes which will in their opinion destroy social friendship: in either case a ban is imposed on whatever tends to disturb this friendship—a friendship which is in the one case already in being and in the other still to make. But what is beyond dispute is that all these dangers are linked with the absolute primacy conferred on the end which the political authorities must pursue and the citizens must, in so far as they take part in the government, keep in view, over the ends pursued by individuals. No less clear is it that these dangers are dissipated the moment that the roles on society's stage are shared between those with and those without official position.[3] When men, either as individuals or as

[1] This implies admission of the classical thesis that Socrates was prosecuted for undermining religious beliefs; but it is quite possible that the real reason for his prosecution by the victorious democratic party was his intellectual training of the Athenians who had collaborated with Sparta after Sparta's victory, even though his own conduct under their regime, that of the 'Thirty Tyrants', had been irreproachable.

[2] For a denunciation of the oppressive character of the institutions conceived by Plato, see my *Power*, Book III, ch. VII (Geneva, 1945; London, 1948). Almost simultaneously there appeared in London a work of vast erudition and great intellectual vigour by Professor Karl Popper, *The Open Society and its Enemies*. The ideas developed in the present chapter often join hands with those of Professor Popper's fine book.

[3] Or, in the case of direct democracy, between the different capacities of the same men acting now in an official and now in a private capacity—though this is something which it is easier to conceive than to realise.

groups, are free to pursue their own ends, the only function of the public authorities is to repair the damage which is continuously being done to public cohesion.

Social friendship and mutual trustfulness can be looked on as the essential framework, or the network of roads, which each member of society uses for his own ends, and tends to spoil by the use he makes of it. The task of the magistrate is to provide continuously for its repair and development. To use this office as a pretext for forbidding the use of the roads would be absurd. So we see that the difficulties we have come against arise from our not distinguishing the 'common good', for which the magistrates are responsible, from the 'collective social interest'.

If I ask myself the question in what the collective social interest of a society consists, I must envisage in answer the well-being of its members present and future under two aspects, their contentment and their perfection. Not that any real answer is possible; the most I can do is to give myself the illusion of answering by some vasty concept, whose fanatical devotee I shall thenceforward be. Be he philosopher or ruler, whoever claims to be the guardian of the collective social interest is a dangerous man. The highest legitimate aim that men can set themselves is to discover what basic conditions are necessary to the continued existence of a society and favourable to the advancement of the well-being of its members. The most obvious and time-honoured of those conditions is avoidance of destruction by some hostile grouping, of wasting away by the exhaustion of material resources, and of break-up by the dissolution of emotional ties. These are the basic conditions which constitute the least indeterminate part of the collective social interest; consequently they are the part which directs the magistrates most clearly to their duty and presents the smallest target for dissension in political debates. Political dissension, indeed, takes on a sharper edge with every extension of the area of public decision to things which respond more readily to subjective appreciation—things about which there is a natural clash between different preferences and interests, so that any common or commonly accepted decision in regard to them is not possible, but only the destruction of one interest or preference of another. Whereas bitterness is absent from debates if they relate to ends desired by all (and can be made so to appear) as being the necessary condition of and foundation for the various interests which rest and flourish on them.

Naturally, these primary ends, which are only the condition and bulwark of the general social interest, should not be taken for the whole of it, and should not necessarily prevail every time that other interests in society conflict with them. Only when and to the extent that they are in danger must they have pride of place. The margin of preference in favour of the common good grows abruptly whenever the whole social structure is in danger—a truth expressed by the maxim *Salus populi suprema lex*. In prosperous times, on the other hand, it may be foolish to prefer some further safeguarding of the common good to the free development of the various interests which form in society.

VARIETIES OF SOCIAL FRIENDSHIP

The notion of social friendship has dominated our discussion. But it has not been clarified—an omission which doubtless largely accounts for the difficulties encountered. Political thought is so deeply marked by its Greek teachers that it is natural for the mind to conceive of social friendship in the form in which the institutions of the Greek city tended to forge it. There everything worked together to create and maintain the greatest possible similarity between the citizens; this was most notably the case at Sparta, the most typical and the most unvarying Greek community—also, paradoxically enough, the one admired by philosophers of more progressive cities. The mill of an education received in common and the unceasing pressure of public opinion made and kept citizens true to the Spartan type, nonconformity to which was thought both ludicrous and culpable.

The attraction held by Sparta for some of the brightest spirits is hard to understand; posterity has generally accepted the theme of its admirers at Athens, which made every deviation from the Spartan type in other Greek cities—Athens especially—a mark of degeneracy and vice. Rousseau strongly adhered to this view. It was a natural consequence that the model of social friendship should be that of Sparta—that, in other words, the citizens must all be shaped in the same mould. This conception of social friendship directly conflicts with the development of the human personality. History is punctuated by the appearance of the mirage of the Spartan, always inspiring systematic attempts to organise conformity—attempts which wear a revolutionary mask. On each occasion, the minds that this mirage leads astray are all unconscious of the affinity between their doctrine and a routine-loving and ignorant conservatism. To listen to them is to institutionalise, for the benefit of whatever new routine they seek to impose, the urge to conformity which is endemic among the mass of men.

The older, wider and more ancient that a society is, the less reason is there to expect to find among its members the frequent repetition of a single type. The less, therefore, is social friendship able to rest on mere similarity. And every effort made to install or restore this similarity will inevitably be tyrannical. For this reason other foundations than similarity must be found for social friendship. Idolatry is a possible one. With every step that numbers and dissimilarity cause men to take away from natural unison, the more the love of one and the same entity may act as a bond, as, for instance, the personification of the fatherland. There is much less difference than is supposed between the national religions of Sumer and Assyria and modern nationalism; in each it is a case of personification of the whole, which becomes the object of a religious cult. It does not always happen that this idolatry invigorates social friendship, for some citizens, who have strong views on the way in which the national god requires serving, may come to hate their compatriots who serve the idol in some other way, whether from lukewarmness or from difference of outlook. National idolatry is particularly liable to sectarian dissension; many internal struggles owe their intensity much less to conflicting ambitions and interests than to the fanaticism imparted to them by contrasted visions of the national idol.

Social friendship is strengthened when all are aware of one and the same framework of loyalties—a framework built of the most complex materials, with as many small rituals as large symbols. The construction of this framework is effected by life in common, it derives from lessons and experiences which all have shared alike; what we are now speaking of may properly be called the culture of a people. But it is one thing to recognise its supreme importance, and quite another to formulate practical recommendations in regard to it. The magistrate, bound though he is to know the worth of this common culture, stands every chance of doing nothing but mischief whenever he aims at enriching or preserving it, for it is a thing too subtle for his competence. It is, in short, no use concluding that social friendship should, more than anything else, engage the attention of the magistrate, when we cannot formulate in the concrete any means open to magistrates for promoting this friendship. Nor is this matter for surprise, for it is something which must grow of itself by way of men's ordinary intercourse, always provided that the intercourse is so regulated that noxious activities are as far as possible restrained. By means of this regulation, which is the essential feature of the art of politics, mutual trustfulness grows apace among men, for now each is used to receiving from his fellows nothing but services, and possible injuries are restrained in advance. To bring this about is the office of the Law.

THE INEVITABLE DIVERSITY OF MEN

The wider and more developed a society is, the less can the climate of trustfulness (such as should always prevail among its members if they are to confer on each other all the benefits possible) be the fruit of a spirit of community; the widening of the circle and the growing diversity of personalities tend to destroy that spirit. For that reason the climate of trustfulness comes more and more to rest on the guarantees provided by the Law. I know nothing of Primus and am emotionally neutral in regard to him. No element of personal sympathy, no feeling of our belonging to each other will induce in him a certain course of conduct as regards me—only the abstract feeling of obligation as such. The different forms taken by this feeling will depend on what in general a man considers that he owes to another, on what he thinks his own honour and dignity require of him, on the prescriptions of positive law, and on opinion.

The word of Primus will, it is clear, be that much the more reliable if zeal on behalf of his neighbour is inspired in him by a universal religion, and if his explicit and implicit obligations are buttressed by a rigorous sense of social honour; also it is clear that clarity and precision in the Law, like everything else which earns it respect, will of themselves furnish social relations with the cement they need. But it has to be admitted that the guarantee of social relations in a very wide circle and a very advanced state of diversity can no longer be the intimate communion which prevails within a small group of people. The ultimate consequences of this are not always deduced.

It should, for instance, be taken as obvious that a circle of men will have more things in common the narrower and more homogeneous it is, and fewer things in common the more numerous and variegated it is. In the narrow circle of the family and household there are only a few things which it is thought necessary to label precisely as belonging to this or that member; there is no need to define in advance who shall at a given moment have the use of this or that tool or appliance, or to what use it shall be put. But the more numerous and disparate that a circle becomes, the more indispensable it is to lay down precisely whose each thing is and with whom in each case the power of decision rests. It becomes inadmissible to suppose that Secundus and Tertius will allow Primus the use of some given tool or appliance just when he needs it, or that they will be in agreement with him in all decisions concerning the allocation of resources to ends. It is important for this reason that the power to dispose and the power to decide should be exactly apportioned. If at any given moment a decision had to be reached as to the right shares in which to apportion all material wealth, then at that moment joint ownership would clearly be the prevailing rule; it is certain, as we have said, that joint ownership would give rise to discord, and disagreement is no less certain on the best way in which to divide up the property so held. It is in consequence vital that general share-outs of this kind should never occur and that everything should be looked on as already divided up, so that dispute only becomes possible on points of detail. This proposition is linked with the one we have already propounded, namely, that the general problem presented by any society does not, as such and in the round, admit of being grasped and solved; this we shall see later in the next chapter.

To wish to return to joint ownership of goods and joint taking of decisions in an advanced society is to aim at applying to it a primitive regime, which works well enough when a small tightly-knit group is content not to lay down precisely to whom each thing belongs and where decision rests. Such a regime is, however, no longer viable when the community's diversity of persons and their variety of conflicting aims make necessary the exact attribution of both things and decisions. The wish for such a return comes under the head of political infantilism; such infantilism is the mortal disease of advanced civilisations, where there is a constant nostalgia for the unity and simplicity of the very small societies for which, according to Bergson, man was intended and in which, until comparatively recent times, he has in any case lived.

THE NOSTALGIA FOR THE SMALL COMMUNITY

We are not here employing the didactic method. Our approach to the subject being that of explorer, not schoolmaster, we have advanced, and brought the reader along with us, rather after the manner of ants which, on meeting an obstacle, look all around for a way past; after a necessary deviation, they go on again in the old direction. What we were seeking was a clear conception of the common good, which might serve the magistrate as a criterion for judging whether a particular decision accorded with or was repugnant to it. Such a criterion would certainly be within our grasp if we had received a vision of the ideal social state, which it was a question of maintaining or creating. But beyond all question every vision of this kind is a disastrous thing, which leads its visionaries on to taking total charge of society so that they may mould it closely to their desire; therein is tyranny.

The very varied benefits which men can in course of time confer on one another by mutual intercourse do not resemble, as has been increasingly borne in on us, a convergent series of which the formula can be found, but a divergent series which cannot be totalled. And the common good has seemed to us to consist in conditions which make possible the development of this indefinite series. Trustfulness between partners struck us as the most obvious of these conditions. But at that point we ran into grave difficulties, just when we were enjoying the satisfaction of joining up with a classical theory.

What we have met with is a contradiction between, on the one hand, the growth of this state of trustfulness and, on the other, the indefinite development of the relations between men, the enlargement of the area which they cover and the diversification of their content. The contradiction is one, clearly, between the effects sought and the condition necessary to their achievement. This contradiction has become steadily clearer; the quest for the climate of trustfulness raises in the mind the picture of a closed, narrow circle of neighbours who are very much alike, who value highly a type which each strives to realise and who are very proud of a common denominator which all wish to maintain. This picture, nourished by two sources, strikes our minds with extraordinary vividness. One source is the classical tradition: the state which almost every Greek and most Latin writers in their turn commended to our admiration was Sparta. It is unnecessary here to recall how, or to ask why, the state whose institutions took the place of battlements became the object of unstinted eulogies,[1] even in Athens which was then its enemy. This 'Laconomania'[2] is met in Plato, Xenophon, Polybius, Plutarch and many others in the 'classical heritage', which in time came to inspire generations of lycée-trained young men; a man like Saint-Just is an obvious product of it.[3]

Political writers and active politicians on both sides, the revolutionary and the reactionary, show affinities in common, the mention of which produces violent irritation in them or their disciples; at the root of these affinities is the vision of Sparta which haunts them all equally.

But we said that there were two sources for the dream of a closed, narrow community. One, as we have seen, is the classical tradition; the other is the psychological requirements of Everyman, who feels a nostalgia for the tribe. No one now agrees with the opinion expressed by Rousseau, that the human species was 'better, wiser and happier under its primitive constitution; as it gets away from it it becomes blind, wretched and evil'.[4] But almost everyone subconsciously wishes to recover the warmth of the primitive group. Psychoanalysts tell us that the unconscious longing of man is for his mother's breast; whether that is true or not, it is certain that he longs unconsciously for the social breast at which he was formed, for the small, closely-knit society which was the school of the species. This unavowed regret is the root of nearly all utopias, both revolutionary and reactionary, and every political heresy, left or right.

Perhaps it is relevant at this point to introduce the myth of Antaeus. This mythological person recovered his strength on touching the soil. And in like manner man, on finding himself again in a small, closely-knit community, displays extraordinary vigour. Therein is a principle common to successes of most varied kinds: those of communist cells, those also of the English aristocracy educated at schools in which the Spartan tradition lingers.

---

[1] A most important book on this subject, which has received insufficient attention, is: *Le Mirage Spartiate. Etude sur l'Idéalisation de Sparta dans l'Antiquité grecque de l'Origine jusqu'aux Cyniques*, by F. Ollier (Paris, 1933). It throws a vivid light on the climate of opinion in Athens at the time of the Peloponnesian War.

[2] The word comes from Aristophanes: 'All the men were "Laconomanes", let their hair grow long, endured hunger, did not wash, did as Socrates did, carried clubs...', quoted by Ollier, *op. cit.*, p. 211.

[3] Stendhal bears marked traces of it.

[4] *Rousseau Juge de Jean-Jacques*. Third dialogue.

We are thus driven to three conclusions. The first is that the small society, as the milieu in which man is first found, retains for him an infinite attraction; the next, that he undoubtedly goes to it to renew his strength; but, the last, that any attempt to graft the same features on a large society is utopian[1] and leads to tyranny. With that admitted, it is clear that as social relations become wider and more various, the common good conceived as reciprocal trustfulness cannot be sought in methods which the model of a small, closed society inspires; such a model is, on the contrary, entirely misleading.

CLOSED SOCIETY AND OPEN SOCIAL NETWORK

These conclusions[2] could have been foreseen. At an early stage in the course of this inquiry we contrasted two schemes of social relations. We had conceived imaginary dashes starting from Primus, to represent all his contacts of whatever kind with other individuals whom, by reason of their contacts with Primus, we called 'neighbours' of Primus. We then conceived other dashes starting from each of these neighbours of Primus, to represent their contacts of whatever kind, and still others starting from the neighbours in the second degree and so on. And we distinguished two possible cases: with the repetition of this process, either the same people tend more than ever to reappear—which marks a closed society—or fresh people are always appearing—which marks an open social network. Let us make the arbitrary assumption that each person has one hundred 'neighbours' in our meaning of the word. At the third degree of my operation, when the neighbours of the neighbours of my neighbours come in, I shall have reached one million contacts; but these contacts may relate either to no more than one thousand people (the case of the closed society) or to many more than one hundred thousand (the case of an open social network). The operation may be complicated and the contrast accentuated by observing the result at several different epochs, in which case the total number of persons covered will remain stable in the case of the closed society, but will rise in the case of the open social network.

[1] In this respect Rousseau displayed a wisdom which his disciples missed: 'His object could not be to recall populous countries and large states to their primitive simplicity, but only to check, if possible, the progress of those whom smallness and situation had preserved from the same headlong rush to the perfection of society and the deterioration of the species.' *Ibid.*

[2] As my awareness of them increased, I realised more fully the force of a work of Bergson, *Les deux Sources de la Morale et de la Religion* (1932).

It becomes clear at once that the situation of Primus is entirely different according to whether he finds himself in a closed society or in an open network. In the first case, because he and his fellows are closely linked together, his actions are known to and discussed by all the others; he lives surrounded by a stable and coherent circle of judges whose good opinion he must earn. This circle, moreover, powerfully suggests to him how he must act as regards each. In this way each individual relation which he has with one of his fellows takes on the character of a relation with the entire circle. Since all his relations lie within that circle, the circle takes on a vital importance in the eyes of Primus; he could not exist outside this milieu.

In a situation like this there is clearly no need to look for the means by which the authorities will have to maintain the regularity of behaviour and the climate of trustfulness. They will be maintained automatically and the difficulty of the authorities will be, rather, as to what they will do to protect, if it appears, nonconformist behaviour (whether good or bad in the eyes of an independent observer) against the violent disapproval of public opinion. By reason of the stability natural to a society of that kind, it may happen that originality in valuable forms can find an entrance only because the authorities wink at it; in that case corruption and progress will appear together, thereby enabling future writers, among whom are Tacitus and Rousseau, to denounce as decadence the conditions from which they sprang.

In an open network the situation of Primus is quite different. His relations with an outsider (whom we will call Alienigenus) interest none of the other persons with whom he has relations, whether habitual or occasional; and these persons themselves are not closely linked. Thus public opinion puts no pressure on Primus as to the use which he makes of his relations with Alienigenus, for no one knows of them. Moreover, Alienigenus may offer no sensible reality to Primus; he may be a name to him and nothing more. Therefore the conduct of Primus on this occasion will have to depend on his own moral sense, which cannot here be the mere reflection of tribal opinion, and on the guarantees furnished by the Law.

But that is not all. The man whose situation was in a closed network had a clear and concrete idea of the society to which he belonged. It was the well-defined microcosm within which all his relations with others occurred. Not to love the microcosm would be not to love the conditions which made possible his own life. Let us now put Primus back in an open network; the society to which he belongs becomes at once an abstract and indefinite idea. The whole of the Spartan society could be seen at its banquets: we could not so see our 'society' and could not even say what the word specifically means. Do we mean French, European or western society? It is impossible to indicate with precision what it includes or how far it extends. In an open network, the relations maintained by Primus with individuals very different from himself do not link up in his mind under the common denominator of 'relations with society'. Another characteristic of our contemporaries which we may notice is a tendency to classify as 'personal relations' those which please them and convey an emotional warmth, and as 'social relations' any which they dislike and find a burden. It is often said nowadays: 'I cannot dine with friends. I have a social engagement.' Thus 'social relations' means for us the unpleasing remnant of the complex of relations from which the pleasing ones have been extracted. For this reason society affects us as a burden, even when it is in reality carrying us.

Thus seen as something heavy and indeterminate, lacking all bodily and visible shape, society may, as with the romantics, be an object of malediction, or may, as with the moderns, be something which owes us a return for its many claims on us. But it leaves in any case no sensible impression on our minds and is not loved; so much is this the case that socialists everywhere have necessarily had to dress it in national costumes. Hence it follows that the conditions necessary to social development do not rouse the mind spontaneously and touch no sensibilities, and that in any large society the common good does not greatly interest more than quite a small part of its members. That is not due to mere egocentricity on the part of the other members; they are on the contrary capable of great devotion to narrower wholes which are more coherent and more tangible.

Our epoch is like Lot's wife. It looks back in time toward certain forms of social life amid which man took on his present aspect; the development of a world-wide social network is a prodigious adventure which cannot but bring grave disappointments in its train. From every side, and under the most diverse banners, the signal has gone forth for a return to the tribal ways of life. Possibly the world-wide adventure will fail, but it is folly not to recognise that in it is progress.

CHAPTER 9

JUSTICE

In every age justice has been called the keystone of the social edifice. By acting towards each other justly, the citizens maintain the condition of trustfulness and friendship which is the basis of an unforced and fruitful co-operation; by acting with justice towards each and all, the public authority wins the confidence and respect which render it effective. Authority finds in its justice, taken as a whole, the end and the means of its activity. The sceptre and the sword of justice are the traditional attributes, closely associated, of the monarch; to be just—to resist the pressures which would cause him to give unjust decisions—he must be strong, and his justice increases his credit, whence he draws his strength.

Preoccupation with justice is, therefore, the political preoccupation *par excellence* and it is no bad thing that 'social justice' should be the obsession of our time. To all appearances, however, it acts as a principle not of concord but of discord. Intellectuals speak of 'realising' or 'winning' it and political groups fight each other for the honour of leading this crusade; for the enterprise is conceived as a struggle against forces hostile to a species of justice the precise nature of which its champions do not doubt. Unfortunately, not all see it alike. Hence comes the spectacle of society splitting and crumbling in the name of the justice which should harmonise it and cause peace to reign.

OF WHAT OR OF WHOM IS JUSTICE THE ATTRIBUTE?

The classical definitions all attest that the place where justice dwells —or should dwell—is the hearts of men. So say the Institutes of Justinian: 'Justice is a firm and unceasing determination to render to every man his due.'[1] Here, then, justice appears as a matter of will. Saint Thomas Aquinas goes a step further: 'Justice is a habit of mind which maintains in us a firm and unceasing determination

---

[1] *Divi Justiniani Institutionum Liber Primus*, first heading: 'Justitia est constans et perpetua voluntas jus suum cuique tribuere.'

to render to every man his due.'[1] So he links up with Aristotle, for whom 'justice is that quality in virtue of which a man is said to be disposed to do by deliberate choice that which is just, when distributing things between himself and another, or between two others'.[2]

Thus justice is conceived as a human attitude of mind which habit strengthens—a virtue. But when people talk of justice today they no longer mean this virtue of the soul, but a state of things. The word no longer conveys to the mind a certain human attribute but a certain configuration of society; it is no longer applied to certain personal attitudes of mind but envisages certain collective arrangements. Whereas it used to be thought that social relationships are improved by justice in men, it is now thought, contrariwise, that the installation in institutions of a state of things called just promotes the improvement of men. This reversal is in the fashion of thought today, which makes morality the creature of circumstance.

We see then that justice today is not a habit of mind which each of us can acquire in proportion to his virtue and should acquire in proportion to his power; rather it is an organisation or arrangement of things. For this reason the first part of the classical definitions, which links justice with the human being, no longer finds a place in modern preoccupations which link justice with society. People no longer say with Aristotle that justice is the moral attitude of the just man, or with the jurists that it is a certain exercise of the will, for these talk of an intimate quality of the soul. The justice now recommended is a quality not of a man and a man's actions, but of a certain configuration of things in social geometry, no matter by what means it is brought about. Justice is now something which exists independently of just men.

Men now seek to establish 'the thing which is just', and it is supposed that the difficulty of doing so is entirely in the execution; no doubts are felt that this conception of the just thing is the true one. Yet very different conceptions of it are possible, and that is why the sages of old treated it as a mental state of moral agents, rather than as an arrangement of things of which the secret was available. In speaking of this arrangement, we must be quite clear what we mean by it: what is the arrangement that can be called just? Let us

---

[1] *Summa Theologica*, Quaestio LVIII, De Justitia: 'Justitia est habitus secundum quem aliquis constanti et perpetua voluntate jus suum unicuique tribuit.'
[2] *Nicomachean Ethics*, Book V, 1134a.

see if the classical definition can help us here, if we drop its relation to man and concentrate on what it tells us about the thing which is just—on, that is to say, 'tribuere jus suum cuique' or 'reddere jus suum cuique'. Anyone determined to see in justice only a state of things may make it consist in the 'suum cuique'; but then the question has to be faced, 'What is this *suum*?' Different answers to this question are possible.

FIRST CONCEPTION OF JUSTICE: RESPECT FOR RIGHTS

The simplest conception of the *suum* is that suggested by the verb *reddere* with which we find it habitually associated; the verb carries the idea of restitution, or restoration: 'If thou meet thine enemy's ox or his ass going astray, thou shalt surely bring it back to him again.'[1] The 'his' which must be rendered to each is, essentially, something which he already had and of which he found himself deprived without just cause.

Justice here appears in the character of preserver or restorer. The dative is determined by the genitive and the ablative: 'this is Peter's, it has been taken from Peter, give it to Peter.' It is a currency which bears the image and superscription of Caesar and comes from his mints: *Redde Caesari*. Justice of this kind may be divided into three parts. It is unjust to assault Peter with a view to taking from him what is his, and it is unjust to covet what is his: 'Thou shalt not covet thy neighbour's house, thou shalt not covet thy neighbour's wife, nor his manservant, nor his maidservant, nor his ox, nor his ass, nor any thing that is thy neighbour's.'[2] It is just to defend what is Peter's against another's aggression, and it is just to restore to him what he has lost. Under this aspect justice appears as an active respect for what belongs to another. We may note in this connection that 'the defence of the widow and fatherless' was understood in former times not as the attribution to them, as widows and orphans, of any new rights, but as an intervention to uphold whatever rights they had already—rights which their weakness made them incompetent to defend by themselves.

This preservative conception of justice was that which was incorporated first in the Covenant of the League of Nations and afterwards in the Charter of the United Nations. These sought to guarantee to each nation, the weak as well as the strong, the tranquil

---

[1] Exodus xxiii. 4.   [2] Exodus xx. 17.

enjoyment of what each had; this was to be achieved by moral condemnation of aggression and by laying on the associated nations the duty of intervening to maintain the nation attacked in possession of what was in dispute, or, if it was taken by force, to restore it.

Justice, then, makes its first appearance as preserver and restorer. Its preservative function is accomplished out of sight by means of its restorative activity. Every time that it puts back landmarks and punishes the act which removed or displaced them, all existing landmarks are made more secure thereby. Thereby it upholds the fundamental condition of social co-operation. The increasing benefits which men derive from the ever more intricate intersection of their activities are completely dependent on mutual confidence and the reliance of each upon the respect of all others for his stated rights. Whoever boldly invades such rights not only offends against his victim but against the general value of mutual confidence. While the preservation of this mutual confidence must rest primarily on moral education, its ultimate warden is the public authority, which never fails more fundamentally in its duty to society than when it is lax to repair the torts which injure mutual confidence. It is, therefore, obvious that any indulgence shown to aggression against rights is a breach of mutual confidence, is an act or feeling directed against society as a whole.

PRESTIGE OF THE PRESERVATIVE NOTION

The notion that justice consists in the upholding of existing rights finds little favour with our time, which considers that it is to be found in the creation of new rights. But what new rights will be just? If each man's existing rights are recognised as a criterion of justice, what is the criterion to be when it comes to creating rights? Awareness of this difficulty shows itself in the form habitually taken by demands for rights.

Throughout the *ancien régime*, the new demands which were proposed for acceptance were presented in the guise of 'restorations of ancient rights, franchises and privileges'. When men desired to change the French constitution, they made reference to the mythical constitutions of Pharamond,[1] mythical himself. And even today

---

[1] Pharamond is supposed to have been the Frankish chieftain who became the first Merovingian king about A.D. 415. He certainly never reigned, and possibly never existed.

demands for new rights are styled 'claims', a word which, in the phrase 'statements of claim', denotes actions in law for the recovery of something which was yours and has been taken from you.

The most daring innovators instinctively use the past as a criterion and present their demands as the re-establishment of what has already been. This instinct sometimes leads to odd results, as in the case of the prophets of communism—evolutionists, all of them, who hold that man has emerged from the animal state to that of conscious co-operation, and have yet thought to make their advocacy of communism more effective by attempts to prove that it had been the primitive way of life. Mental approaches of this kind are evidence for the fact that unconscious search is always made for the reinforcement which comes from presenting a demand as a 'claim' in the true sense. It springs from the deep conviction that the way to get something accepted now is to be able to represent it as having existed in the past, and that acceptance of an inauguration of new rights will be that much the readier the more successfully it can be represented as a restoration of a past state of things.

If there is no known precedent for what is sought, recourse can be had to pre-history. The invention of a 'state of nature' on which to base claims was the great resource of the eighteenth-century writers; the notion of a primitive order to which return must be made—the secular exploitation of the religious conception of the Fall—lacks all positive authority in the spheres to which it is applied.

We have just been observing a very general tendency to present demands for rights in the form of 'claims'. The reason for it is the great difficulty found in defining the just as soon as the customary is no longer available as a criterion. The notion of maintaining as it is what is established or earmarked is a clear one. It is just to respect rights and just to safeguard them. These rights are those which are in force. To do justice in this sense is to maintain in being. So ran the royal oath: 'As for me, I will, so far as I know and can, God helping me, honour and safeguard each one of you, according to his rank and dignity; and I will preserve him safeguarded from all mischief, whether hurt or deception; and I will maintain for each the law and justice which pertain to him.'[1]

Nothing is more necessary to intercourse between men than the justice which preserves—which asks no other title for what is than that it has been. But, it is certain, this is not the justice at which

---

[1] Quoted in May, *Maximes du droit public français* (Amsterdam, 1775), vol. I.

innovators aim. The justice of their seeking is a more perfect kind, in which rights are founded, not on long possession, but on reason. The difficulties involved lead to a search for support in the 'conservative' fiction: let us see what these difficulties are.

SECOND CONCEPTION OF JUSTICE: THE PERFECT ORDER

Today, reasoning on justice is focused on the distribution of rights, the existing distribution being thought unjust. But how, on our argument so far, can any given distribution of rights be assessed in terms of its justice? If justice exclusively consists in preserving established rights or restoring them as against the aggressor, such an assessment is impossible. Today, however, this is not the model on which justice is conceived; injustice consists not only in the neglect or invasion of existing rights but also in their existing distribution. What is now sought is, in short, an order which is just absolutely. But now comes the problem: how can we tell what order is just absolutely? In this second conception of justice, as in the first, what is involved is a conformity. In the first, justice was what conformed with the existing order, which was the touchstone; in the second, the existing order is just or unjust according as it conforms or fails to conform with a model entertained in the mind. In other words, the existing order will be called unjust in so far as it falls short of the vision of a just order which haunts our spirit and has become our touchstone.

There is no obscurity about our second meaning of the word 'just'. It is a question of adjusting what is to what it is considered ought to be. Thus, for everyone to know what the just is, two conditions only must be fulfilled: that the same scheme of what should be is present in the minds of all, and that what is should be seen by all in the same colours. In that event the changes which must be effected in the existing order to realise the ideal order will have received perfect definition.

Unfortunately, opinions differ both as to how what is should be viewed and as to the merits of the scheme of what should be. If rights are regarded not as already assigned but as still available for perfect distribution, it is impossible to expect unanimity on their next assignment, for different minds entertain different models of the ideal order. The sense of justice bids each one of us change the existing order that it may conform with the just order. But the just order is not identical for all minds, and any presumed identity, so long as we confine ourselves to generalities, dissolves when it comes to application. For this reason, agreement to discard the existing order for a just order is an agreement in words only, for our agreement on movement towards the just order implies no agreement as to wherein this just order consists. All we are agreed on is the need to change—not the goal. The past is repudiated as a criterion and there is no agreement as to what to put in its place. It is something which Montaigne notes time and again: 'It is easy to bring the charge of imperfection against a polity, for all mortal things are full of imperfection; it is easy to engender in a people contempt for its ancient usages—no one ever attempted it who did not succeed; but to establish there a better order in place of the one destroyed is a task in which many of those undertaking it have failed dismally.'[1]

Pascal, too, is sceptical and couches his scepticism in much more positive form: 'Justice is what is established; and so all our established laws must necessarily be accepted as just without examination, because they are established.'[2] Beyond that, agreement is impossible: 'Justice is subject to disputes.'[3] 'The art of factious opposition and revolution is the disturbance of established customs, exploring them to their source in order to bring to light their defect of justice. We must, they say, return to the fundamental and primitive laws of the state, abolished by an unjust custom. That is a game leading straight to ruin; the scales are quite untrustworthy.'[4] Pascal leaves no doubt as to his meaning: 'If we follow reason alone, nothing is just in itself; everything changes with time.'[5]

Even though nothing is just in itself, it does not follow—and let us note this—that an individual or a ruler cannot act justly. The virtue of justice is not hit by this scepticism; but the idea of a particular order incarnating justice is hit hard. The authority of Pascal avails to dissipate the illusion that the just order comes naturally to the mind. But we are not bound to concede to him that justice is undiscoverable, though we will admit that it must be sought. For many of our contemporaries it will be a discovery indeed.

---

[1] Montaigne, *Essais*, Book XI, ch. 17 (ed. Hachette, 1951).
[2] *Pensées*, art. VI, pensée 6 (ed. Havet), p. 73.   [3] *Idem*, pensée 8.
[4] *Pensées*, art. III, pensée 8.   [5] *Ibid.*

SHOULD JUSTICE BE IDENTIFIED WITH OTHER QUALITIES
OF SOCIAL ARRANGEMENTS?

If justice is a quality which we look for in social arrangements, and if we find it difficult to form a clear idea of it, it is very tempting to identify it with other good features of social arrangements—features of which it is easy to form a clear picture.

For instance, are there not among the various social configurations some which present a natural stability, so that a configuration of this kind tends to reassemble of its own accord on any attempt to pull it apart? We see in it a condition of stable equilibrium. Having this property, it is, other things being equal, certainly preferable to a configuration which is without it. If we forbid ourselves to choose among arrangements based, each of them, on subjective preferences, we may ascribe an objective superiority to an arrangement having the property of stability, and we may be tempted to say that such a configuration is 'just'. But its quality is in fact sufficiently denoted by the word 'stability', and there is neither rhyme nor reason in making the word 'justice' play the part of a useless synonym.

Yet another conception of justice can be put forward; it too is objective in character, though its objectivity is merely instrumental and conditional. Provided that we have an idea as to what the good of a whole is, that internal configuration will be the best which will carry the whole to the fullest achievement of its particular good. Take, for example, the case of an army as to whose end, victory, there is no dispute; the configuration which fits it best for realising its end is the best for it. The realisation and the maintenance (or the restoration) of this configuration or shape should be the desire of anyone aiming to promote the good peculiar to this particular whole, and this desire is a manifestation of the virtue of justice in relation to the given whole and its pre-determined end. But, all the same, what the man serving this whole and this end will desire—and rightly desire in his capacity as their servant—may be deemed unjust by one who is not their servant, or by one who, in his capacity as servant of this whole, does not see clearly what is necessary to its end.

It may happen, for instance, that a general employs severity against insubordinate elements, thereby serving the cause of victory, and that his conduct may then be deemed unjust either through ignorance of its necessity in relation to the end pursued or through indifference to this end—these being, of course, two very different cases, of which the second is much the most interesting. If the justification of an act lies in its power to steer a given whole to a given end, the acceptance of these data creates, it is clear, the frame of reference within which those who would appraise the justice of the act must place themselves. Judge the act from within another frame of reference and its justice may be denied, because, for instance, the critic is thinking of the soldiers not as members of an army whose business it is to win or be in good shape to win, but as mainstays of a family. The conclusion is that appraisals of justice are most unlikely to coincide, unless they are founded on a feeling of belonging together for a common purpose.

JUSTICE AS MERE CONFORMITY TO THE RULE LAID DOWN

Many authors have considered that all pursuit of the just outside the sphere of positive law is a vain thing. Just, in their view, is what conforms to the published rule, unjust is what does not. The rule is the criterion of the just and the unjust, and the criterion itself defies measurement. A rule cannot be called just or unjust, for to decide the point there must be something to measure it against.

This intellectual standpoint may have quite different consequences, according as it is adopted by theologians and accepted by believers, or as it is applied by philosophers and jurists who are not believers. Let us examine the two cases in turn. All theologians agree in saying: 'Just is what accords with the commandments of God, unjust is what is contrary to them.' But whereas some think that what is commanded by God is just because God's will has made it just, others consider that God commands it because it is just. For the latter, the just is older than any command, even God's; for the former, only the will of God gives it meaning. On the second view God's commandments are not confined to giving us knowledge of good and evil, but determine, what was till then indefinite, what good and evil are to be. These decrees of his He can issue as He pleases, and their purport might as easily have been to bid us do what is forbidden and to forbid us do what is bidden; in the precepts of the Omnipotent there is no element of necessity, for there is nothing to bind Him who binds everything. We see, then, that theology makes room for two points of view, the contrast between which has been clearly expressed by Leibniz; on either view God commands what is just, but on the first view something has been commanded because it is just, and on the second it is just because it has been commanded. Both points of view have been maintained in their time by Doctors of the Church, but the Christian point of view *par excellence* is certainly the first one,[1] whereas in Islam the second prevails.[2]

In a society of believers which is religious through and through, the general idea that justice is conformity with the rule laid down will shape, necessarily and unequivocally, the positive laws stemming from the divine commandments—the laws will receive an induced respect from the commandments. But the same idea will have very different results in an unbelieving society, or one in which social life has been secularised to its roots. If justice is no more than conformity with the rules, there will be no place in the social order for discussing the justice of the rules. Just as a religious society conceives morality as obedience to the rules laid down by the Omnipotent in the plenitude of His power, so in a secularised society morality must be conceived as obedience to the rules laid down by the prince of this world in the plenitude of his sovereignty. But in the latter case, instead of the just being unchanging and surely ascertainable by the exercise of casuistry on the divine decrees, it will be infinitely variable at the good pleasure of the sovereign introducing changes into it. This was the thesis maintained by Hobbes and criticised by Leibniz.[3] This is not the place to expatiate on so large a subject, which is not the one under consideration here; our purpose is only to emphasise the fact that there are high authorities for the proposition that anyone saying that 'some rule

---

[1] Cf. the discussion by Bayle in 'Réponse aux questions d'un Provincial', *Opera*, vol. 3, pp. 408–9, and in Gierke, *Les Théories Politiques du Moyen Age* (ed. Jean de Pange), pp. 229–31. Cf. also the important work of Georges de Lagarde, *La Naissance de l'Esprit Laïque au Moyen Age*, 6 vols. *passim*.

[2] Or so I understand.

[3] 'The justice of God, says Mr Hobbes, is merely the power which he has and exercises of bestowing blessings and misfortunes. This definition surprises me; it is not in the power of bestowing them but in the will to bestow them reasonably,—in, that is to say, goodness guided by reason, that the justice of God consists. But, says he, justice is not with God what it is with man, who is made just only by observance of the laws made by his superior. Mr Hobbes is wrong there too, as is Mr Pufendorf who has followed him. Justice turns not on the arbitrary laws of superiors, but on the eternal ordinances of wisdom and goodness, in men as much as in God.' Leibniz, *Essais de Theodicée: Réflexions sur l'Ouvrage de M. Hobbes*.

or other is unjust' is talking nonsense, the reason being that the rule itself is the only criterion of justice.

Yet it is an observable fact that every day of the year men direct criticism at the existing rules, which they tax with injustice. The answer made by contemporaries is that men call unjust the rules which they dislike, that what they represent as just is what suits them, that 'just' is the high-sounding title which they give to their preferences, and that their notions of the just are as various as their preferences. From this it is concluded that the search for justice is the pursuit of a will-of-the-wisp, with each man calling just whatever happens to attract him.

THE FEELING FOR THE JUST

But before we conclude, as modern positivists invite us to do, that the word 'just' is merely a term of approval applied by each man as suits his taste, we must examine whether there is nothing in common to be found between the various opinions held of the just. To bring home to us the ambiguity surrounding the just, an ingenious author points out that a fiscal measure may be called just in so far as it places the burden of tax on those who are at the moment best able to support it, but unjust in that it penalises those who have in the past been energetic and thrifty.[1] Now is it not evident that we have here two evaluations of the same measure by a single operation of the mind, applying itself to different aspects? On the one hand, unequal incomes in the present should, it is considered, support unequal burdens; on the other, unequal efforts in the past should ensure unequal results in the present. Always it is a case of ensuring the equality of proportion of one thing to another.

If there is no agreement among men as to what is just, at any rate the ways in which different minds work when it comes to appraising justice in a particular aspect are identical. What they find just is to preserve between men as regards whatever is in question the same relative positions as exist between the same men as regards something else. One man says that the wage of Primus should be half as much again as that of Secundus, because Primus does that much more work; another man says that the wage of Secundus should be half as much again as that of Primus, because Secundus has to feed a family larger by half than that of Primus. So far as the solution is

---

[1] T. D. Weldon, *The Vocabulary of Politics* (London, 1953), p. 29.

concerned, the opinions of our two advisers, call them Black and White, are diametrically opposite. Out of a total wage of 250, Black would give 150 to Primus and 100 to Secundus, White would give 100 to Primus and 150 to Secundus. Black and White certainly do not see eye to eye; but can we fail to note that Black and White have used exactly the same mode of reasoning, though their starting points are different properties in the persons compared? Let us call in a third adviser—call him Red; he may argue that Primus and Secundus should receive precisely the same wage, because he has considered them under some aspect in which they are demonstrably equal, as, for instance, their having worked the same number of hours. The disagreement between Black, White and Red is a disagreement as to what solution is just, but it is important to stress that their common manner of reasoning implies that the sense of justice is in fact the same in all three advisers.

Let us represent Primus and Secundus as two points in space, situated by reference to three axes; on one of these axes is set the work accomplished, on the second, family requirements, on the third, hours worked. The relative positions of Primus and Secundus will be differently ranged on each of these axes, and anyone who measures the rewards due to them by reference to their positions on one axis only, just though he may aim at being, will seem unjust to anyone measuring on another axis.

It will be noted that the concept of equality, which plays a basic but far from simple role in the appreciation of justice, enters into all three judgments. It seems worth our while to labour the point. A total payment of 250 is to be divided between Primus (40 hours of work, two mouths in the family, 150 units produced) and Secundus (40 hours of work, three mouths in the family, 100 units produced). Of the total payment of 250, 150 should go to Primus, says Black, only 100, says White, 125, says Red. It is immediately clear that if the Red solution is chosen (i.e. 125 paid to each), it must offend equality in the eyes of Black because Primus is paid only 0·83 per unit produced while Secundus is paid 1·25 per unit produced. But also it must offend equality in the eyes of White because the Primus family obtains a payment of 62·5 per mouth and the Secundus family a payment of only 41·7 per mouth. In the same manner, the Black and the White solutions must each seem inequitable to the two other judges. Black's solution will displease Red because Primus is to be paid 1·5 times as much per hour of work as Secundus, and will scandalise White because the Primus family will obtain 0·75 per mouth as against 0·33 per mouth in the case of the Secundus family. White's solution (100 to Primus, 150 to Secundus) will result in rewarding Primus one-third less than Secundus per hour worked, and per unit produced less than one-half as much.

The identical aim of all our three disputants is to treat equal things equally and proportional things proportionally; only the proportions which serve as starting-points are different for each of them. Light has been thus thrown on the relations between equality and justice; justice, as Aristotle said, is an equality of proportions. Every allocation of reward which is, as it must be to be just, founded on equality under a certain aspect, will be hierarchical and contrary to equality under another aspect. Take a very simple example; the case of a man with orders to spread among different factories with very different capacities. If he shares them out equally, the time of the factories will be the less taken up by the orders the more important that the factories are, and the factories will from this angle have been treated unequally; if on the other hand he shares out the orders in proportion to each factory's capacity, this division of them, though aiming at equality, will be unequal. Complications may be introduced into the problem. Unequal in capacity, the factories were, before the orders were given, in a state of unequal activity by reason of other orders; does justice demand that the new orders should bring them all to a state of equal activity, or will doing so penalise unjustly those which had by their own efforts made themselves busier?

Justice is thus seen to be as simple in principle as it is varied in application. A simple algebraic analogy will perhaps make the point clearer. Let us postulate points in a multi-dimensional space. Each of these points is distinguished by its own set of co-ordinates, and there are as many co-ordinates as there are dimensions. The problem now set us is to project these points on to a single vector in such a way as to preserve the relations existing between them in the multi-dimensional space. To this problem there are an infinite number of possible solutions. We may, to start with, arrange the points on the vector according to the values of one of the co-ordinates affecting them—an arrangement which produces as many solutions as there are dimensions in the space in question. These are the simpler solutions, each of which neglects all but one of the co-ordinates with which our points are endowed. But all the co-ordinates may more plausibly be taken into account. In order, however, to combine the several or many co-ordinates which together fully characterise one point into a single value for this point, we must use a set of 'weights', or parameters. The single value will be the sum of the co-ordinates each multiplied by the specific parameter we shall have seen fit to assign to it; provided we apply to each set of co-ordinates of each point the same set of weights or parameters, our single values will be comparable. But, quite obviously, the adoption of the same set of weights is arbitrary, and, as different minds use different sets of weights, the single values arrived at will be different.

Each solution offered will be an answer to the problem set, but each will be different from the rest and none will be more valid than another in terms of the problem. For there to be one, and only one valid solution, we must be told at the start one of two things: either that classification is to be based throughout on a single specified co-ordinate or on a combination of specified co-ordinates by means of a specified set of parameters or weights.

As the single values of these points in space can stand in innumerable different orders, according to the co-ordinate or the weighted combination of co-ordinates retained for their ordering, so also it is with men, who can be regarded under a great many different aspects and present under each aspect different relations of inequality. It is, therefore, impossible to classify these different relations unless it is stipulated either that only one aspect or a specified combination of specified aspects is considered. Only if such a condition is made can a definite classification be achieved; but this classification is not valid absolutely, it is valid only in relation to the particular criterion applied. Change the criterion, the classification changes. Take the example of a competitive examination: it cannot be said that it selects the best men absolutely, but only those who do best at a given set of tasks; these tasks, which have different values assigned to them, furnish each single man with a general co-ordinate which makes classification possible. But the classification produced by the competition is not the only one possible; there is an infinity of possible ones to be had by varying the tasks themselves and the value to be assigned to each. All that the defenders of the competitive test say for it is that the classification obtained thereby is the most relevant to their particular purposes.

THE NOTION OF RELEVANCE

Suppose that I am a millionaire and that I have the benevolent idea of establishing a fund to enable young people to visit the picture-galleries of Italy. Suppose further that I lay down the following criterion for choosing fifty annual beneficiaries: the committee of selection must choose the applicants with the fairest heads of hair. This being the rule laid down by me, the donor, the members of the committee will have to arrange the applicants by degrees of blondness; they will be just if they follow this rule exactly, they will be unjust if they depart from it (so that a less blond man is admitted into the annual contingent to the exclusion of a more blond man). Yet everyone will concur in saying that the rule which they are applying is an absurd one; the journey to Italy can be looked on as a reward for merit, but what merit is there in being blond? Or, more plausibly perhaps, the journey to Italy can be looked on as a means of cultural advancement which should be awarded to those who will derive most profit from it; but blondness indicates nothing as to artistic or cultural propensities. Thus the criterion which I have laid down is not a relevant one.

This notion of relevance is fundamental to all problems of justice. If I have to effect a distribution of something among a series of individuals, I must, if I am to be just, found my classification and proportions on the serial order of these individuals in another plane; this serial order is my standard of reference. And if my final share-out does not conform to the serial order of reference, I show myself unjust. But, in addition, the serial order which I make my standard of reference must be relevant to the final share-out. If, for instance, it is a case of leaving my goods at death and I take as my standard for their share-out the serial order of degrees of relationship with myself, this standard of reference will be thought relevant; but if, as head of a government, I take the serial order of degrees of relationship as my standard for nominating to high office, my choice will be thought scandalous, because the standard of reference is irrelevant for the purpose.

There is injustice whenever the mind is scandalised by false proportions—a thing which happens either when the serial order laid down is not respected or when that serial order is clearly irrelevant. Let us take a concrete case. An industrialist, compelled by a falling off in orders to discharge several members of his staff, dismisses not the most recently engaged but those who are the least useful to him in his business; this choice may seem just to him and unjust to his employees, who consider that he ought to apply the seniority rule, under which he would discharge those who had least service with him—the latest arrivals. There is in this case a clash between two conceptions of the just. Now let us suppose that the employer acts in the same way but that there is a general contract laying down the rule of seniority; in this case the conduct of the employer is unjust because it does not conform to the rule laid down. Lastly, let us suppose that the employer himself enunciated the rule of seniority, which he claims to apply but in fact violates; in this case there is injustice of a radical and absolute kind.

Analogous instances to the last two cases frequently occur in social life, and cause reactions which are as violent as they are legitimate; they involve, however, no intellectual problem. The intellectual problem is directly posed by whatever has affinity with the first case; for here there is a clash between two conceptions of the just, each of which is solidly founded.

THE PROBLEMS OF JUSTICE

There is no problem of justice when those who have to make a share-out know by reference to what serial order, whether agreed or by common consent relevant, this share-out must be made. The just share-out is that which conforms to the relevant serial order, and the man who aims at applying it conscientiously displays the virtue of justice, since his purpose is to assure to each his due. On the other hand, there is a problem of justice when there is doubt or dispute as to the serial order relevant to the occasion. More than that, and this is what makes for trouble, two or more men may be in conflict as to what is just in a case in which each of them displays the virtue of justice, each being determined to apply conscientiously the serial order which he thinks relevant. So we see that the thorny problems are those concerned with the choice of a criterion relevant to the occasion.

The choice of the relevant criterion is particularly easy in the case in which the thing to be shared out is seen by everyone as means in the service of an end on which everyone is agreed. Suppose, for instance, that on a given day I have ten pairs of skis at my disposal and that there are fifty young men all anxious to put them on; the allocation will be quickly made and accepted by all if one of their friends is lost on the mountains and it is essential to bring him back before nightfall—the skis then go to the best skiers. When action has an obvious end, the just share-out is that which maximises the particular action's chances of success. If we take up again the example of the fund for visiting the Italian picture galleries, there will be a simple criterion of allocation if its aim is to draw up a systematic catalogue of these galleries. Mistakes of fact are, of course, always possible; for instance, if I am the selector of the French team for the Davis Cup and I have chosen and sent off four tennis players, one of whom plays much below the level of someone else who could have been chosen, I can be charged with an error of judgment but not with injustice, if I had in fact taken the four players who were generally considered to be the best and classed as such.

The imperative of the end governs the share-out of what are seen as resources directed to that end. And it leaps to the eye at once that all sorts of contradictory judgments are possible. For instance, the French Prime Minister needs to designate three delegates for an international conference of the highest importance; the end which he has in mind is a successful issue to the conference for his country, the places which he has to fill are regarded by him as resources to this end, and he is careful to choose the three men who will, he thinks, be the most effective for the purpose. His principal adviser criticises this choice, pointing out to the Prime Minister that his primary consideration should be to stay in power (an alternative end) and that the nomination of three delegates who will be away for some time gives him the chance of getting out of the way three individuals whose intrigues are harassing him. The secretary of the party now appears on the scene with yet another opinion; the three places are eminently desirable and should be given as rewards to the three people who have done most for the victory of the party. (Here the notion of end takes flight and what is to be shared out is looked on as means of satisfaction.) This example comes from the daily realities of politics; it will be generally agreed that the first point of view impresses itself irresistibly as the only just one for the occasion.

When there is agreement on an end to be achieved and all are united in thinking that certain resources should be put to the service of that end, the right and necessary share-out of those resources is by reference to the serial order of competence for the purpose among those dedicated to the end. The only point on which disagreement could then be possible would be as to the internal structure of the serial order adopted, for the classification of those dedicated to the end is not necessarily the same in the eyes of different judges; but these judgments are various rather than conflicting, for all are concerned to measure one and the same objective competence and it will be possible to reach agreement on some particular classification as the most likely to be right. Very different is the case when two rival groups of opinion regard the resources to be shared out as having to serve two different ends, in relation to which the recipients are drawn up in two different serial orders; or, again, when the two groups admit the legitimacy of both ends but are divided as to their relative importance. And the problem gets more complicated with every addition to the ends to which the resources are applicable and the more the degrees of importance attached by different minds to different ends become differentiated.

In considering the resources to be shared out as means of action which must serve the realisation of some given end of action, we have equated the problems of justice with the problems of action. But men admit justice of this kind only so far as a particular end of action obsesses them, and not otherwise. A newspaper publisher, for instance, has profits to allocate, and ascribes this success to large-scale reporting; his obsession is to make his paper more successful, and to that end he decides, having now more to spend, to spend it on more reporting. But his editorial staff, on the other hand, not sharing the preoccupation which governs his conduct, want him to disburse his surplus in salary increases to them. In their eyes, the resources arising from a common undertaking are not means for advancing the fortunes of the common undertaking, but should rather, being the consequences of the undertaking, serve as means for enriching individual lives. Anything to be shared out, whatever it is, is always liable to be looked at under two different aspects: as means of action to be shared out by reference to the criterion relevant to an end of action, and as means of existence to be shared out by reference to a different criterion. Each of the two points of view has its validity, varying according to circumstances. If, for instance, I am commanding a company of infantry on an important march when the nation is at war, and on coming to a township I requisition all the bread available, the mayor will back up my action; nor will it seem unjust to the inhabitants whose minds are attuned to the end of what I have done. Yet the same requisition, if made on peacetime manœuvres, will seem unjust to them, because the end to which it is directed is not looked on as of sufficient importance.

Thus, the amount of resources which it will be thought just to devote to an end will turn on the importance attached to that end. But men are very unevenly taken up with distant ends necessitating collective action; thus a minority of promoters with a lively sense of ends requiring action, who therefore regard resources as first and foremost means of action, is naturally bound to come into conflict with a majority whose nature it is to regard resources as means of existence.[1] The result is that tension underlies every process of share-out; it is the more serious with every rise in importance of the blocks of resources to be divided. That is the reason why it is wise to break up the general process of share-out into as many small, disconnected share-outs as possible. The more comprehensive the process the more serious the tension.[2]

[1] A minority of promoters, seeking means of action, must naturally be hostile to too great a whittling away of the available resources in the form of individual means of existence, and is bound to aim at clawing back a part of these resources with a view to using them as means of action and thus raising the undertaking's potential. It must also, and for the same reason, view with the greatest disfavour the use made by a leisured class of large chunks of resources under its control; for here are means of action ready to hand which the class puts to use as means of enjoyment. Social history, indeed, presents us with two almost chemical processes taking place side by side more or less intensely; on the one hand promoters, agents of catalysis, tend to synthesise scattered means of existence into concentrated means of action, and on the other hand those in possession and enjoyment, agents of decomposition, tend to drag down into means of enjoyment means of action which come all ready for use into their possession. It is clear that, so long as an idle class succeeds in cornering an important part of social resources, there is no room for the application of another important part to the service of distant aims by a constructive élite; consequently, society has no more obvious interest than the speedy liquidation of the chunks of resources not applied to ends of action, as a waste of what society could put to good purpose. The following picture of the way things go may serve: the rich cells, which do not use their wealth to be enterprising, are attacked by the poor cells who would like to be enterprising in combination with the great mass of poor cells who lack all spirit of enterprise. The rupture of the envelope protecting the rich cells, call it their right or their privilege, causes dispersal of their substance throughout the body of society; immediately the poor cells who want to be enterprising apply themselves to the absorption of this scattered substance with a view to carrying out their own programmes.

[2] In reality the conflict is threefold: in what proportions should resources be regarded as means of action or as means of existence; how to distribute the means of existence;

The simplest method of effecting this fragmentation of share-out is to attribute every new element of resources to its owner as it appears. As, with exceptions, new elements do not appear of themselves but as the result of determined efforts, it is generally allowed that they should go to those whose efforts have produced them. This leads us to an examination of the problem of the just in regard to the share-out of the fruits.

THAT RESOURCES ARE FRUITS AND WHAT FOLLOWS FROM IT

It is of the greatest importance to recognise that resources are fruits; we are about to see why this is so. Let us imagine any gathering of men whatsoever among whom I am empowered to share out all resources as I see fit. As I am free to do what I like, I shall draw up my decree of allocation by reference to my own serial order of choice, whatever it is. The share-out which I enjoin may be made either equally or by reference to the amount of affection which I feel for particular people or in some other way. Anyhow, here is my allocation made and the shares fixed proportionally. This share-out of mine represents a settled policy, and applies as much to the resources that will be available in the future as to resources which are available in the present. But the resources of the future are themselves contingencies of the future. At some future moment, which we will call the 'second day', these shares of mine, though they accord with the proportions laid down, are found to be each of them smaller than on the 'first day', because the total resources are smaller, and everyone is then heard complaining of his diminished share. Alarmed by this discontent, I go for advice to Mentor, who adresses me as follows:

'From the earliest times, all peoples have regarded increasing plenty and the proliferation of resources as the mark of a good government; naturally, therefore, yours stands condemned. You should have taken thought for what economists in every age have called the maximisation of the future product. You ought to have foreseen that Primus, a generic name for any single one of your

---

how to share out the means of action among different ends as to the relative importance of which there is disagreement. That is why St Thomas Aquinas said: 'Unde videmus quod inter eos qui communiter et ex indiviso aliquid possident, frequentius jurgia oriuntur' (*Quaestio* LXVI, art. 2).

citizens, would read your edict as meaning that his livelihood in future would depend not on his own activity but on the collective activity, in which what he does himself cuts a most diminutive figure and which he regards as being in essence the activity of other men; and that Primus would for the future do no more than is enough to satisfy custom and opinion. It is that spirit which has diminished the collective livelihood.'

Much upset by what I hear, I deplore to Mentor that justice and collective utility should be at variance. But he will have none of it:

'You say they are at variance because I have made you see that what you considered your just edict is contrary to collective utility. But are you sure that you were just? Ask Primus what he thinks. Justice for him meant that the fruits available to him should be proportional to his activity; he finds it unjust that this relationship should be disturbed. I have still another answer in my locker to give you: in an ensemble of men nothing should be considered just which sets it in the path of its own decline, for justice is essentially constructive.'

From this I draw the conclusion that, on the one hand, I have no discretion at all as regards the share-out of future benefits—it must follow the serial order of the contribution made—and that, on the other hand, it will be a task of immense difficulty to apply this serial order. But what Mentor says next to a large extent relieves me of this task:

'The great pile of fruits which haunts your mind exists only in your imagination; it is in fact a thing of modest fractions, each of them the product of a specific team which carries out its own process of share-out within itself. Your part is merely to be called in to arbitrate the disputes which constantly arise on these occasions.'

It now seems to me that what Mentor is recommending is that I should concern myself with share-out as little as possible. But on my exposing to him the way my mind is moving he contradicts me: 'Certainly not. You can effect all sorts of improvements. All that I have sought to bring home to you is that the idea of regulating from on high the entire share-out was a presumptuous chimera.'

THE SHARE-OUT OF THE FRUITS WITHIN
THE TEAM

Now that we are clear that what is to be shared out should be looked on as fruits and that the primary process of share-out should take place within the team which produces them, let us address ourselves to the problem as so defined.

Let us suppose that it is of capital importance to me to have the manuscript of this book copied in a single day, that for this purpose I get together ten typists who are unacquainted and belong to different milieus, and that I offer a very high total reward for the achievement of the task in a single day. When it comes to sharing out this total reward, the just allocation will seem to be that which is proportional to the number of pages typed and initialled by each typist. Objection to this share-out can be made only on the ground that it has been possible to finish the work within the time laid down —thus earning the total reward—only by reason of the individual contributions which were of more than average merit, whereas the collective success was endangered by the individual contributions which were of less than average merit; for that reason the typists should be paid, not simply by reference to the number of pages completed by each, but on a progressive tariff graduated by reference to that number of pages. Probably, however, this solution will enter nobody's head, and, if it is suggested, will certainly be rejected as being hard of comprehension for the less intelligent; a rule of justice must always be intelligible to all. Therefore the share-out of the product will be proportional.

If, however, my intention in committing to them this work of copying was merely to employ workless people with a view to giving them a helping hand, the principle of share-out will be a quite different one: equal rewards or rewards proportional to the number of mouths to be fed. This example brings out clearly the contrast between share-outs made with a view to a practical object and those made with a view to the subjects.

In social life this contrast tends to fade out. In my example I made it clear that the typists did not know each other and did not belong to the same milieu. Now let us make the hypothesis that they are used to working together and that each is aware of each other's personal needs, which are like her own. In that case repugnance will be felt to the inequality, clear cut and sharply angled, in wages, which is based on the contribution of each to the common task. This psychological tendency will make for the flattening out of the angles, and will be the more pronounced the more that the workers are used to coming together on the same sort of task.[1]

The newer an action-group, the less linked by habitual co-operation its members and the more exceptional its fruits, so much the readier are those engaged in it to agree on the justice of a share-out of these fruits by reference to the individual contributions. Contrariwise, the more that members of the team see each other as 'neighbours' and the more that the team gains in social coherence, the more the idea of 'all alike' gains at the expense of that of superior and inferior performance. But this is a tendency which, though it may be accounted common to all those taking part, has naturally more force with those with whose personal interest it runs than with those to whose personal interest it runs counter. It is, in consequence, a safe prediction that, in a first stage, all the participants will agree in favouring unequal share-out of fruits by reference to proportional equality, that, in a second stage, they will agree in favouring a moderate rounding off of the angles, but that, in the end, they will no longer be in agreement, with some wanting to carry the process of levelling down further and others not. If a conflict of this kind is settled by counting heads, levelling down will always win, for it is certain that the number of performances which are below the average will be greater than the number of those which are above the average. A settlement on these lines will be the more readily borne by those whom it damages the stronger their emotional attachment to the group. It will, in other words, be borne with unequal complaisance, and there will be those who leave the group from a desire to seek elsewhere fruits which are proportional to what they do.

This scheme of thought suggests a way of classifying a society's teams of action. If we arrange them in order of age, we shall find, on the assumption that the scheme is valid, a rounding off of angles of share-out as we proceed from newest to oldest; this gradual process of levelling down itself starts off a process of escape from

[1] It has often been noticed that differences in remuneration are easier to maintain the more the recipients are strangers to each other; whereas, for instance, they will tend to disappear within a pool of typists, it will be possible to maintain them in the case of someone who, being outside the pool, applies to obtain copying work.

old groups and formation of new ones—tends, in other words, to create centres of unequal share-out in proportion as it tends to equalise share-out. This would explain why, in sum, the margins of inequality introduced into society by the process of share-out always present a fairly constant general profile.[1]

Thus, at the same time that society is continually maintained in resources by the functioning of work teams (or action groups), it is continually maintained in inequalities by those resulting from the processes of share-out of fruits which go on within the teams of work. But, society being itself a large milieu of existence, the same tendency to the erosion of inequalities shows itself there as in small milieus; in the result the inequalities produced by action groups undergo a certain flattening out *a posteriori*.[2] Thus we see that contrary influences are forever at work in combination. The work teams, which provide society with resources, affect it, so far as equality is concerned, like some hot spring which breeds inequalities, whereas society, which uses the resources, functions like a cold spring which attenuates these inequalities.[3] The state of inequality, photographed at any given moment, is the product of a crowd of

[1] As is well known, Vilfredo Pareto drew attention to the remarkable degree of constancy in the distribution of incomes before taxation—and his statement has been subjected to full and lively discussion ever since. Our argument, founded only on a hypothesis, tends to make predictable a certain stability of profile in the rewards for work and enterprise, if the revenues derived from 'scarcity-rents' due to the unequal appropriation of natural resources are excluded; unequal appropriation of this kind should be regarded as a phenomenon unrelated to the process of actual production.

[2] Such is the intention of the budgets of our time: progressive rates and allocations of revenue for raising the incomes of the poorer.

[3] We are here dealing only with the effects of flattening out within the society, as shown particularly in the democratic societies of our time. It should, however, be mentioned that social arrangements may be such as to introduce inequalities which are not the natural result of the process of creation of resources. This is what happens when social elements allot themselves, or get themselves allotted, important blocks of resources either because of the power they wield or in consideration of services which they are thought to render but do not render—or no longer render effectively. This is the phenomenon to which the word 'exploitation' is properly applicable; it is applied improperly to the larger shares taken by the leaders in the processes of creation or in socially beneficent activity. This phenomenon has played a large part in social history, where the inequalities created by it tend to be perpetuated almost indefinitely when the resulting privileged positions have taken the form of concrete rights over natural resources. Thus we see that rights created in the Middle Ages have governed down to our time the possession of certain lands on which stands the City of London. The example evokes the possibility of like effects resulting from the direct appropriation of natural resources, as in the case of the land on which Manhattan stands. Here we have causes of inequalities of a non-structural kind, in which the intervention of authority is not illegitimate.

phenomena, on each of which certain actions can no doubt be brought to bear; it is, however, utopian folly to seek to annul *en masse* all their consequences with a view to creating a condition of share-out which is the result of mental choice and transcends the phenomena of social life.

However high may be my place in society and however great my authority, it is never my affair to share out everything among all, but only, at a given moment, certain things among certain people. If, when the moment comes, I use reflection and counsel to seek out the serial order relevant to the occasion, and if I apply that order, then I have acted with justice and have displayed the virtue of justice; and that is all that can be asked of me. If I hold a military command and consideration of the part played by a particular officer in a battle leads me to recommend him for an important decoration, no-one will reproach me for not having taken into account the fact that there were already many decorations in his family. If I am president of a selection board and the insufficiency of marks to a candidate's credit leads me not to choose him, no-one will reproach me for not having taken into account the fact that the situation of the candidate's family made it particularly important for him to get the post for which he has been turned down. It has often been said that justice is blind; let us go so far as to agree that to be just she must be myopic. Just as the situation of the family of the unsuccessful candidate is not a circumstance which could lead me to pass him notwithstanding his inadequacy, so, if I am an official administering public assistance, I am not to rebuff him when the needs of his family cause him to seek help on the ground that he would not have needed help if he had worked harder for his examination. In every share-out what has to be considered is its particular end, which is sometimes to select the most promising candidates and sometimes to assist the most necessitous families: categories must not be confused.

Sadly and too frequently found together are the presumption which claims to have found a formula of overall distributive justice and indifference to the immediate obligations of commutative justice.[1] The scrupulous practice of commutative justice by the

---

[1] It is, for instance, a manifest failure to observe the elementary obligations of commutative justice when a debt is repaid in depreciated currency, for then less is repaid than had been in the minds of the two parties to the transaction. The state which authorises this failure and the citizens who profit by it show themselves unjust.

citizens, the backing of public opinion for its observance and its forcible endorsement by the government—these do between them more for the common good than is done by proposals for overall distributive panaceas. It is, moreover, a product of barren and lazy thinking to picture distributive justice as the work of a supreme legislator. Rather it is the duty of each single person, for there are none so free of ties that they do not have to take decisions on share-out to others, even if, as in the case of the mother of a family, what is to be shared among others—her children—is only work, patience and love. Each of us in his efforts to render the equivalent of what he has received practises commutative justice, and each of us, in making conscientious share-out and in lining-up our fellow-recipients in the order relevant to the occasion, practises distributive justice.

To suppose that the just authority is one which inaugurates an impeccably just order at all points is the broad way to follies of the most dangerous kind. An authority is just when it gives an example of justice in all the activities proper to itself—and that it finds hard enough. The logical end of the illusions now in vogue is the quite absurd one of a society in which everything would be arranged justly and no-one would have to be just.

THAT IT IS IMPOSSIBLE TO ESTABLISH A JUST SOCIAL ORDER

No proposition is likelier to scandalise our contemporaries than this one: it is impossible to establish a just social order. Yet it flows logically from the very idea of justice, on which we have, not without difficulty, thrown light. To do justice is to apply, when making a share-out, the relevant serial order. But it is impossible for the human intelligence to establish a relevant serial order for all resources and in all respects. Men have needs to satisfy, merits to reward, possibilities to actualise; even if we consider these three aspects only and assume that—what is not the case—there are precise *indicia* which we can apply to these aspects, we still could not weight correctly among themselves the three sets of *indicia* adopted. The attempt comes up against a basic impossibility.

Is it, on the other hand, necessary to call attention to the fact that nothing is more absurd than the defence of an existing social order as just? What is this serial order of yours that you should make me see the reflection of it in the existing order? There is no such thing. Your proposition merely is that whatever is, is just.

Must our conclusion be, then, that justice cannot rule in society? It must be so if justice is found only in an arrangement of things which coincides with some intellectual prepossession, whatever it is. But our conclusion is that justice is not there.

IN WHAT DOES THE RULE OF JUSTICE CONSIST?

Justice is a quality, not of social arrangements, but of the human will. The cardinal phenomenon in the positive history of human societies is the successive mastering of new processes, which call for operational reorganisation. Thus, new goals become attainable by new modes of co-operation and new relationships come about. There is no once-for-all scheme of things to be established and preserved; our own conceits in this respect should be abated by our poor opinion of the different conceits held by our forefathers. Therefore what we should be concerned with is that the whole ceaseless process of change should be increasingly permeated by the quality of justice in our individual wills. Every immediate field of choice open to us, in either our private or public capacity, offers us opportunity for the exercise of justice. Whenever we miss this opportunity we feed the sum of social injustice—a sum which it is comfortable but untrue to regard as the product of some single institution or mode of arrangement.

PART III

THE SOVEREIGN

CHAPTER 10

ON THE DEVELOPMENT OF THE IDEA
OF THE SOVEREIGN WILL

The object of this work is not to prime the reader with documentation, but only to call his attention to a problem which I think has been too neglected, namely, the content and substance of decisions couched in the imperative. The more comprehensive the power of decision and the more unbridled the authority wielded by the sovereign, the greater becomes the importance of this problem.

The reader must not expect from me a history of the concept of Sovereignty. I had indeed begun such a history, when I became aware that I was treading again the same road as when I was studying the development of Power; and this was to be expected, for the idea which men form of the rights of political command on the one hand, and the powers in effective exercise on the other, are two phenomena which give each other mutual sustenance and react on each other. For that reason it was not possible to treat of the growth of Power without treating of the growth of the idea of Sovereignty, and my attempt to handle the second brought me back to the first. With this difficulty facing me when I embarked on Sovereignty, I have preserved only those fragments of my labours which had, I thought, something to contribute to the present work, whether because they bring home the extraordinary progress and emancipation of the Sovereign Will in the course of European history, or because they disclose a notable effort, too little remembered, to impose degree on what threatened to be a law to itself.

THAT ABSOLUTE SOVEREIGNTY IS A MODERN IDEA

The Sovereign Will which modern writers ascribe in principle to the people, and which issues before our eyes from constitutional organs by various procedures, is conceived as a will capable of exercise on every subject-matter whatsoever without limitation by any subjective right. It is a command from on high which its form validates whatever its substance, and which has neither limits nor rules governing its subject-matter.

This will makes the law and there is no law other than this will. *Quidquid populo placuit legis habet vigorem.* The general view in our own times is that human societies have always acknowledged an authority which, as Jurieu puts it, has no need to be right for its acts to be valid—an authority which creates and destroys rights to any extent and has nothing but its own will to regulate it: *sit pro ratione voluntas.* Current belief is that this authority was formerly in bad hands and today rests in good hands, and that to have put it in good hands is the only safeguard as to its use which can be given to the citizens. But it is a mistake to suppose that over time Sovereignty has merely changed masters. More than anything else, history records the actual erection of this boundless and unregulated Sovereignty of today, of which our ancestors had no conception.

Today the monarchical state seems incomprehensible: claims on behalf of wielders of power to a boundless and unregulated right vesting in a single man would not be tolerated. But in olden days this right never existed: it is a quite modern growth. This conception, by which theorists of an extremist kind thought to serve the royal authority, in fact killed it; the notion did not, however, die along with the royal authority, but has on the contrary come to full bloom in the service of a new authority. That any human will whatsoever possessed an unlimited right to command the actions of subjects and change the relationships between them—that, for a whole thousand years, was something which was not only not believed but was not even imagined.

My intention is to outline here how the modern idea of sovereignty was slowly built up, how the right of the sovereign, which was a limited right standing guard over other rights, was transformed into an unlimited right, author of other rights at will. Two major stages, both of them clearly marked, can be discerned in this process. First is the transition from the limited feudal monarchy to the absolute monarchy of the seventeenth century. Then comes a further advance of the despotic idea, the transition from absolute monarchy to arbitrary regimes. The present study deals with the first stage only of this grand transformation.

THE MONOPOLISATION OF SOVEREIGNTY

In the Middle Ages men had a very strong sense of that concrete thing, hierarchy; they lacked the idea of that abstract thing, sovereignty. The word 'sovereign' was in current use, but not in the modern sense. In its then significance it simply meant 'superior,' which is the etymological meaning. And any superior was, in relation to his dependants, their 'sovereign'.

Sieur, sire, seignior have the same root; *sovereign* and *suzerain* have another one, closely related to the first. 'Seignior' comes from *seniorem*, 'sire' and 'sieur' come from *senior*; all three words derive from *senex* and carry the idea of superiority linked with the idea of age. On the other hand, popular Latin *superanus*, based on *super*, is responsible for 'sovereign', while 'suzerain' stems from the root *susum* or *sursum*; the idea of both words is the same, that of being over or superior.

In common usage all these words were employed indifferently. A father was called the 'sire' of his son, as in England he still is in the case of thoroughbred horses and pedigree dogs; a husband was called the 'sovereign' or 'seignior' of his wife, while a king was addressed as 'mon Sieur'.

What the Middle Ages felt and expressed was that each man had a superior, whether he was called his seignior, his suzerain or his sovereign. And the superior too had a seignior, a suzerain or a sovereign. In this way society appeared as what Augustin Thierry has magnificently called 'a great chain of duties'.

THE LADDER OF COMMANDS

Each vassal owed obedience to his suzerain, but this duty was no indeterminate debt, such that the suzerain could vary as suited him the obligation of the inferior. On the contrary, this obligation was specified in detail, a detail such as in our own day is not to be found in even the most advanced of collective labour agreements. Carefully studied, the expression 'accountable and liable to forced labour at pleasure' (*taillable et corvéable à merci*) implies something that should not be rather than was, somewhat as we use the word 'proletarian' today. It was recognised as something wrong, as something which was inconceivable for a freeman and was undesirable even in the case of serfs—whose obligations were in fact effectively laid down for all to see, so that these unfree men themselves had their right reserved to them as against the right over them possessed by their superior.

The medieval mind was unendingly concerned to define in the most detailed fashion the obligation of the inferior and to leave to command as little latitude as possible outside the powers accorded it. Attempts were made to set this obligation down in writing, but, written or not, it could always be verified by the testimony of peers—the peers not of the creditor but of the debtor for obedience. What made the condition of serf a wretched one was that he alone could not claim the judgment of his peers.

Under these conditions, command was never sovereign in the meaning which this word has come to have in modern times; never was it entitled to alter the content of the obligation which fell on the inferior, or to whittle away the right retained by him. In actual fact, no doubt, the lord was always on the move as regards his dependant, struggling to increase his right by acquisitive prescription which custom would verify. But, conversely, the dependant struggled to cut down his obligation by the same method, namely, the heaping up of precedents. In the struggle the inferior had the help of a still higher power to whom he could always make appeal. This appeal to the authority of higher degree is of the essence of the feudal regime. It is, I believe, from the feudal regime that this right of appeal, which seems to us almost a fact of nature, comes. And when the seigniors claimed to bar all appeal to the king, they were going against the very nature of the feudal type of organisation and justifying its eventual overthrow.

That there was a sovereign from whom all rules issued, the *solus conditor legis*, the source of all private rights—that was the idea to which the evolution of Roman thought came in the end and which the commentators unearthed in time in the *Institutes* of Justinian. But this first 'renaissance' took place only in the twelfth century; before the reappearance of this idea the monarch was looked on only as judge and not as legislator. He made subjective rights respected and respected them himself; he found these rights in being and did not dispute that they were anterior to his authority. The attitude of the sovereign toward rights is expressed in the oath of the first French kings: 'I will honour and preserve each one of you, and I will maintain for each the law and justice pertaining to him.' When the king was called 'debtor for justice', it was no empty phrase. If his duty was *suum cuique tribuere*, the *suum* was a fixed *datum*. It was not a case of rendering to each what, in the plenitude of his knowledge, he thought would be best for him, but what belonged to him according to custom, which could be attested by the juries of custom. Subjective rights were not held on the precarious tenure of grant but were freehold possessions. The sovereign's right also was a freehold. It was a subjective right as much as the other rights, though of a more elevated dignity, but it could not take the other rights away.

The Middle Ages could admit a tiered system of rights even as regards an arable field, so that the superior could always be checked by the inferior, sometimes to the point at which his 'right' was emptied of content; *a fortiori* they could admit as regards a people a tiered system of authorities where the highest in dignity was the poorest in substance. There we see the natural bent of the medieval genius; the conception of later Roman times—a single master monopolising all authority and enjoying the plenitude of power—had become foreign to it. It was to no purpose that Marsilius of Padua pleaded for an imperial restoration in this sense and that Dante praised its merits.

To concentrate the entire substance of authority in the higher command was a herculean task, and the medieval emperors failed in it. The emperor was recognised as the suzerain of suzerains and the seignior of seigniors—as, it may even be said, the king of kings. The last title sounds a superlative but is not so really, for it implies command over those who were best placed to disobey. And it was not long before each of them, starting with the kings of France and England, proclaimed himself emperor in his own kingdom.

It was these lesser emperors who succeeded in monopolising authority.

THE PLENITUDE OF POWER

Eugenio d'Ors brings home by a striking image the process of concentration of sovereignty:

Let us suppose ourselves on a hilltop from which are simultaneously visible a medieval township and a Renaissance city. The former is a little forest of spires and towers: does it not represent in plastic form the principle of feudalism? Perhaps the spire of the cathedral, being higher and more tapering, dominates the other spires, but that makes little difference. In like manner the sovereignty of the emperor in feudal times dominated the others. But what the life of feudal times stood for in juridical outline was plurality and profusion in plurality—and that was what the township stood for in architectural outline.

But the Middle Ages are over. The kings have subjugated the seigniors. At the same time, in the same spirit and for the same reasons cupolas replace spires. A cupola crowning a great public building seems as though it were its soul. It gathers up all the structural lines of the building, draws them together and makes them meet at a single point. It subsumes the entire life of the city and crowns it.[1]

Analogies must be used with discretion. They are only useful for giving a general impression; if they are put to further uses they do harm. The point made by this one is that the royal power really did tend to become something like a cupola, resting evenly on all the various parts of the popular edifice and making its weight felt everywhere.

But it was not in the temporal order that the idea of a single, concentrated authority, which made its immediate presence felt at every point, first carried the day. Its first victory was in the Church and the beneficiary was the pontifical power. The way in which the bishops of Rome transformed a mere pre-eminence in the church into a plenitude of authority over it is a great transformation on which little is known, because it happened in ages of historical obscurity. But one thing is clear, that this concentration of authority served as model for those which came about in the temporal realm. The notion of majesty, full and entire, was brought back by the popes.

Writing of the papal authority about A.D. 1280 Aegidius Romanus Colonna uses these terms: '*Tanta potestatis plenitudo, quod ejus posse est sine pondere numero et mensura.*' Alvarius Pelagius develops this idea of a power which cannot be weighed, counted or measured; he affirms that it knows no exception, embraces everything, is the basis of every authority, is sovereign, unlimited and immediate.

Not only by its example, but also because of the threat of domination which it constituted, the ecclesiastical authority, in monarchising itself, drove the royal authority in the same direction. The researches of the Roman lawyers brought back to life the image of the all-powerful emperor, master of the laws. The kings of that day were reluctant to give currency to this image so long as its prestige would have profited the emperor, and for that reason they discouraged in

[1] E. d'Ors, 'Coupole et Monarchie', *Les Cahiers d'Occident*, VI, 2nd series (1926).

earlier times research into Roman law. But the imperial power, enfeebled by the popes, could not turn to its own profit a majesty which was destined to descend on the various kings. Thus Edward the First, the English Justinian as he has been called, is found introducing Roman law into his country at the end of the thirteenth century; and Philip the Fair covered with his authority the Norman jurist, Pierre Dubois.

The *plenitudo potestatis* became the goal towards which the kings moved consciously. To reach it, a long road stretched before them, for it was necessary to destroy all authorities other than their own. And that pre-supposed the complete subversion of the existing social order. This slow revolution established what we call sovereignty.

THE ROLE OF PARLIAMENT IN THE CONCENTRATION OF AUTHORITY

Nothing is less natural than a concentration of authority which keeps it far away and out of sight. For that there must be a mystical outlook such as in western man is poorly developed; or else the authority, if it is to make its weight felt under such conditions, must bear a sacred character of a very pronounced type.

The natural thing is an immediate authority which is present bodily and asserts itself spontaneously in every human grouping. All those peoples whom the Germans call *Naturvölker* (living in a state of nature) know this immediate authority. They know as well another authority of higher degree and yet another above that one— these too no less based on human relations of a most concrete kind. Everywhere what may be called the natural hierarchy is the same: head of family, headman of village, leading man of district and so on up to the supreme chief.

These headships do not fit easily into our modern categories. It can no more be said that their powers come from below, like those of a municipal council, than that they come from above, like those of a prefect; they are not so much handed down as forged for themselves by their holders. And when a succession takes place, they are more truly taken over by a new holder than entrusted either to an elected person from below or to a nominee from above. Membership of the same family is everywhere an important factor in determining the new holder.

For his dependants, the chief is the man who can talk to the man above; and for the man above he is the man who can get himself obeyed by his dependants. These possibilities are not open to him because he is chief; it is truer to say that their being open to him is the reason for his being chief. As no one but he will set his little group to work on the execution of decrees from above, it is of the greatest importance that he should approve of these decrees. They must remain lifeless if he does not see to it that they are executed, and this he will do more readily if they have been decreed in his presence, with his participation; it is because headmen or chiefs are the natural executive that it is natural to summon them to a part in making the laws.

So it comes about that no other organ than 'the king in parliament' enjoys any great extent and intensity of authority. Among primitive peoples a parliament is needed to take any decision of importance. The reason is not that the king is 'not entitled' to take decisions without parliament, as has been said by travellers imbued with western principles, but that he is under the practical necessity of convoking this assembly, because it consists of the men whose goodwill and entire support are necessary to the success of any plan whatever.

That should not seem strange to us. For the only executive agents that the king had were the local magnates. Experience shows that even with modern officials, used by long tradition to treat as their first duty obedience to the orders given to them, orders which they find distasteful get badly executed. With these local magnates, who had not been bred in the same discipline, such orders would not be executed at all.

At the beginning of the Middle Ages kings were but poorly equipped with means of getting themselves obeyed; they had for that reason to seek consultations with their powerful vassals and make opportunities for discussing with them matters of public interest. The great hall of the palace where the king held his assizes —in this resembling every other great seignior—was all the better furnished if some powerful feudal lords were sitting there with him. Their presence, as the king wrote in his writs of summons, would give more weight to his decisions.

It is a well-known fact that at this period the seigniors did their best to avoid coming, disliking the loss of time and the enfeeblement of their authority which might result from their leaving home. Worst of all, they knew that something, often a financial or a military aid, would be demanded from them before they were allowed to return.

Whenever the authorities of the realm, of which the king's was only the most exalted, came together, the resulting physical concentration created something which began to resemble what we understand by a sovereign power. Under these conditions, and with the names of the seigniors as well as the king's appearing at the foot of documents, it was possible to promulgate a general edict.

Others besides the notables could present themselves at the royal assizes—not indeed 'representatives of the people' in general, but mandatories of this or that group, demanding justice and the exercise of authority. At first it was the thriving bourgeoisie of the cities, whose presence was no less useful to the king than to themselves, whether they claimed his protection against the arbitrary power of the great nobles or granted him subsidies.

In this way these gatherings (*colloquia*), which had the triple character of a session of justice, a council of state and the timid beginnings of a legislative assembly, were the means by which the affairs of the realm came more and more into the hands of the king. The council of the king and the courts of justice progressively developed an independent life, the assembly remaining under the name of Parliament in England and States-General in France.

The English historian Pollard, passing in review the result of these assemblies up till Tudor times, concluded that these *colloquia* and parliaments had contributed greatly to the growth of sovereignty. It would be absurd to suppose that parliaments came into being to exercise a check on sovereignty, for before their time sovereignty did not exist: 'The crown had never been sovereign by itself, for before the days of parliament there was no real sovereignty at all: sovereignty was only achieved by the energy of the crown in parliament, and the fruits of conquest were enjoyed in common.'[1]

The erection of sovereignty into a right of concentrated command was marked by certain transformations of the civil law. During the Middle Ages, the dependant of a seignior who killed his 'sovereign' was guilty of something much more than murder—of 'petty treason'. With the disappearance of this idea of 'petty treason' and the limitation of treason to an offence against the king alone, the monopolisation of sovereignty had made great strides.

Colloquia were necessary to achieve this great transformation. The kings who were most ambitious of authority made most use of

---

[1] A. F. Pollard, *The Evolution of Parliament* (London, 1920), p. 230.

parliaments. It was, for instance, Philip the Fair who admitted the Third Estate to the States-General, and Henry VIII, a great authoritarian, was one of the most 'parliamentary' of English Kings.

MONOPOLISATION IS ACHIEVED

The long feebleness of the sovereign or, to speak more accurately, the monarch's lack of 'sovereignty' as we understand it today, can best be illustrated by public finance. State expenditures, as we now call them, were thought of in feudal times as the king's own expenditures, which he incurred by virtue of his station. When he came into this station, he simultaneously came into an 'estate' (in the modern sense of the word); i.e., he found himself endowed with property rights ensuring an income adequate to 'the king's needs'. It is somewhat as if a government of our own times were expected to cover its ordinary expenditures from the proceeds of state-owned industries.

It was the duty of the king's servants to see to it that his assets brought in the necessary means, a task in which they often failed not only because of over-spending but also because it is never easy to combine political leadership with good husbandry; and indeed old documents relating to the falling away of net income from the king's assets sometimes have quite a modern ring. Extraordinary resources were often needed; but the king's servants had no warrant to exact in his name contributions from subjects—in fact our word 'exaction' was coined in protest against attempts of the kind. The king could not exact contributions, he could only solicit 'subsidies'. It was stressed that his loyal subjects granted him help of their free will, and they often seized this occasion to stipulate conditions. For instance, they granted subsidies to John the Good (of France), subject to the condition that he should henceforth refrain from minting money which was defective in weight.

In order to replenish his Treasury, the king might go on a begging tour from town to town, expounding his requirements and obtaining local grants, as was done on the eve of the Hundred Years' War; or he might assemble from all parts of the country those whose financial support he craved. It is a serious mistake to confuse such an assembly with a modern sitting of parliament, though the latter phenomenon has arisen from the former. The Parliament is sovereign and may exact contributions. The older assemblies should rather be thought of as a gathering of modern company directors agreeing to turn over to the Exchequer a part of their profits, with some trade union leaders present agreeing to part with some of their unions' dues for public purposes. Each group was called on for a grant, and each was thus well placed to make conditions. A modern parliament could not be treated like that, but would impose its will by majority vote.

The Hundred Years' War was needed to accredit finally a permanent tax, which made possible a standing army and the development of an executive to carry out the royal will. The history of sovereignty is linked with the history of administration. When he had his officials everywhere the king became something quite different from the distant suzerain he used to be. His authority thereby acquired a new immediacy.

The growth of his own apparatus made him regard as tiresome the advice tendered by social authorities which were, administratively, no longer necessary to him. We see how in the seventeenth century the States-General were no longer summoned in France, and how in England Charles I tried to dispense with parliament: it was absolute monarchy.

In England, after fifty years of revolutions, the king found himself defeated. That is not to say that sovereignty was weakened, but only that the part of the king in sovereignty was much diminished. Thenceforward parliament, under the formula 'the king in parliament', became more and more the effective holder of sovereignty— the principal beneficiary of the monopolisation of sovereignty which king and parliament had effected jointly.

In France, on the other hand, after the frightful disorders of the League, in the course of which the royal authority had been shattered practically and challenged theoretically by each of the two parties in turn, it was in the end generally agreed that the king's authority could not be too wide. Here is a remarkable fact: at the States-General of 1614, the Third Estate sought to have it made a fundamental law of the realm, to be sworn to by all officials and schoolmasters, that it was forbidden to shake off the yoke of obedience to the monarchy 'on any pretext whatsoever'.[1] It demanded the express condemnation of the opinion that there existed a right of resistance to the royal authority, and those who had to oppose this motion were the Ministers of the Crown! This

---

[1] This remarkable motion is cited in my book, *Power*, English translation, 2nd edition (London, 1952), p. 167.

shows the great advance made by the idea of sovereignty and demonstrates clearly that this idea was at that time entirely comprised in that of royal power.

VARIOUS TYPES OF SUPERIORITY
DISTINGUISHED BY L'OYSEAU

Let us see how the idea of sovereignty looked to a great jurist, Charles L'Oyseau, who was contemporary with Henry IV. We find it in a state of late transition.

L'Oyseau is far from confounding the different species of superiority. He meticulously distinguishes ownership (*sieurerie*), seigniory, suzerainty, sovereignty. All have the juridical aspect of dominion and power, but of different dominions and powers.

'Private seigniory', though a dominion actual and apparent, is no longer conceived as capable of exercise over persons—we are far removed from any justification of serfdom—and is summed up as '*the right which each individual has in his property*'.[1] L'Oyseau would like this right to bear the name of *sieurerie*, to distinguish it from 'public seigniory' which is '*an authority possessed over freemen and another's goods*'.[2]

But there are two sorts of public seigniory. The one is suzerainty, exercised by those who are generally called today 'the seigniors'. To this species of superiority L'Oyseau evinces a strong repugnance. The other is sovereignty.

Sovereignty is the seigniory of the state. For all public seigniory should remain with the state, notwithstanding that individual seigniors have usurped suzerainty. But sovereignty is entirely inseparable from the state. Were the state deprived of it, it would no longer be a state and whoever had it would have the state inasmuch as he would have the sovereign seigniory. For instance, when King Francis abandoned sovereignty of Flanders, Flanders was in consequence torn away from the state of France and became a separate state. For sovereignty is the form which causes the state to exist; indeed, the state and sovereignty in the concrete are synonymous. Sovereignty is the summit of authority, by means of which the state is created and maintained.[3]

Let us note this definition: 'summit of authority'. And let us note that L'Oyseau allows in substance only two species of authority

---

[1] C. L'Oyseau, *Traicté des Seigneuries* (Paris, 1609), p. 1.
[2] *Ibid.*   [3] *Op. cit.* p. 24.

—that of a private individual over his property and that of this 'summit'.

How great a change is here from the medieval outlook! In place of the graded superiorities which characterised the feudal regime, with each superior having some power and right over his inferior and thus being vaguely entitled to be called his sovereign, there are now only two powers and two rights—or at any rate no more than two tend to get recognition.

ALLIANCE OF BOURGEOIS OWNERSHIP
WITH THE ROYAL POWER

The medieval chain of duties is now broken, or at the least so worn out that only traces of it remain; the entire substance of powers and the whole force of rights have been concentrated in the two extremities. On the one hand is the individual, who is free and has power over himself (the *potestas in se ipsum*), and is conceived as owner, exercising a private *sieurerie* or *potestas in re*. On the other hand is the monarch who exercises a sovereign right over the whole kingdom.

The plenitude of individual powers is the ideal of the bourgeoisie which is rising and the condition of the commercial civilisation which is beginning. The bourgeois, now free of personal servitude, wishes to free his property as well. This individualist urge requires the reinforcement of the public authority, which alone can break what remains of the feudal chains.

The plenitude of the public authority is, therefore, necessary to the bourgeoisie, as efficient cause of the plenitude of individual powers. That is why the bourgeois Third Estate was anxious to strengthen the absolute monarchy which worked on its behalf. It wished and hastened the coming of what would be called 'absolute monarchy', something undreamt of in the Middle Ages.

What are the implications of this 'summit of authority' of which L'Oyseau speaks?

DESCRIPTION OF SOVEREIGNTY

It consists in absolute and entire authority at every point, what the canonists call plenitude of authority. There are in consequence no degrees of superiority in it, for whoever has a superior cannot be supreme and sovereign; nor is it limited to certain times, otherwise it would not be absolute authority, or even seigniory, so much as an authority held in reserve. It is without exception as to things or persons pertaining to the state, for any exception would no longer pertain to the state. It is, finally, of unlimited power and authority, because a superior would be needed to uphold any limitation.[1]

'Of unlimited power and authority' is an affirmation of capital importance; we shall often come across it again. L'Oyseau maintains this idea of an unlimited right by an argument which was to serve many others and notably Rousseau:[2] 'Of unlimited power and authority, because a superior would be needed to uphold any limitation.' The jurist concludes in lyrical vein: 'And just as the crown cannot be if its circle is not complete, so sovereignty is not if anything is lacking to it.'

The writer is, we feel, carried away by the idea of perfection, of 'roundness' which is its synonym. Clearly what he has in mind is no longer the concrete relations existing between men, but an ideal entity, a plenitude of authority which misses the characteristics of plenitude if it is incomplete at any point.

NATIONALISM AND 'MAJESTAS'

When the idea of an authority which is absolutely without superior is developed logically and in abstract terms, it leads inevitably to the idea of an authority without limits. For, if there was anything able to control or check it, that something would be superior to it.

This dialectic is apparent in an author who wrote in England at about the same time, Albericus Gentilis. Those are supreme, he said in substance, to whom none is superior and they are not supreme if there is the slightest doubt as to their complete independence. 'For this reason, only he is supreme who recognises nothing above him except God, and who has to give account to God only— and sovereignty consists in there being nothing, neither man nor law, above the ruler. This power is absolute and knows no limits. The prince, said the law, is absolved from the laws; therefore the law is what pleases the prince.'[3]

It may be that the emphasis with which the independence of

---

[1] *Op. cit.* p. 25.

[2] Rousseau said: 'For if any rights remained vested in individuals, then, as there would be no common superior to pronounce between them and the public (meaning 'sovereign'), each man would be in some matter his own judge and would soon claim to be it in everything.' *Contrat Social*, I, ch. VI.

[3] Albericus Gentilis, *Regales Disputationes Tres* (London, 1605).

the sovereign power is affirmed—an absolute independence which is the source of that power's absolutism in other respects—is a result of the religious conflicts of the time. Gentilis, for instance, was a member of the Reformed church from Pérouse, who had sought refuge in England, and his is an affirmation which upholds the complete autonomy of the English king as regards papal interference. The personal circumstances of his case were very similar to those of Marsilius of Padua; the latter's too led him to speak in terms which were absolutist because autonomist. The astonishingly absolutist motion of the Third Estate in 1614 was a reaction against the interference of the Jesuits, under whose theory the power of kings was subordinated. The independence even as regards the law of which Gentilis was the spokesman was meant to justify the unprecedented measures taken by the Tudor kings against the institutions of the church.

The exaltation of sovereignty is linked with the rupture of medieval internationalism and clericalism. Even those who, having nothing to hope for from the sovereign, were unwilling to allow to him an unlimited right, lodged this right in an abstract thing which was set over him under the name of sovereignty. Hotman seems to have been the first man to divorce sovereignty and the prince and to regard the former no longer as an attribute of the latter but as an independent entity. With Bodin too it is an entity, bearing the name of *majestas*. There must be, says Bodin in substance, in every political society some supreme power to make the laws and invest the magistrates—a power which is itself subject to no law other than the laws of God and Nature.

LIMITS OF SOVEREIGN POWER

However addicted our authors were to an entity without seam, they did not carry their thought to its logical conclusion; what held them back were the concrete images of sovereign authority which formed in them.

Though it is an overall right, it is not, explains L'Oyseau, a right of unlimited intensity:

We must boldly note that there is a most important difference between the users of these two seignories (the public and the private). We may use the private seigniory at our own free will and caprice (for, as the law says, everyone may do what he likes with his own), because, as it consists of what is ours, it can hardly happen that we wrong another whatever use we make of it. But the public seigniory must be used with reason and justice, because it is concerned with things which belong to others or with people who are free. Anyone who uses it capriciously usurps and encroaches on the private seigniory which is outside his sphere. If he so uses it against persons, he makes slaves of them; if he so uses it against goods, he takes what is another's.[1]

It leaps to the eye that the *potestas in se ipsum* and the *potestas in re*, liberty and property, are here conceived as antecedent (whether in time or in logic does not matter) to the public authority. Usurpation and encroachment are terms which can be used only in respect of something which has an anterior and absolutely independent existence. This property of absoluteness conferred on liberty and property, which was to have consequences of vast importance in the eighteenth century, weakens the absoluteness of sovereignty.

Moreover, L'Oyseau finds in sovereignty 'very important limits'. After having said that nothing must be outside it, he corrects himself by adding:

However, as it is only God who can be all-powerful and the authority of men cannot be completely absolute, there are three sorts of laws which limit the authority of the sovereign, without affecting sovereignty. They are, the laws of God, because the prince is no less sovereign for being subject to God; the natural, as distinct from the positive, ordinances of justice, because, as we said above, it is right that the public seigniory should be exercised justly and not capriciously; and, finally, the fundamental laws of the state, because the prince should use sovereignty according to its own nature and under the powers and conditions on which it is established.[2]

Let us consider in succession each head of restriction. The state is inscribed in the Christian republic, and the prince is a subject of God—a subject with a special mission: to this he must be faithful. In other words, he is not at liberty as regards either the end which he pursues or the means which he employs; religion points out to him the end and does not leave him full liberty of choice as regards the means. This restriction was worth as much as the piety of the king and the religious convictions of the people, for by then the spiritual power had lost the right of oversight and control which was its prerogative in the Middle Ages. When it ceased to be part of the understanding between ruler and ruled that both should be followers of the Christian Faith, this restriction collapsed of itself.

[1] L'Oyseau, *op. cit.* p. 9.   [2] *Ibid.* p. 9.

The second restriction is the obligation to respect the natural law and natural rights, private property counting at the time as much as personal liberty. This restriction, however, could be upheld only as long as natural law and natural rights were believed in. Never were they more loudly proclaimed than at the time of the Revolution; they were then to serve as a self-supporting philosophy. But a rootless philosophy of natural rights was sure to wilt, and not long after its most solemn proclamation the thought grew that there was no such thing, but only positive law and rights granted by the state. With that the second restriction crumbled away.

Now comes the third: the fundamental laws of the state. The prince may use sovereignty only in the form in which, and on the conditions on which, it was established. That presupposes a contract, real or notional, between the sovereign and others, whether the people itself or the estates of the realm. The whole of medieval thought had conceived political society as a two-way affair, a conception which naturally led to reciprocal obligations; the prince was tied down by his obligations towards his subjects. But these obligations, which restricted the liberty of the sovereign, necessarily disappeared when the two ways joined up in 'sovereignty of the people'. Once the people is sovereign, it is a contradiction to speak of its tying itself down, as Pufendorf had already seen and stated:

As the sovereign assembly is composed of all the citizens, and no-one in consequence has acquired any independent right by its decisions, nothing prevents the people from revoking or changing those decisions as often as it thinks fit, unless it has sworn to observe them in perpetuity; and even in that case the oath only binds those who have actually taken it, as we showed earlier. In some popular states, in an attempt to render an ordinance perpetual, a penalty has sometimes been laid on any who should propose its revocation; it is, however, as easy to abolish the penalty as the ordinance.[1]

So we see that sovereignty, as L'Oyseau presents it to us in 1609, is already a prodigiously healthy plant. The only obstacles in the way of its indefinite growth are three orders of laws, all of which came to be abrogated by three historical facts: irreligion, legal positivism and sovereignty of the people.

---

[1] Pufendorf, *The Law of Nature and Peoples*, Book VII.

CHAPTER 11

THE SOVEREIGN AS LEGISLATOR

It is paradoxical that the seventeenth century should excite the admiration of the conservatively minded, for it was a highly revolutionary time—much more profoundly revolutionary than the eighteenth century—and its upheavals entailed those of 1792 as a mere consequence. Louis XIV in all his glory was no more than a successful revolutionary—an earlier Napoleon who turned to profit an earlier Jacobinism no less simplifying and terrorist than its successor. This Jacobinism, by overturning the rule of law which preceded it, emancipated the sovereign.

Liberty for the sovereign, that was the badge of the seventeenth century. For the sovereign it meant that he was no longer bound by rules; thenceforward he made the rules as he saw fit. Very likely he used this power with great moderation, but that is not what matters. That he should have acquired it at all, therein is the evil.

THE CONCRETE ADVANCE OF POWER

Historians have never sufficiently brought out the importance of the Fronde, the reason being that they have not correlated it with the comparable crises which shook the Spanish and English monarchies at the very same time. The root of these disturbances was everywhere the same: taxes imposed by governments. It was against the exactions of Richelieu that Normandy rose in 1639, it was against the exactions of Olivares that Catalonia rose in 1640 (even going to the length of seeking union with France) and that Portugal broke off from the Spanish monarchy. It was the exactions of Charles I which brought about the trial of the refractory Hampden —the spark to the fuel of the English revolution. It was again the exactions of Olivares which caused the revolution at Naples in 1647.

Contemporaries were well aware of the correlation of events. In the early days of the Fronde, a crowd of women collected in front of Notre Dame when Anne of Austria had gone to hear Mass and shouted at her: 'Naples! Naples!' And the refugee queen of England warned her against annoying the populace.

It was not only the aggravation of fiscal burdens which stirred men to revolt or revolution; it was also the new claim put forward by the state to tax as it saw fit. Its exercise of that right was not acknowledged by all; many opposed to it the time-honoured principle that every subvention was in the nature of a treaty between the groups who paid it and the monarch who received it. Time-honoured to the point of being obsolete! The sovereign asserted his right to tax. It was a decisive victory from which the democratic sovereign would one day reap the benefit.

This right to tax was but one aspect of the right of sovereignty—a right which waxed ever stronger. Instead of the right to supreme authority being, as in the Middle Ages, one right among many possessed by others—a right checked by all the other rights, with which it must come to terms—the right of sovereignty now became for progressive minds the right *par excellence*, the source of all other rights which it was thus at liberty to control as it saw fit and abolish at its good pleasure. In our own time this idea has such an ascendancy that we can now hardly conceive what it was for which Henri de Montmorency and de Retz were fighting.

THE ADVANCE OF THE ROYAL PREROGATIVE

What they fought for was in essence the natural equality of subjective rights, whether they were those of the monarchy or of other bodies or individuals. When Bonaventura described all the authorities within a society as deriving from a single source (for him, the Pope)—as being one and the same authority broadening down from step to step—he was depicting an ideal system. The opposing reality was something far more complex; a host of agents, princes, cities, communities of every sort, had woven into a web their very different rights which, though they had been acquired by very different means, were all attested by treaties, charters and contracts. And these rights were all equally sacred.

Once groups or individuals of any kind had won recognition that certain rights belonged to them, they could then oppose those rights to all comers—to the prince no less than anyone else. The complex of honours, privileges and liberties—the rights, in short—of a group determined its status. The status (*estat*) of either a person or a group

was the whole bundle of legitimate interests and consecrated rights
—something that had to be respected by all and could be opposed
at need even to the sovereign himself.

Therein is the point of capital importance. If the prince had to
summon the 'States' whenever there was an important decision to
be taken or, still more important, a law to be passed, the reason was
to prevent injury to the status of those with well-attested rights;
therefore their consent was necessary. When Philip the Fair asked
his subjects to defend 'the state of the realm', he meant thereby
the whole corpus of the very different rights belonging to very
different titularies—in a word, the existing state of things.

The status of the king was at that time something limited and
closely defined: the honours and rights which were his due. His
rights extended over the entire realm, but at every point and in
every matter they encountered rights of other members of the
realm; these he was in no position to destroy or change as pleased
him. On the contrary, his office was, as medieval writers never
tired of reminding him, to do justice and render to each his due.
This did not mean that the monarch should decide arbitrarily what
each should have, but that it was his duty 'to maintain each in his
right'.

As seignior, the king had certain rights which were entirely
analogous to those of other seigniors. As supreme seignior, he had
rights which were proper to himself; to these the English jurists
gave the name 'Royal Prerogative'. This prerogative never stopped
growing, and, in the reign of James I, Cowell defined it as 'this
special power, pre-eminence and privilege which the king has in all
matters over all persons, and out of the ordinary course of the
common law, by right of his crown'.[1]

This prerogative was necessary to the fulfilment of his office, but
it was limited by the nature of its end, and, before the seventeenth
century, it did not mean that the sovereign could alter the status
of his subjects—as the modern state does every day.

---

[1] In the legal dictionary of J. Cowell, called *Interpreter*, in the article 'Prerogative'
(1607). Quoted by J. R. Tanner, *Constitutional Documents of the Reign of James I*
(Cambridge, 1930).

ABSOLUTE SOVEREIGNTY

The progressive advent of absolutism can be thought of as consisting essentially in a great change of balance between the rights of the monarch and those of the subject. The much-cited anecdote of Frederick the Great and the miller of Sans-Souci faithfully represents the ancient state of affairs. The king's rights have incomparably greater scope than those of the miller; but as far as the miller's right goes it is as good as the king's; on his own ground, the miller is entitled to hold off the king. Indeed, there was a deep-seated feeling that all positive rights stood or fell together; if the king disregarded the miller's title to his land, so might the king's title to his throne be disregarded. The profound if obscure concept of legitimacy established the solidarity of all rights. When a new king was enthroned, his subjects acknowledged his right, and, at the same moment, he confirmed and promised to uphold their diverse rights. No change in these rights could be effected without the consent of their holders. To take a most striking instance, Louis XIV's own 'officers of justice' rebelled when his financial secretary, Emery, proposed to levy on them a tax to which they had not given their assent. This was the beginning of the Fronde; that was what the Fronde stood for.

More than financial interests was involved, and the devaluation of subjective rights in general caused profound reactions. In our day we are used to having our rights modified by the sovereign decisions of legislators. A landlord no longer feels surprised at being compelled to keep a tenant; an employer is no less used to having to raise the wages of his employees in virtue of the decrees of Power. Nowadays it is understood that our subjective rights are precarious and at the good pleasure of authority. But this was an idea which was still new and surprising to the men of the seventeenth century. What they witnessed were the first decisive steps of a revolutionary conception of Power; they saw before their eyes the successful assertion of the right of sovereignty as one which breaks other rights and will soon be regarded as the one foundation of all rights.

As the reaction to this claim mainly showed itself in the sphere of encroachments on the right of property—because this right was deeply entrenched and because the bourgeoisie was in the saddle—it is often wrongly thought that the principal encroachment of the sovereign was in the sphere of property. In fact, it was in this sphere that the sovereign encountered the hardest resistance. The opposition was feebler and he made more progress at less cost and with less outcry in the work of destroying public rights in opposition to his own, such as the privileges of provinces, bodies and communities.

The actual events nourished an idea which outgrew them and cast its shadow on the centuries to come: the idea of absolute sovereignty. Enlarged budgets made possible enlarged administration. The proliferation of its immediate agents made Power more and more able to get itself obeyed. The phenomenon was a general one. It was the period in which appeared—what had long been building up—the *Beamtenstaat*, the bureaucratic state.

By raising its capacity to get itself obeyed, Power gained in consideration. It was then that the absolutist theories made their appearance. It would be a mistake to regard these theories as causes; they are, more truly, consequences. Absolutism is not a consequence of the distortion inflicted by theorists on the medieval doctrine of divine right; it is truer to say that growing absolutism attracted to its service a theory which the medieval theologians would have found unrecognisable. Justifications poured in on it from every side; that of Hobbes, though founded on the quite opposite principle of sovereignty of the people, led to the same absolutist conclusions. This was because the prestige of triumphant Power had graven in men's hearts the same feeling for sovereignty; ratiocination, inspired by this feeling, followed later. Respect and admiration were directed less to royal persons than to royalty itself. It was not only Louis XIV who was named the *Roi-Soleil*; Louis XIII, a much less radiant figure, had been called this before him. Not the man but the thing—that was what mattered. In England, for instance, the talk was more and more of the thing—the Crown itself. The notion of 'sovereignty in itself' was everywhere in the air.

SOVEREIGNTY AS ATTRIBUTE

So far the word sovereignty had had only a subordinate existence. What was recognised was a fact, the sovereign—a fact of more and more imposing aspect. Sovereignty was conceived as the character belonging to the sovereign. The essential was the sovereign and sovereignty was the shadow which he cast—or, to put it more precisely, his attribute.

No doubt the sovereign was not in all cases one man, but the picture formed of him was so much that of a single person that even a regency council was reduced to an artificial unity. Thus we find Aegidius Romanus writing in the Middle Ages: 'Plures homines principantes quasi constituunt unum hominem multorum oculorum et multarum manuum', and Occam writing: 'Plures gerunt vicem unius et locum unius tenent.'[1] From about this time, moreover, senatorial governments had begun to wane, especially in Italy, and the rule of a personal sovereign had become the most frequent form of rule. Only in the Low Countries had an evolution in the opposite direction been set in motion.

In speaking of the sovereign, therefore, what was in mind was a man, or at the very least a narrow and clearly defined group. It was a clearly understood thing that what acted in sovereign fashion was a human will; this will, being human, was necessarily disfigured by imperfection, it was capable of insubordination as regards the divine will from which it claimed title and of insolence as regards the subject of its rule, namely, the people (thought of as individuals and groups, not as an entity).

Clearly, therefore, it needed to be continually recalled to the service of its end, the common good, and continually enjoined not to violate the natural law. In the Middle Ages the Church in general and the Papacy in particular had performed this office. With the Papacy weakened, the Church continued to perform it in diminished measure even in the age of absolutism; with accents of respect was mingled a tone of rebuke in many a sermon preached even before Louis XIV—and Louis accepted it.

This fallible human will needed to be prevented from injuring legitimate interests. It was for that reason that the 'States', a true representation of those interests and not of different opinions, had to be convoked. The sovereign could err and for that reason it was a duty incumbent on the king to take counsel. Sovereignty, as Bacon put it, was wedded to counsel; before any decision was taken, the matter must be laid in the womb of counsel, where it took shape, even though in the end it was the office of the sovereign to present it to the public.[2] If notwithstanding all precautions it happened

---

[1] Aegidius Romanus (1315), III, 2, cap. 3; Occam (1347), *Dial.* III, vol. 22, lib. 3, cap. 17.

[2] The metaphor of Bacon, following the taste of the period, is more elaborate: 'The ancient times do set forth in figure both the incorporation and inseparable conjunction

that this will became corrupted, it should be obeyed at first 'to avoid a yet greater disorder', but its perseverance in error justified in the end a right of resistance, which could develop into a right of insurrection, deposition or tyrannicide.

Such were the correctives of sovereignty, in days when it appeared as an attribute of a person of flesh and blood and was clearly seen to have devolved on a human will capable of vice and error. They were correctives rooted in the nature of things and were required by logic for every human will exercising rule; they were in large part preserved even under the absolute monarchy itself—or at any rate every effort was made to maintain them. On the other hand, the need for them was no longer recognised when men took to reasoning on sovereignty in itself without regard to concrete realities.

THE SOVEREIGN AND THE LAW

Liberty of the sovereign was as much outside the philosophy of the Middle Ages as was radical liberty of the individual. The period during which emancipation of the individual made progress was the same as that in which emancipation of the sovereign was achieved.

This statement invites challenge: could the man who had no superior have been anything but free? Assuredly he was not, if he felt himself, and was considered by others, to be in thrall to a rule. In the Middle Ages, the law, which it was the duty of the sovereign to serve, was such a rule. For anyone who understands 'the law' in the modern sense and thinks of commands formulated by a body, the statement that the sovereign was subject to the law seems

of counsel with kings, and the wise and politic use of counsel by kings: the one, in that they say Jupiter did marry Metis, which signifieth counsel; whereby they intend that sovereignty is married to counsel: the other in that which followeth, which was thus: they say, after Jupiter was married to Metis, she conceived by him, and was with child, but Jupiter suffered her not to stay till she brought forth, but ate her up; whereby became himself with child, and was delivered of Pallas armed out of his head. Which monstrous fable containeth a secret of empire; how kings are to make use of their council of state: that, first, they are to refer matters unto them, which is the first begetting or impregnation; but when they are elaborate, moulded and shaped in the womb of their council, and grow ripe and ready to be brought forth, that then they suffer not their council to go through with the resolution and direction, as if it depended on them; but take the matter back into their own hands, and make it appear to the world that the desires and final directions, which, because they come forth with prudence and power, are resembled to Pallas armed, proceeded from themselves.' Bacon, *Essays Civil and Moral*, xx, Of Counsel.

contradictory. A prince in subjection to such commands is in a subordinate position to their formulating body, and then it is not he, but this body, which is sovereign. And this other sovereign is not in subjection to the laws because it makes them. But to the Middle Ages law meant something quite other than commands formulated successively. For them it was a code of rules anterior to and co-existent with the sovereign—rules which were intangible and fixed.

The king of feudal times was a supreme judge enthroned by the law, and exercising his power, as Bracton put it, *sub lege*. On the continent 'the law' now means nothing but the decrees promulgated by competent authority; in the English-speaking world it still comprises the three elements of principle, custom and the decrees of authority. In olden days custom was the supreme binding force. What a man had a right to was what he had held within living memory; what a man should do in a given position was what it had long been regarded as proper for a man so placed to do. Hence came the great importance of the jury, a group of knowledgeable men who could say what custom was and what it required. This over-riding importance of established rights and obligations was an obstruction to reform as well as to encroachment; it can be criticised as well as praised. Strangely enough, the country where this conception of the law was most enduring has proved itself the most progressive.

In such a system subjective rights had guarantees which they have never found since. The fixity of 'the law' limited naturally the right of the sovereign—a right which was itself based on and delimited by the divine law and custom. Magna Carta in England was nothing other than a vigorous reassertion of this rule. The greatest difficulties confronted anyone who sought to change it, and Christendom was scandalised when Emperor Frederick II, the first 'enlightened despot', asserted the right to suppress ancient privileges, annul contracts which formed the bony structure of society and forge new laws by which every relationship and status was changed.[1]

In the end the time-honoured credit of custom collapsed before the intellectual thrust of the Renaissance in combination with a social thrust against acquired rights, while at the same time the hitherto accepted interpretations of the divine will were overthrown by the Reformation—along with its priestly interpreters. The

[1] Cf. E. Gebhardt, *L'Italie Mystique*; and B. Landry, *L'Idée de Chrétienté chez les scholastiques du XIIIe siècle* (Paris, 1929).

frameworks which determined and delimited the role of the monarch were attacked from two sides. The right of monarchs to regulate the lives of subjects by decisions of vast extent came to be admitted and even desired.

In a word, monarchs assumed the legislative power. Law, that is to say, with time became more and more something built instead of something given. It is at once clear that there is here a change of capital importance.

JUSTICE AND WILL

The traditional view of the king was in effect that of a will at the service of justice. We find St Isidore of Seville invoking an old proverb: 'If you do justly, you will be king, if not, not', and Bishop Jonas of Orleans writing: 'Rex a recte dicitur.' The monarch was pictured as holding the scales; that was his essential attribute, and his most majestic aspect was that of president of a court of justice. So much did he seem the justiciar *par excellence* that of all the functions which feudal decentralisation had spread widely the first which he succeeded in bringing back into his own hands was the judicial, and the artisans of the reinstatement of Power were, above all, the judges.

How is justice done? By rendering to each his due: *suum cuique.* The idea of justice implies the idea of rights which justice notes, weighs, conciliates—rights which are pre-existent and fixed so that justice is the more just the more respectfully it treats them. This was what justice meant, to the end of the monarchy, to the magistrates of the French 'parlements', and herein lay, besides more squalid reasons for quarrel, the deeper cause of the struggle which they waged throughout the seventeenth and eighteenth centuries against the government—or, as they put it, the 'ministry'. The ministry purposed to enact laws—to replace custom, that is to say, by novel prescriptions and alter subjective rights. The 'parlements' refused to register many of these edicts. They found it paradoxical, in effect, that the sovereign, called on to weigh rights in the scales of justice, should have been able to alter those rights beforehand by his legislative power. From then on what had been just before the promulgation of the law had ceased to be so after it. Instead of the decision being guided by fixed criteria, it was guided now by shifting criteria. And if the royal justice was just to the extent that it conformed to the established code of rights, what did it become if the royal will changed that code? The answer was—a mere handmaid of the will.

Today it is hard to understand the proud resistance of the ancient magistrature, for it is accepted now that the only function of judges is to apply the variable prescriptions of the sovereign. But this was a condition to which the magistrates of former days did not tamely submit. They were well aware that the legislative will was capable of improving law, but only in so far as it let itself be guided by higher criteria. Another demand made in their representations and remonstrances was that the reasons for the edicts should be explained and justified by bringing them to the touchstone of true principles and real necessities. The monarchy made the fatal blunder of ignoring their pleas and of maintaining that what made its laws valid was the royal will—therein recalling the later Roman Empire: *quidquid principi placuit.*

Thus will and justice were still in harness, but with will now giving the lead to justice and no longer justice to will. An idea had been born which was destined to fill all future centuries with the disorder it caused—that right issues from a will which has power to establish it. It was an idea which was bound to prove fatal to the monarchy, for, if right is the creation of will, why of the will of a single man?

WHY DID WILL COME TO THE FRONT?

It is possible to follow in successive ordinances the remarkable change in the language put in the mouth of the king, with its growing insistence on his will.

The change is too often explained by the theory of divine right, which underwent at that time a complete subversion and tended to represent the monarch as the image of God rather than as his servant in the cause of the common good. 'To hold his realm from God only' had been at first an expression of humility, and the clergy had countenanced it in their efforts to combat the Germanic tendency of both Carolingian and Merovingian kings to treat realm and empire as so much heritable property for ultimate division among heirs. As Bishop Jonas of Orleans taught in the ninth century: 'No king should say that he holds his realm from his ancestors, but he should *humbly* believe that he holds it in reality from God.' In the seventeenth century 'to hold from God only' had become an expression of pride.

But even that would not explain why the 'image of God' should have put his will forward as sufficient explanation of his decrees. For in terms of true theology the laws of God himself are not the fruit of his will but of his reason, which is regarded as logically antecedent to his will, so that the just is not just because God has willed it but because God is just. Anyone holding that it was imitation of the divinity which brought the royal will to the forefront is bound to relate the phenomenon to an intellectual influence of the Reformation, which gave out in set terms that only the will of God was the source of the divine laws. But the theory of divine right, in its monstrously distorted seventeenth-century shape, was much less the principle than the justification of an attitude. And logic applied to the concept of sovereignty in itself would in time extract from this attitude a quite different justification, at once more durable and more dangerous.

SOVEREIGNTY IN ITSELF

Descartes shared with his contemporaries the need—which it is his claim to fame to have felt—of re-thinking reality in novel terms.

There takes place in the order of ideas a certain wear and tear which deprives notions of all definite outline, as happens to a coin which has passed from hand to hand for too long. Whether, around 1640, this wear and tear justified the demonetisation of the traditional notions of political science, is something which should not be asserted too lightly. These notions continued in vogue up to the Revolution and are found current during the constitutional crisis provoked by Maupeou. But in the seventeenth century certain bold spirits had felt the need of rationalising the social structure, taking as their point of departure (as Descartes did in another sphere) their only certitude—an individualist one like his own.

The word 'I' is as much the point of departure in the political work of Hobbes as it is in the philosophical work of Descartes. And that alone patently opposes the thought of both of them to medieval thought in general. It was Hobbes's achievement to deduce logically the necessary structure of political society from the characteristics and needs of the 'I'. His thought, like that of Descartes, owed nothing to previous thinkers. *La Méthode* opens with the words 'Je pense', and *Leviathan* might well have opened with the words 'I desire'. Hobbes in effect takes man from the point of view of the appetite which leads him to seek material things; those who delight to relate modes of thought to social forms could say that Hobbes thinks like a bourgeois, not only of acquisitive, but of possessive and fearful temperament. What was going to happen if the appetites of all took the bit between their teeth? Hobbes drew the most terrifying picture of the resulting anarchy.

And therein is the reason why the 'I' submits itself to a power which bridles its conduct; it is secured by that means in its goods and person against the appetites of others. The public authority is seen as surety for liberty and property. Without that authority, reasons Hobbes, I should be a prey to insecurity. My rights would cease to be because there would be no force guaranteeing them. This feeling of the utter nullity of right in the absence of a police force guaranteeing it would have been no less unintelligible to a grandee of feudal times than to a popular commune. It leads Hobbes on to reflect that, since only the public authority validates subjective right, it is also its only begetter; that it is for that reason the source of all rights—that the only rights are those which it creates and consecrates.

The behaviour of the 'I' is now different from that to which its appetite inclines it, for now it weighs the benefits for which it hopes against the punishments which may overtake it. There can be no other source of these punishments than the public authority. And as it can reward one behaviour and punish another, thus making one desirable and another undesirable, its position enables it to dictate behaviours.

The result is that 'every law, written or oral, draws its force and authority from the will of the state'—that is to say, from whoever has at his disposal means of constraint. In this horrific conception everything comes back to means of constraint, which enable the sovereign to issue rights and dictate laws in any way he pleases. But these means of constraint are themselves but a fraction of the social forces concentrated in the hands of the sovereign. Why have they been left with him? Because he is the source from which there comes to each man the practical advantage of seeing himself protected and assured in his individual life. All begins with the individual, all comes back to him. Doubtless, too, the sovereign is now well-placed to make war on individual rights.

But the sovereign of Hobbes's conception is one which is essentially favourable to the individual—is his ally against privileged bodies. What he fears is not the sovereign but anarchy. He is far from unaware that Power is capable of committing on its own account the very aggressions which by definition it is its office to prevent. But this consideration seems to him negligible. In his eyes the individual is in urgent need of the safety afforded by the public authority. The public authority, in which individuals put their trust, is explained by its usefulness in that respect; so it comes about that men take the public will for their own and reckon the momentary harm which that will may inflict on them of less account than the permanent benefit conferred on them by it.

The inspiration of this conception is a fearful and atheistic individualism. It owes its vast *réclame* to its perfect logical structure. In the whole social edifice it makes room for two persons only: the individual, cut down to the measure of his essential characteristic of seeking pleasure and avoiding pain, and the sovereign, cut down to his essential characteristic of disposer of force—who can for that reason either punish and make painful, or reward and make pleasurable, any behaviour whatever, as seems good to him.

Thus, the sovereign is no longer the crown of a complex social edifice, but rather the pivot of an edifice which has undergone arbitrary simplification. What makes this doctrine pleasing is the drastic curtailment of social forces to a single pair, individual-state— a curtailment which responded too well to the tendencies of the time not to leave its mark. So it was too with the affirmation that individuals lay the foundations of the public power, that the latter concentrates in itself all their natural right (which is nothing else than the individual power of each), and that it redistributes to them their civil right, which is merely what the public authority guarantees.

Locke as well as Pufendorf, and even Rousseau, were to feel the lure of this mechanically perfect construction. Though their thought differs in some respects from that of Hobbes, its starting-point is Hobbes; they think in terms of Hobbes. The idea of an entity completely empowered to regulate all behaviours made a resounding entry into political science. It was the hour of *sovereignty in itself*, whose existence hardly anyone would thenceforward have the hardihood to deny; the efforts of all would be directed merely to its division, and to such attribution of it as seemed to promise its least dangerous use. But it is the idea itself which is dangerous.

CHAPTER 12

THE THEORY OF THE REGULATED WILL
AND 'FORTUNATE POWERLESSNESS'

Man is no great inventor of ideas. The good ones are far from new, and the bad ones are no less antiquated. The band-waggon of heresy, though done up in new colours, runs back into the thousand-year-old ruts. Our intelligence, it might be said, holds certain models, which serve as the skeleton to the flesh of all its theories. The doctrines of today are but a silhouette of yesterday's, in a new dress.

Thus, the theory of sovereignty of the people, as generally advanced in our own time, is but a new version of the theories of despotism advanced in the seventeenth and eighteenth centuries to the profit of the Stuarts and Bourbons—theories which did not then win the same approval as they receive today. The claim advanced three centuries ago (and admitted today) is that the will of the sovereign makes the law for the subject, whatever the will may be and subject only to the condition that it issues from the legitimate sovereign. The king (or the people) has only to formulate a command, whether general (a law) or particular (an order), for the subject to be bound in conscience to obey, whether by doing or by refraining from doing. And the sovereign, whether king or people, is completely free as regards its wishes. It may command whatever pleases it: *quidquid principi* (or *populo*) *placuit legis habet vigorem.*

The least reflection makes it clear that, once the principle of the unchecked and unbounded sovereignty of a human will is admitted, the resulting regime is in substance the same, to whatever person, real or fictive, this sovereign will is attributed. The two systems thought to be the most opposed, that which attributes to the king an unlimited and arbitrary sovereignty and that which attributes to the people precisely the same thing, are constructed on the same intellectual model; they confer the same despotic right on the effective wielder of power, who is seldom the king and can never, by the nature of things, be the people.

The system is, in truth, the same in either case; it receives support in both for the same reasons, principally the lure offered lazy minds by over-simplified ideas.

THE 'ANCIEN REGIME' REJECTED THE DESPOTIC IDEAS IN VOGUE TODAY

The surprising thing is that so vulnerable an idea should have so great a vogue in our own time. The men of the seventeenth century were not so simple, and the despotic idea had not at that date won for itself general acceptance. It was, on the contrary, everywhere denied that it lay with the sovereign will to lay down rules as it pleased; it was not believed that its wishes, whatever they happened to be, had power to bind. Everyone knew that the ordinance of a temporal power was not morally binding in virtue of its form, if its substance did not satisfy certain conditions.

In a word, the sovereign, or his spokesmen, were less free under the *ancien régime* than they are at present, and command was less arbitrary. The more we cite the authors who advocated a change of sovereign, the more we forget (unjustly) the authors, and still more the magistrates, who applied themselves to disciplining sovereignty. Yet it is from them that we might learn today to moderate the transports of the wishes attributed to the fictive person in whose name we are governed.

What we are going to see is that from the sixteenth to the eighteenth century a theory of sovereignty held the field which I do not hesitate to call admirable; it was the doctrine of the old 'parliaments' of the monarchy, which survived the storms of the Revolution and took fresh life from Royer-Collard.

WHEN IS THE COMMAND LEGITIMATE?

Two preoccupations will always obsess the minds of men who reflect on politics.

First, in any organised society or state, there must be a supreme authority which all admit. This authority mobilises the subjects in the event of danger from without, and quells and appeases internal disputes. The state of a country in which there is no authority able at need to issue commands and get them obeyed is one of misery, desolation and ruin. At certain times persons of an authoritative temper become completely obsessed by the vital need for a sovereign, and by the need for him to be an absolute sovereign if he is to quell disputes. Their obsession gets to a point at which they overlook the second problem presented by sovereignty.

A legitimate sovereign is necessary—that is the first point. But, secondly, he must command nothing which is not legitimate, and not every order which issues from a legitimate source is legitimate. For the sovereign authority to be able to bind in conscience by its mere commands, it would be necessary that its every command should become just by the mere fact of its having been commanded; the implication of this is that there is no antecedent idea of justice for the new justice to clash with. This is an opinion which was open to Hobbes, but which is not open to Christian thinkers.

In Christian eyes there are, on the contrary, wills which are just and wills which are unjust. The wills of rulers are as much liable as those of others to go astray; their will, which is for subjects an order, may be a rebellion against God. The Christian view is that it is the duty of rulers to eschew such rebellion and that the possession of political authority does not confer on those holding it any right either to follow their own wishes or to make others follow them. On the contrary, authority carries with it the obligation to command the thing that should be commanded. *Regum timendorum in proprias greges, Reges in ipsos imperium est Jovis.*[1]

It follows that the sovereign will must not be arbitrary. But how can it not be arbitrary in fact, if it is also absolute? Bossuet brings out the difficulty:

It is one thing for a government to be absolute and another for it to be arbitrary. So far as power of constraint is concerned it is absolute, for there is no authority able to constrain the sovereign who is in this respect independent of every human authority. But it does not follow from this that the government is arbitrary.[2]

In other words, a government has not the right to act in ways contrary to reason. But, even so, supposing it commands what should not be commanded?

Théodore de Bèze has given the only answer open to the Christian

---

[1] Horace, *Odes*, III, I.
[2] Bossuet, *Politique tirée de l'Écriture Sainte.*

conscience. It would be wrong to call his answer a Protestant one, for all the Fathers of the Church can be cited in support of it:

> Only the will of God, which is the rule of all justice, is eternal and unchangeable. Therefore it is to Him alone that we are bound to give an invariable obedience. As for the obedience due to princes, we should have to admit that as invariable an obedience was due to them as was due to God if in their commands they always acted as the voice of God; but, since only too often the contrary happens, obedience to them is subject to the condition that what they command is not contrary to religion or morals. I call contrary to religion those commands which order to be done what the first Tables of the Law of God forbid, or which forbid to be done what they order. I call contrary to morals those commands obedience to which involves a man in injuring his neighbour or not rendering to him his due, according to his public or private vocation.[1]

THE PRACTICAL PROBLEM

It is not difficult to see the practical problem here posed. On the one hand, the sovereign power, if it is to be effective in its role of *defensor pacis*, must have an authority which is uncontested and supreme; it does not therefore admit of any controller, for a controller would be in some sense its superior. But this sovereign power should for all that lack the strength to do what it should not do. In Bracton's famous words, *Rex debet esse non sub homine sed sub deo et lege.*

How in practice can an all-powerful sovereign be prevented from willing what he ought not to will? There is no juridical solution to the problem.

Yet to our ancestors it presented no insurmountable difficulty. The reason was, perhaps, that their minds were less imbued with the insolence of rights than with the consonance of duties. They realised that the right of the subject and the right of the sovereign were in conflict, but their stress was on the duties which are in harmony. 'Truly it is a misfortune for men to have to be ruled by a king, who is only a man like-minded with themselves. . . . But kings are in no better case, in that, being men (which is to say weak and imperfect), they have to rule a countless multitude of corrupt and deceitful men.'[2]

Kings and peoples, being under a common obligation to serve God and obey him, have much less cause to quarrel about rights

---

[1] *Du droit des magistrats sur leurs sujets* (1581). De Bèze (1519–1605) was one of the leaders of the Calvinist party.

[2] Fénelon, *Directions pour un roi*, Supplément.

than to give each other mutual help by means of reasonable command and reasonable counsel; the subject is not so wise that he has no need of being commanded, the prince is not so wise that he has no need of counsel. We shall now see how this division of labour operated in the institutions and manners of the *ancien régime*.

NEEDED PRECAUTIONS

That we may not lose ourselves in the maze of old ideas, we must first utterly discard the writers who refused to admit that sovereignty belonged to the king indivisibly. The idea of sovereignty of the people dawned, it is true, not long after; more truly, it never lacked a few adherents. But, in the *ancien régime*, it is clear that, unless the king is looked on as holding sovereignty absolutely and immediately, discussion of the limits of the royal authority is really discussion, not of the limits of sovereignty, but of the way in which its various attributes were parcelled out.

Here what interests us exclusively is to know how sovereignty appeared to those who felt no doubt that it was concentrated in the hands of the monarch who owed it to no human authority. In other words, how did the absolutists conceive of absolutism?

We must also take a second precaution. It is not merely in our own day that the language of politics has been loose and cluttered with equivocal expressions. The unceasing attempt of the politician to influence men naturally commits him to the use of words with an emotional content; so far as he can, he enlists them in his service as mercenaries of proven worth. The verbal draperies of any political thought are inevitably misleading, for the object is not to bring understanding but to seduce.

The legal texts of the *ancien régime*, just as the legal texts of today, are full of misleading ritual flatteries. But we must not stop at the hyperbolical language in which the greatness of the royal authority was depicted, but look to see how, in the substance which follows, it was kept within bounds. These textual contradictions, moreover, are not mere formal hypocrisies. The theorists of the royal authority and even the monarch's own mouthpieces were in actual fact forever contradicting themselves, and there are no better guides to the understanding of their thought than their own *démentis*.

The kings 'exercise an absolute dominion': how does it happen then that their officials can, and on occasion should, prevent the execution of the royal orders? The right of making the laws 'belongs to the kings alone, independently and indivisibly': how does it happen then that they find themselves in a state of 'fortunate powerlessness' (*heureuse impuissance*) in the matter of changing the laws? Their will regulates all things: by what right, then, can their entourage 'cut down this will to the needful size'?

The doctrine involved seems quite incomprehensible until its hidden principle has been discovered. Let us approach it in stages.

THE FORTUNATE POWERLESSNESS OF KINGS

The same Chancellor d'Aguesseau who asserted that 'kings exercise an absolute dominion which resides in themselves and for which they are accountable to themselves alone' made Louis XV say: 'The fundamental laws of our realm put us in a condition of fortunate powerlessness to alienate the right to rule from our crown.'[1] The same Chancellor Maupeou who declared in the name of Louis XV that 'the right to make laws for the guidance and government of our subjects belongs to us alone independently and indivisibly'[2] also made him say: 'They have tried to frighten our subjects as to their status, their dignity and their property rights, even as to the future of the laws which establish the succession to the crown, as though some occasional edict could extend to these sacred immutabilities—to these institutions which we find ourselves fortunately powerless to alter.'[3]

Powerlessness in one who is all-powerful is a paradox. But would it not be an absurdity for command to liquidate itself? And if a specific powerlessness prevents it from doing so, does it not deserve the word 'fortunate'? This line of thought appears in a well-known pamphlet of the fifteenth century:

Command must necessarily be regulated by law, for law tends to the preservation of commander and commanded alike.... And therefore those who repeat, as though it were a commonplace, that the prince is above the law say what is true but give it a wrong sense. For what they mean by it is that he can break and abolish the law at will; whereas its true meaning is that he is above the law as much as a building is above its foundation—tamper with the foundation and the building collapses. In

[1] Declaration to the *Parlement* of July 1717, in Isambert's *Recueil des anciennes Lois françaises*, vol. XXI, p. 146.

[2] Declaration to the *Parlement* of December 1770, in Isambert, vol. XXII, pp. 506–7.

[3] Declaration to the *Parlement* of February 1771, in Isambert, vol. XXII, p. 513.

the same way, whenever the fundamental laws of a kingdom are tampered with, the kingdom, the king and the royal authority which are built above them collapse at once.[1]

Whatever tends to destroy sovereignty is beyond the competence of the sovereign, and estoppel of suicide constitutes no diminution of his authority. The powerlessness is fortunate because it serves the interest of sovereignty itself.

The maxim that 'the king can do no wrong' is usually given an incorrect meaning. The interpretation of it by the friends of despotism is that whatever the king does is right. But the true meaning is very different: that the king cannot do what ill accords with the end or aim of royalty. To be thus bound takes nothing from his majesty:

If evil counsellors seek to dazzle your eyes with mirages of greatness and omnipotence, telling you that you should not let your hands be tied but do and order all things at your good pleasure, you must then remember your brave words, divine as much as royal—that your liberty and greatness consist in being so straitly bound that you cannot do evil; for, in truth, ability to do evil is a mark of powerlessness rather than of real power.[2]

Leibniz, we may observe, applies the same reasoning to the sovereignty of God. It is not abridged, he says, by His being under the necessity of choosing the best:

Rather it is the truest and most perfect liberty to be able to make the best use of His free will, and to use this ability unceasingly, and without being deflected either by external force or internal passions, the former of which enslaves the body and the latter the soul. Nothing is less servile or more conformable with the highest degree of liberty than to be drawn always to the good, willingly and gladly.[3]

But the man who is king cannot have a high degree of perfection. He is not subject to external force, since all force belongs to him, but he is under the sway of the passions. Those who help him combat these passions act as precious auxiliaries to him in his mission on earth, which is that of the salvation of his people; they also serve his own eternal salvation, which will be his reward for having truly fulfilled his duty.

[1] *Briève remonstrance à la noblesse de France sur le fait de la déclaration de Mgr. le duc d'Alençon* (1576), pp. 13–14.
[2] Arnaud de Pontiac addressing Henry III in the name of the clergy of France on 3 July 1570.
[3] Leibniz, *Abrégé de la controverse avec M. Bayle* (ed. Janet), vol. II, pp. 367–8.

Nothing, therefore, is taken from sovereignty when it is constrained to walk in good ways. In his *La Grande Monarchie de France*, published in 1519, Claude de Seyssel exalted the royal authority sufficiently to please Francis I. Yet he said, among other things:

> Though he has full power and authority to command and do what pleases him, yet this great and sovereign liberty of his is tied down and bridled by good laws and ordinances, and by the number and diversity of the officers of state who are both near his person and quartered in all parts of his kingdom. Everything is not permitted him, but only what is just and reasonable and prescribed by the ordinances and the opinion of his council. Thus, kings would find it hard to do anything too violent or which inflicted too great hurt on their subjects; for they have about them various princes and other illustrious personages who serve as axes to lop off from the royal will whatever is superfluous and injurious to the public.[1]

THE REGULATED WILL

How is this? Did not the king's own officers owe to him an obedience that was prompt and perfect? Was it permissible for his entourage to lop something off from the will of the sovereign? The answer is that it was indeed permissible, and the doctrine of the *ancien régime* never varied in that respect.

Even under Richelieu's ministry, Le Bret, in his treatise *De la Souveraineté du Roy*, asserts that, in the event of the king wanting to have bad edicts put out,

> ...the sovereign courts owe it to their reputation to offer to the prince grave remonstrances and to try in every sort of way to turn him from his course. For just as it must always be presumed that the decisions of the prince are based on equity (as Solomon says, *voluntas regis labia justa*), and that when he makes ordinances he is convinced of their usefulness to the public, we must hope also that he will consent to listen to the remonstrances of his officers who seek to undeceive him and make him see the unhappy consequences both for himself and for his people, which may follow from the registration of bad edicts.[2]

This passage puts its finger on the true conception of absolute monarchy. It implies a royal will of an ideal character, whose principle is the common good, *cura salutis alienae*; as Bishop Jonas wrote in the time of Charlemagne, *rex a recte vocatur*. This royal

---

[1] C. de Seyssel, *La Grande Monarchie de France*.
[2] Le Bret, *De la Souveraineté du Roy* (1632), ch. VII, pp. 195–6.

will serves as model for the will of the man who is the king. It is this ideal will which is sovereign; it makes without qualification for the best and must therefore receive unqualified obedience. It is just and reasonable that, so far as the 'royal will' is concerned, there should be no bounds or limits to obedience. But as human weakness makes it impossible that the decisions of the man who is king should always have this 'royal' quality, the royal will is encased within certain forms, chosen with a view to making it as probable as possible that it will live up to what it should be. It follows that an ill-conceived and capricious decision of the man who is king does not partake of the 'royal will', but should be looked on as an inconsequent decision of the moment which it is the duty of good counsellors to hold up. It is not so much a right which belongs to them as a duty which falls on them.

'The object of all these things', says Seyssel, 'is so to restrain the disordered will of a wilful prince that in the long run it necessarily happens that, before his command is executed, there is time and opportunity to make him change his mind or to check it.'[1] If the king has to reach his decisions in council, if he has to have them registered and promulgated by his 'parliaments', it is not in the least because he shares his sovereignty with counsellors and officers who hold their authority from him alone, but because it is their duty to recall his will to the model of a royal will.

When our contemporaries are told of institutions which act as brakes on the expressed wish of the sovereign, they immediately ask 'what right' a Senate or a House of Lords can oppose to the un-limited right of the sovereign. But that is not the proper question to put. So viewed, it is wholly incomprehensible that the council, to which the king summons whom he pleases, and the courts of justice, whose authority issues from the king alone, should be able to oppose to his will any retarding or restricting influence. Beyond all question neither council nor courts have any 'right' as against the king. The situation should not be analysed in terms of separation of powers; perhaps Montesquieu has some responsibility for the obstinate tendency of so many today to see everything from this point of view.

Rather we must take the opposite view: that these filters to the monarch's authority are so much organs of himself that he only acts as monarch in acting through them. And this is very well expressed

---

[1] Seyssel, *op. cit.* part I, ch. XII.

in the famous argument made by Oliver St John in the Hampden case. There are, he says in substance, two wills in the King's Majesty. One is the *voluntas interna* or *naturalis* which is to be found in every man, king or knave; the other is his *voluntas externa* or *legalis*, which is peculiar to the sovereign and declares itself according to the occasion either in council or through legislation. This objective will, which is the sovereign will, is the product only of the observance of forms, but for which it is no more than an individual will.

To instance: His Majesty is the fountain of bounty; but a grant of land without letters patent transfers no estate out of the King, nor by letters patent but by such words as the law hath prescribed. His Majesty is the fountain of justice; and though all justice which is done within the realm flows from this fountain, yet it must run in certain and known channels.[1]

VICAR OF GOD—AND A MINOR

Under the *ancien régime* these two sayings were equally current: 'The king is God's vicar' and 'the king is always a minor'. How are they to be reconciled? One asserts that the king occupies on earth the place of God—that is to say, he has an unlimited right of command. And the other ranks him among those whom lawyers call 'unable to plead', except through a proxy. There is, however, nothing illogical in this.

Let us suppose, playfully and improperly, that it is necessary to replace God in the government of the universe, and that a vicar has been put in to manage this exalted office. The latter must now act with the divine wisdom and justice of God himself. But he is still not God. Are there not grounds for fearing that he may disturb the order of the world? Is not this imperfect lieutenant bound to feel sudden caprices which he will be unable to reconcile with the general laws maintaining the harmony of the whole?

'The wiser a man is, the less he is prone to unrelated decisions and the more comprehensive and connected are his views. Each particular decision is conceived in relation to all other decisions, to the end that their integration may be the best possible.'[2] These characteristics of the divine government, as Leibniz sets them down,

---

[1] Argument of Oliver St John in the case of Ship Money (Howell's *State Trials*, vol. III).

[2] Leibniz, *Nouveaux Essais sur l'Entendement* (ed. Janet), vol. I, p. 507.

are not found in the rule of the vicar. Therefore, so that he may not wreck what God has built, the fundamental laws which regulate the course of things must be placed beyond his reach.[1] The general providential order is thus stabilised by reason of the 'fortunate powerlessness' of the vicar, who must then be constrained to exercise his special providence reasonably and virtuously. This requires that he be protected as far as possible against the disorders natural to his fallen state. Wisdom requires 'that the monarch do nothing by sudden and disorderly caprice, but act advisedly in all things'. We are back to the formula of Seyssel.

Rightly aghast at his responsibilities, to which it is the duty of his spiritual guides and experienced counsellors to recall him continually, the vicar will himself desire 'to maintain in working the checks by which absolute power is regulated'.[2] Those who constrain him to follow the path of right will not be for him obstacles to his authority or rivals to his power, but rather the indispensable auxiliaries of his royalty, since they will help him to remain everything which a king should be.

THE ABSOLUTE AND THE ARBITRARY

We see then that the conception of sovereignty in absolute monarchy is at the antipodes to arbitrariness. The definition of arbitrariness has been given by Juvenal: *sit pro ratione voluntas*. The will of the sovereign takes the place of reason. Arbitrary government, says Bossuet, is that in which there is no law other than the will of the sovereign.[3] In his *La Science du Gouvernement*, Réal carried the definition further: 'There is no recognised law other than the will of the prince and this will exalts itself above laws natural and positive, divine and human.'[4]

The perfection of absolute monarchy may be defined by turning the Latin formula around: *sit pro voluntate ratio*. It is a government in which the sovereign will is absolute, but in which every precaution, moral or material, has been taken to ensure that this will coincides with reason. In theory, the monarch can do whatever he wills; but

---

[1] Leibniz, *ibid.* 'I hold that there are but few freely taken decrees which can be called universal laws such as regulate the course of things...just as but few hypotheses are needed to explain phenomena.' Pp. 525–6.

[2] Seyssel, *op. cit.*   [3] Bossuet, *Politique tirée de l'Écriture Sainte.*

[4] P. F. Réal, *Science du Gouvernement*, vol. I, p. 299.

he is allowed to will only what is just and reasonable—he cannot do what is unjust and unreasonable because he is deemed not to have willed it. In this way he is held in check without violation of his majesty. Whatever different forms it may take, the intellectual conception is basically the same in different authors. They hold in common the conviction that there are natural laws which can be known by reason and that it is the royal duty to apply them.

If, by reason of their infirmity, the ordering of men must take the form of a will, in substance it is not a will: it is reason. What right would a will which was not reason have to force the moral allegiance of men? Men can be constrained physically to do what a particular man wants them to do: they cannot be bound in conscience. Their moral allegiance is to what is best, and command is valid for them to the extent that it enjoins what is best—that is to say, to the extent that it is itself 'subject to reason', as Bossuet puts it: 'First, the royal authority is sacred; secondly, it is paternal; thirdly, it is absolute, by which is meant independent; and fourthly, it is subject to reason.'[1]

It is essential that it be independent of every human will, so that it may render complete obedience to reason alone. And it is the degree of its submission to reason which justifies the degree of its authority over men.

Guizot has expressed this very well:

> Royalty is something quite different from the will of one man, though that is the form under which it appears. It is the personification of the sovereignty of law, of a will which is essentially reasonable, enlightened, just and impartial, which rises above all individual wills and is for that reason entitled to govern them. That is what royalty means in the minds of peoples, therein is the reason for their allegiance.[2]

It thus appears that the sovereign will is not in the least the subjective will of the sovereign. It is, rather, an objective will, the product of reason, of which the sovereign should be the bearer.

The perfect sovereign is, therefore, perfectly unfree, if I may so put it. At each single moment he is tied down to doing whatever maximises the common good. This way of thinking presupposes that there is in every sphere, the useful no less than the just, a 'best'. The entire conception breaks down if we say, with Hobbes, that nothing is good except what is desired. In that case anyone with

---

[1] Bossuet, *ibid.*

[2] Guizot, *Histoire de la civilisation européenne*, near the end.

the power prescribes the best to his own taste—it ranks as best only from having been so prescribed. In that event the sovereign has complete liberty instead of being tied down to complete submission. It is then the reign of arbitrariness: *sit pro ratione voluntas*.

This way of thinking, under which the sovereign can prescribe and do anything he likes, is at the other extreme from the doctrine of the monarchists of the *ancien régime*. The French magistrates repudiated this idea with the utmost energy.

In order to attribute to the prince this unlimited authority, it is necessary to adopt the system of Hobbes, who knows no other rule of good or bad, just or unjust, than the civil laws; who regards as good everything which the prince commands and as bad everything which he forbids. From this he concluded that sovereigns are impeccable and can never rightly be blamed. Their will makes the just and the unjust; therefore they can never encroach on what is another's because it becomes theirs the moment that they want it.

How is it possible for them to act unrighteously? There is nothing unrighteous except what they have forbidden because they have forbidden it, and they forbid themselves nothing.[1]

THE TWO DOCTRINES OF RESISTANCE TO ROYAL ARBITRARINESS

There is, it is clear, a fundamental difference between the conception of a royal authority whose conduct is predetermined both by pre-existing moral imperatives and ever-present rational imperatives and that of a despotic authority without guiding rule.

Under the first system, governmental action should follow the line of a curve which can in principle be plotted; when action departs from the curve, it is a duty owed to the sovereign himself to recall him to his prescribed course. Under the second system, governmental action has no other rule than the will which animates it. In the struggle waged throughout the *ancien régime* against the lapses of power, the first doctrine was constantly invoked—especially in the great battle between the *parlements* and Maupeou, the Chancellor, in 1770–1.

And at various other times war was waged against arbitrariness; it was denied that sovereignty belonged to the king alone, or even that it belonged to him at all. For instance, during the wars of religion, according to the shifting interests of the parties at strife,

---

[1] *Maximes du droit public français* (2nd ed. Amsterdam, 1775), vol. I, pp. 141–2.

first Hotman, the Reformer, and then Jean Le Boucher, the Leaguer, set up sovereignty of the people against sovereignty of the king.[1] It was a Catholic pen which wrote:

> It is in the Estates of the realm that the sovereign power and public majesty which make and establish kings reside naturally and originally; kings exist in virtue of popular approval and not of divine or natural law. When the Estates have established a government, it always remains within their competence to change it.
>
> The power of establishing and disestablishing in this respect dwells with the people and Estates, who are the eternal guardians of sovereignty and judges of sceptres and realms; of these they are the origin and source, for it is they who have made kings not by necessity or constraint but by their own free choice.[2]

To say that the sovereign will is subject to reason is one thing; to say that it is subject to the people is another. And it is a natural reaction to an arbitrary will to say: 'What you are doing is not reasonable and we do not want it.' But there is a world of difference according to whether or not it is added: 'And the reason why we do not want it is that it is unreasonable.' If this addition is omitted, if the rejection is not the sanction laid on the immorality or absurdity of the thing ordered and is founded only on a superior right belonging to the people, it is clear that this superior right can itself become justification for immoral or absurd commands. Jurieu said just this in speaking of the English Revolution:

> It is not even important to know whether in all this the nation has on the whole acted rightly. For even when it is wrong, there must still be in every society some authority which need not have acted rightly to have acted validly; and that authority resides only in peoples.
>
> It is certain that if peoples are the primary seat of sovereignty they have no need to act rightly for their acts to be valid.[3]

We see here the start of the landslide in ideas which was to convert the struggle against arbitrary acts 'in the name of the king' into the unlimited authorisation of arbitrary acts 'in the name of the people'. All the care that had been taken to keep the commanding will subject to reason was to prove wasted effort the moment that it was said that the commanding will should be subject to and identified with the will of the people; all the guarantees of social conservation

---

[1] Hotman, *Franco-Gallia* (1575).
[2] J. Le Boucher, *Sermons de la simulée conversion* (1594).
[3] Jurieu, *Lettres pastorales*.

and individual liberty which were given by a sovereign will subject to reason disappear the moment that the sovereign will is merely the will of another sovereign whose larger numbers do not render him any less subject to moral infirmities than was the king.

Those men were right who refused to admit that law was the expression of the subjective will of the king. They might have said with Montesquieu that it is the expression of the necessary relationships which stem from the nature of things; or they could have borrowed the more precise language of St Thomas and called it the *dictamen* of practical reason. What they in fact said was that it was the expression of the general will. This expression, which, as Rousseau meant it, still denoted an objective will, was quickly understood as signifying the subjective will of a majority. The entire labour of the old jurists in their attempts to formulate the limitations on sovereignty was then thrown away, notwithstanding the efforts of men like Benjamin Constant, Royer-Collard, Guizot and Tocqueville to train the artillery of ideas onto a new arbitrariness.

The 'majoritarian' will knows no 'fortunate powerlessness', and it is not subject to the condition of being 'regulated' in the exercise of its sway. And yet, if it was ever true to say in other days that the will of the king was ill-contrived and capricious, that it had been overwhelmed by bad counsellors and that it must be recalled to just and reasonable courses, how much more applicable now would be this same system of thought, when it is a case of an unwieldy mass whose means of information and expression are incomparably worse.

THE 'FEED-BACK'

The theme of this chapter could be expressed in language of the most modern kind. We apply today the generic term, 'feed-back', to any organ found in an organism or to any mechanism installed in a machine, which registers the fact that some activity or impulse is going too far or getting out of gear; the 'feed-back' signals to the centre from which the activity or impulse comes messages which effectively check or adjust the process, so that it does not go further than is needed for the effective functioning of the organism or the machine. It would be unscientific to suppose that these regulative mechanisms hinder the perfect working of the machine or organism.

The attentive reader will certainly not have concluded that it is a simple problem to regulate satisfactorily the governing will—still less that it can be resolved in terms of constitutional procedure. It would be childish to think that, once a body had been set up with orders to be reasonable, it could not help being reasonable, and that, once it had been given the task of influencing sovereign wills, the only decrees ever issued would be good ones. The experience of the old *parlements*, who allotted themselves this role but sometimes played it far from satisfactorily, would be enough to give the lie to this optimistic conclusion. We cannot assume in any body of men either perfection of virtue or infallibility of judgment.

All that can be said with certainty is that we form a puerile and dangerous idea of the good 'polity' when we suppose it to be one in which the sovereign will meets with no check in the body politic; on the contrary, the presence of adequate checks is the condition on which every organ functions well and is preserved.

PART IV

LIBERTY

CHAPTER 13

THE POLITICAL CONSEQUENCES
OF DESCARTES

It is as much outside my subject as it is beyond my capacity to discuss the nature of science. But my argument demands that I should venture a few remarks on the form in which knowledge is communicated.

We say to a small child that 'the fire burns'. Philosophically, this way of speaking, which attributes an action to what is not even properly an object, may be held incorrect; but it is natural, and necessary for the imparting of information. What we, the unlearned, ask of a savant in a given science is simply that he should ascribe to the objects of his study tendencies the knowledge of which will enable us to predict events—and eventually to modify or produce these events. The proposition: 'Opium has a narcotic property' is a sure and useful piece of information; it is a good thing to know, even though curiosity ought not to stop there.[1]

Science, in its aspect of immediate and useful knowledge, may be conceived as a vast collection of propositions relating to tendencies of objects. Research penetrates far behind the veil of visible objects and the properties which they display; but from these great voyages of exploration it always returns with a further batch of affirmations concerning the activities of visible objects. It is fascinating to reflect that Einstein's theory won approval in our own time for the special reason that it made possible accurate prediction of the visible movements of Mercury, just as in earlier days the accurate prediction of the movements of Venus won approval for the theory of Galileo. In the end the conquests of science resolve themselves into verifiable predictions—'a particular object will act in a particular way'—and at the level at which discoveries are put to practical use it does not matter that the said object dissolves on analysis and

---

[1] To avoid confusion, we hasten to add that the proposition that 'opium sends to sleep because it has a narcotic property' is, by reason of its claim to make an explanation out of a tautology, ridiculous. But to say that 'opium has a narcotic property' is not tautological; the statement announces a piece of concrete information.

its action is caused by something else. Moreover, such is our need to think in terms of tendencies ascribed to these objects (subject and attribute), that this way of speaking turns up again at the threshold of modern physics. To explain certain subtle phenomena of radio-activity, scientists have posited a species of 'thing' called the 'neutron' and have assigned to it properties and tendencies.[1]

My meaning is that the fruit of every science, however far its researches are pushed, is always expressed in the form of the ascription of tendencies to objects. It is the indispensable method of communication with the practical man, and one which is, perhaps, natural to our intelligence—but my purpose does not require me to go so far. I will conclude these general remarks by observing that progress in every science is by way of better ascriptions, which are more conformable to experience and make possible more exact predictions; and that the theorist who goes further, and seeks to find behind the qualities of objects the primary and simple principles of which these qualities are the various manifestations, is always subject to the condition that his theory throws light on the qualities of visible objects and makes it easier to foresee the events which may be expected to flow from them.

MAN IN GENERAL

In early childhood we find persons the most visible and important of 'objects'; there is no object whose tendencies it is more necessary for us to know. So much is this the case that it is possible to wonder whether our very idea of object is not derived from our idea of person; but this is not the place to go into that.

It is universally agreed that to be a good judge of men is a very valuable accomplishment. But what precisely is it? The judge of men knows how to ascribe to each the tendencies which are proper to and characteristic of him—the tendencies which he will manifest in action and which another must for better or worse take into account. During the Waterloo campaign, Napoleon did not realise the need to protect himself against the economical spirit of Soult, who sent to Grouchy many fewer despatch-riders than Berthier (his previous chief of staff) would have done. Our instance itself indicates a vast difference between knowledge relating to men and knowledge relating to things.

[1] Cf. G. Bachelard, *L'Activité rationaliste de la Physique contemporaine* (Paris, 1951), pp. 118–21.

Things which are in the same sufficiently defined category all display exactly the same properties and are interchangeable; it is not so with men. The knowledge of things is by species, the knowledge of men is by individuals.

The great ambition of the political scientist is, however, to be like other scientists. To this end he looks for basic characteristics and common tendencies which he can ascribe to all men—to Man as such. Certainly this is an honourable ambition, but it needs remembering that in no science whatever is theory an end in itself. If some theory is erected on a foundation of observation and experience, what will come out of the theory are tentative ascriptions of tendencies to sensible objects; and, according as the event does or does not verify these imputed tendencies consequent on the theory, it will be thought right to keep or reject the theory. But, for more than three centuries now, ideas have been put forward and discussed of the basic characteristics and essential tendencies of Man in general, without any attempt to find for them an empirical verification. Notwithstanding which, all our political and social institutions have been reconstructed on the basis of these ideas.

This last remark prompts the answer that these ideas cannot have been false and inadequate, seeing that the aforesaid institutions function not too badly; to this answer reply may be made that the reality of the institutions is greatly different from their principle and that this impurity in them, for which they are taken to task, is really due to the relaxation of intellectual imperatives under the pressure of social necessities. The institutions 'made for Man', which have been adjusted to some general idea of Man, have been remade on coming into effective contact with men.

THAT EVERY 'IDEA OF MAN' IS NECESSARILY AMBIGUOUS

There is a long history behind the discussion touched on in the last paragraph, but it is an unprofitable discussion. For any idea that is entertained of Man can never be true in the sense that an idea entertained of a thing can be true. No doubt 'the nature' which we ascribe to a thing is never more than a projection of the mind, but we are allowed to forget that fact in the case of a nature which lends itself to every sort of verification by observation and experience. We may make successive corrections in our mental image which we call 'nature of the object', so as to obtain an ever growing correlation between the predictions based on this nature and actual events;

thereby, instead of saying merely that we have a more and more useful image of the object, we are enabled to say as well that our knowledge of the nature of the object is always improving. Language of this kind brings no disadvantage in practice, for, as far as we are concerned, everything goes on as if the object really had a nature which we understand better and better—a nature which passively awaits, as it were, the progress of our intellectual conquest in its regard. By means of this nature, we think, the object can be grasped in its entirety. Once we know this nature, then the behaviour of the object in all sorts of circumstances and under pressure from all sorts of forces seems to us predetermined and altogether predictable.

But every idea of Human Nature (or even of the nature of a particular man) which we can construct on this model is hopelessly false. Man is an object which has no 'nature' in the sense in which we have just been using the word; no definition of his properties is so comprehensive as to make possible the assertion that his behaviour will necessarily be of a certain kind. And that, not because our knowledge is not sufficiently advanced, but because there is no constancy of nature by which man may be grasped in his entirety. Whatever idea we may form of the nature of a man cannot be true in the sense that an idea of the nature of a thing is true, that is to say, wholly verifiable by the event and certainly predictable. And it would be a logical absurdity to suppose that such an idea of human nature can ever be acquired.

The very fact that we do not think it a waste of time to address advice, exhortations and appeals to someone shows two things: first, that he may act in a way which we deprecate, and next, that it is possible for him to act in another way which we approve. The invariable attitudes of men to each other attest that we mutually ascribe to one another this faculty of choice. And this bars the idea of complete predictability, and with it the notion of a 'nature' which subjects a man to the same determining necessities as a thing.

Language discloses the fundamental ambiguity which underlies the concept of 'human nature'. For we invoke 'human nature' indifferently both to excuse Primus, whom we condemn for having behaved badly, and to stimulate Secundus to behave well. In saying of Primus that he has 'obeyed human nature', we represent it as something which has necessarily determined his behaviour, as though what was in question was a thing and not a man; whereas we tell Secundus that his natural duty is of a certain kind, that the natural law requires him to behave in a certain manner—which he may or may not do. 'The natural law' of an object leaves it with no option as to the course which it will follow; there is no need to instruct the object in its law. Different indeed is the 'natural law' which we teach Secundus, to which it is, in our view, his duty to conform though we fear his possible failure to observe it!

It could be plausibly advanced that each of the two 'natures' invoked is the same in kind as the nature of a thing, and that what differentiates a man from a thing is his possession of two natures. He has a fallen nature, which he obeys just as a thing obeys its nature, and another nature which, though mislaid for a time, can be recovered; by means of this other nature, whenever he returns to or is recalled to it, he fulfils 'the natural law' by a process which is as inevitable as the first, or as that operating in the case of things. The argument presents the freedom of man as a choice between two natures, both present in him, each of which, whenever he has recourse to it, determines his actions just as inevitably as its own proper nature determines the actions of any object whatsoever.

This way of conceiving man as the bearer of two natures, *homo duplex*, turns up in the most varied quarters,[1] for human thought employs only a few models. Only the most clear-sighted of these authors have seen that this conception is a two-storey 'materialisation' of man; he is like a thing when he obeys his lower nature, but even when he attains obedience to the law of his higher nature he is still only another thing, as irresistibly ordered about by his higher nature as formerly he had been by the nature from which he has escaped. In fact, what makes him a man is only his continual capacity to choose the nature which he will obey. This view of man as both brute and angel but as free in neither capacity—as free only to be brute at some times and angel at others, or at any rate one rather more than the other—has played an immense role in human thought.[2] Whatever its merits and drawbacks, I doubt that it plays a profitable part in political science.

---

[1] Am I wrong in thinking that it dominates the thought of Marx? Think of the world of difference he supposes between the conduct of man in bourgeois society and what it would be in socialist society! Can so much pessimism on the one hand and optimism on the other be explained except by postulating that the predominance of private property or its extinction entails in a man the operation of one or the other of his two natures? I hesitate to impute so foolish a view to so eminent an author.

[2] It is a curious feature of our times that duality of nature has been ascribed to light: sometimes it is corpuscles and sometimes waves.

Without prolonging further a discussion which is not indispensable to our argument, we will merely observe that nothing else but man raises in the mind two images, the one drawn from experience and the other ideal. Our everyday life makes useful and necessary to us forecasts as to the behaviour of objects entering our lives, the chief of which are men themselves. We form particular judgments on the individuals with whom we are regularly brought in contact, and from these judgments we draw generic judgments applicable to those whom we know little or not at all. Practical judgments of this kind are conditioned by our milieu, and we infer 'human nature' from the behaviours which are familiar to us, so much so that a *sansculotte* was as completely beyond the imagination of a *philosophe* of eighteenth-century salons as Hitler was beyond Mr Neville Chamberlain's. Thus, the man of our practical judgment is the man of our group, who resembles us and acts very much as we do—perhaps rather better, as was well said by Bergson.[1] This starting point for common sense is also that for every study of social science which deserves the name.

To speak thus is not to say that every ideal image of man is a vain thing. So to think would be the height of folly, for it is the special attribute of man to wish to, and to be able to, acquire resemblance to an image which is presented to him. But, if social science has to recognise the power of the image to modify behaviour in the milieu in which it gets diffused, its true premise is still the behaviour (as modified) and not the modifying image.

The ideal image must, however, be allowed to enter as such into a whole host of concrete attitudes. Let us illustrate this fact with an example taken at random: in our deeply christianised society, an individual whose life has been a long succession of crimes is not as such a 'criminal', but a man who has committed crimes—a quite different thing. It is well understood between us that he is not wholly defined by his proven activities, and that there is still something else in him which remains worthy of respect.

The Christian idea of man has lost none of its power over minds which have rejected the faith; striking proof of this is found in the failure of these minds, while accepting as true the hypothesis of natural selection, to give practical effect to it. If it is true that matter, having received life, progresses from lower to higher forms of organism, two conclusions seem to flow from the fact. First, the

[1] *Les Deux Sources de la Morale et de la Religion*, p. 4.

progress of our species will be the better assured the more care and advantages that we lavish on the higher types without bothering about the lower types, whose reproduction it will be reasonable to prevent. Secondly, human societies being themselves regarded as living organisms, it will be reasonable, as in every other complex organism, to make the less developed cells serve to maintain and foster the higher forms of life. Natural selection logically demands an inequality of rights favouring the human specimens who carry the best chances for the future of the species. At one time, when individualism was in vogue, it was said that the new view of biological history (made necessary by evolution) required that individual initiatives should be left to take their course freely, thus bringing natural selection into play. But, more than that, this view justifies as well a socialism which steers social resources to the most gifted individuals, thus favouring their development at the expense of other people's. Yet, during the century in which natural selection came into its own, all the social institutions of the West evolved in the opposite direction to that called for by this inegalitarian logic—such was the force of Christian ideas.

It is a curious thing, moreover, but true, that political applications of the Christian idea of man grew and multiplied at the very time that Christian theology was rejected. So long as this theology prevailed, its metaphysical affirmations about man played but a small part in political institutions. Over the whole field of temporal organisation, the image of man most regarded[1] was the predictable, as we have called it, and not the ideal. And this was reasonable enough; an engineer does not base his installations on the ideal output of the motors which he employs but on their probable effective output. The improvement of motors is one thing, the best use of those available quite another. This distinction will be lost to view if dummies based on 'the motor in itself' are erected; the real start of this over-simplification was in the seventeenth century—it is already visible in the arguments which accompanied the English Revolution.

In the following pages we will pay attention to the consequences which ensued on the Cartesian theory of man; that theory no longer

[1] It was not often that political thought regarded an *idea* of man; for ultimately the glossarists wielded more influence than the theologians. It is only with the Jesuit doctors of the late sixteenth century that we begin to find philosophic thought about man applied to political conclusions. They are perhaps the real fathers of modern political thought.

opposes a man who is predictable to a man who is possible ideally, but pictures a man 'in himself' who is by hypothesis the single image of a source of phenomena.

THE CARTESIAN DICHOTOMY

On the one hand I have a clear and distinct idea of myself as being only a thing which thinks and has no extent, and on the other I have a distinct idea of the body as being only a thing which has extent and does not think.[1]

I distinguish two sorts of instincts. One is in us in our capacity as men and is purely intellectual: it is the 'natural light' or *intuitus mentis*. The other is in us in our capacity as animals and is a certain impulsion of nature to the conservation of our body and the enjoyment of bodily pleasures—which ought not to be followed invariably.[2]

The admirable clarity of Descartes' style leaves no room for doubt. He ascribes to man two 'natures', which are at work in him simultaneously. This conception has striking merits: it accounts perfectly for the phenomenon, so often encountered, of heterogeneity of judgment and action. The words of Ovid, attested as they are by innumerable other quotations, are in perfect agreement with Cartesian thought. *Deteriora sequor* evokes by the choice of verb the pull of my animal nature which I obey, as a thing obeys its nature; *video meliora proboque* evokes on the contrary the static and contemplative attitude of the spectator and judge, which is that of my intellectual nature.

The dangers of this conception, which so much preoccupied Leibniz, are not slow in appearing. It is admittedly conceivable that these two natures are entirely distinct and that each is pure of its kind. The more apt for knowledge Descartes made our intellectual nature, the more legitimate it is to suppose by analogy that our animal nature is entirely subject to influences proper to itself; the logical conclusion is to conceive of man as thinking like an angel and acting like a beast. The hypothesis of the two distinct natures at work simultaneously then raised the question of the link between them—a question which has never been satisfactorily resolved in the Cartesian system.

But let us ignore the latter problem, for what we are concerned to

---

[1] *Méditation sixième* (ed. Gibert), II, 157.
[2] Letter to Mersenne of 16 October 1639, quoted by Laberthonnière, *Autour de Descartes*, I, 77–8.

do here is to examine our intellectual nature as Descartes conceived
it. He saw that nature as limited, but as perfect within its limits.
'Whatever we conceive clearly and distinctly to belong to the nature
of something can truly be said and affirmed about that something.'[1]
The clear idea is true, and our errors come only from extending our
intuitus mentis to objects which are not accessible to it: 'What is the
source of our errors? It lies here only that, my will being much wider
and more extensive than my understanding, I do not confine it
within the same limits as my understanding, but extend it to things
which I do not understand.'[2] We may picture this conception by
saying that the mind sees truths by means of a light which comes to
it from God but that its own disposition allows it to reflect only on
certain objects. These are those which it is free to see; it goes astray
when it tries to see those which are outside its angle of reflection.
Descartes writes:

> Whenever I restrain my will within the bounds of my knowledge so
> that the only things on which it passes any judgment are those which are
> clearly and distinctly represented to it by the understanding, I cannot be
> mistaken; because every clear and distinct conception is beyond question
> something definite, and cannot consequently derive its existence from
> nothingness but must necessarily have God for its author. And God,
> being perfect, cannot be cause of any error.[3]

These few citations will sufficiently recall the Cartesian episte-
mology to those who have ever studied him; it carries the important
corollary that the ideas which are clear are, potentially at any rate,
common to all men. For, as the understanding is conceived as
seeing what it sees illumined by a light which comes from God,
this light is the same for all men. This explains the apparently
paradoxical proposition that reason is naturally equal in all men,[4]
who have the same intellectual nature. What appears to me clearly
and distinctly is true not only for me but absolutely.[5] In consequence
others should see it as I do. Very often they do not so see it, but that
is because of their failure to pay attention[6] or because they are
encumbered with prejudices.[7] Therefore the more they have cast off

---

[1] *Réponses aux deuxièmes objections* (aux Méditations), ed. Gibert, II, 219.
[2] *Méditation quatrième*, II, 140.
[3] *Ibid.* 143.
[4] *Discours de la méthode*, at the beginning.
[5] *Principes de la philosophie*, 43. 'It is certain that we shall never take the false for the true so long as we are judging only of what we see clearly and distinctly.'
[6] *Ibid.* 45.　　　　　　　　　　[7] *Ibid.* 50.

prejudices and learnt to exercise their intelligences, the more they will agree.

This consequence of 'more agreement' flows logically from Descartes' thought and is of the greatest importance. We may reasonably expect history to be the register of the continuous and inevitable advances in harmony between men if, with every exercise of intelligence, they cannot help becoming more unanimous in the recognition of common truths on which each of them will base his particular judgments.

No doubt it is true that each single man will not discover these truths for himself, since everyone does not pay the same attention; but men's intelligences, once trained, will be quick to receive the truths presented, and the self-evidence of those truths will, as Mercier de La Rivière puts it, take in the end absolute possession of them.[1] And there will be important truths for the body social as well as necessary truths for the mind, so that, in an educated people, it will be possible to make laws with unanimous approval.[2]

Descartes did not go to the length of saying this and there is no indication of his having thought it, and I would hazard the guess (if speculations of the kind were not always out of place) that he would have seen in it just that extension of the *intuitus mentis* beyond its proper limits, which he made the source of our errors.

---

[1] He asks us 'to consider what our ignorance would be without the help of instruction, and what is, after instruction, the irresistible force of self-evidence—the absolute possession of us which it takes'. (*L'Ordre naturel et essentiel des Sociétés politiques*, London, 1767.) The following extracts from vol. I, pp. 98–101, complete the picture.

'Beyond all doubt there are truths which sufficient examination has made so clear and obvious that it is no longer possible for the mind to conceive reasons for doubting them, once it is aware of the reasons which have caused it to accept them.'

'Our minds move naturally along the path of self-evidence, and doubt is a state which we find tiring and disagreeable. We may, therefore, look on self-evidence as the mind's repose; the mind finds in it a species of well-being much resembling that which physical repose brings to the body.'

'We may, therefore, regard self-evidence as a beneficent divinity which rejoices in giving the earth peace. You do not see geometricians at war about truths which are self-evident to them; if any momentary disputes do arise among them, it is only in so far as they are still at the stage of research, and the only aim of such disputes is the task of creating certainty. But as soon as self-evidence has pronounced for or against, each lays down his arms, and gives himself over to the peaceable enjoyment of this common good.'

[2] It should be noted that this final unanimity of an instructed people is at the opposite pole to the original unanimity of an ignorant people—of which Rousseau speaks. Rousseau believed not in growing convergence but in growing divergence.

'THE POLITICAL CONSEQUENCES OF DESCARTES'

The title of this chapter gives me some scruple which it is time to explain. The enthusiastic reception accorded Cartesianism has given an immense vogue to the notion of self-evidence; it has received applications which Descartes himself would have disavowed. It is the fate of the thought of all great writers to undergo extensions and developments, some of which are veritable distortions. The resulting whole may be regarded, historically speaking, as the consequences of the original thinker, so long as it is realised that the link of some of these consequences with his thought is logical and the link of others only psychological.

It flows, I think logically, from the Cartesian system that an idea which is for a given individual clear and distinct, and is true if it is clear and distinct, must always be capable of being made clear and distinct for other understandings as well; that unanimity on this idea, even if it has not been actually reached, is potentially available and that approach to such unanimity will in fact always be in progress. So far, I think, Descartes is personally responsible.

But he is not responsible when ideas which are not clear and distinct are endowed with the virtue of self-evidence. The language is, it is true, a Cartesian language; had Descartes not lived it would not have been used, and we may certainly see in it the consequences of him, but he cannot be held responsible for it. This may seem a subtle distinction, but I am often struck by our tendency to treat great thinkers rather after the manner of the Chinese, who praised and blamed ancestors according to the behaviour of their descendants.

CONCEIVING AND UNDERSTANDING

Descartes has perfectly distinguished Conceiving and Understanding. Conceiving is seeing with the mind's eye a clear and distinct image which is in the mind. Understanding is to have a full knowledge of all the properties of any object to which thought applies itself. But we can have full knowledge only of our own concepts. When I think of a right-angled triangle, I have only to consider this image with sufficient attention to draw from it, beyond the possibility of contradiction, all the properties of such a triangle. In short, every clear and distinct concept carries with it its entire comprehension—implicitly at any rate.

Very different is the case of images of concrete objects. However hard I apply myself to thinking 'tree', the attention which I devote to my representation will never give me a comprehensive knowledge of the properties of trees. I am, to start with, unable to form a distinct idea of the tree, for my memory presents to me in succession the image now of one tree and now of another without my mind feeling compelled to settle on one rather than another. But suppose I succeed in abstracting from this flux of images a representation of 'tree in itself'; what I think about it will have no significance, and I shall know nothing of what researches into plant biology can teach me. So far as concrete objects are concerned, the generic concept that can be formed of them results from a process of reducing to a common denominator the objects of the class of which we have sensible experience; the concept consists merely of the contribution made by our sensible experience—a contribution diminished by the elimination of the known elements which we have found not to be common to all the objects of the class. A concept of this kind is merely a cul-de-sac; there is nothing to be got from reflection on it—no increase of understanding.

Where concepts are concerned, self-evidence is a valid notion; once the concept of 'circle' is given, it is self-evident that the radii are equal. But it is not self-evident that the earth is (more or less) round; that is a piece of knowledge which is acquired and communicated. And I cannot deduce from this acquired knowledge even approximately that all the radii of the earth are equal; it is not strictly provable.

Thus we see that the notion of self-evidence has been extended beyond the area in which Descartes allowed it validity. It has no application to concrete objects. We may observe, however, that it becomes less inapt when applied to objects which are really more in the nature of concepts than objects; it is reasonable to say 'it is self-evident that the fire burns', just because 'fire' is not an object in the true sense but rather a human concept which includes the property of burning. This concept as such, however, teaches us nothing about the cause of 'fire'.

SELF-EVIDENCE IN POLITICAL THEORIES

One is always entitled to deduce from a concept the affirmations which belong to it. But to extend such affirmations to an object to which the concept is ill-related is a very different thing. Let us take a simple example: the proposition of Adam Smith that each man is the best judge of his own interest. In itself, this proposition is incontestable; indeed the interest of Primus only provides a clear concept if I understand by it what interests Primus and what he prefers—in short, his own choice. None, it is clear, can know his preferences as well as himself. But let me once substitute for the concept 'interest of Primus' a defined objective, such as extracting the largest possible profit from his farm, and the proposition loses all certainty.

We conceive of a planet revolving in a circle around a central body, and we can then affirm with certainty that it will always be at the same distance from the central body. But convey this affirmation to the case of the Earth and the Sun, and we shall have said something false, because the Earth does not move in a circle. In all the natural sciences we adopt concepts as hypotheses and we draw from them logically valid deductions, but when the deductions are belied by experience we reject the hypotheses themselves.

In politics this does not happen because political concepts have a transcendental value ascribed to them, so much so that if the example just given were of something political we should even try to make the Earth revolve in a circle. The reason for this is, no doubt, some compulsion on the mind which makes it unwilling to submit to reality in the political sphere, willing as it is to do so in others. The truth is seen to be that the forms dear to the mind are not always those actually taken by things; the mind longs for the simple and is forever confronting the complex. An illustration will show this.

THE PROBLEM OF THE ORCHARD

Let us suppose that the following problem is put to a hundred pupils at school: 'There are in an orchard one hundred thousand apples to gather. How many heaps must be formed and how many apples should be put in each?' There are an infinite number of possible solutions to the problem, but the pupils will envisage two answers only, the first one hundred heaps of one thousand apples, the second one thousand heaps of one hundred apples.

If now, instead of posing this question as a problem to one hundred children, we send the children into the orchard in question with orders to construct heaps of apples, we shall find, when they have finished the job, several large heaps and several small, built to no apparent shape or size. Thus the solution reached by activity will be very different from that conceived by the mind.[1]

This very simple example brings out a fundamental feature of politics, namely, the contrast between the structures conceived by the intelligence of man and those realised by his activity. There being such a contrast—a theme which cannot be developed here—it is clear that, if the legislator is animated by ever stronger intellectual compulsions, then the more numerous are the social ties and the more varied the social combinations, the greater and more continuous must be his reformist activity; yet he will never succeed in reducing the gap between the thing conceived and the structures actually found, so that his fine words will always seem a mockery.

DEMOCRACY OF THE UNDERSTANDING

But it is enough for our present purpose to note the consequences of the extension (justified or not) of Cartesianism to the political and social field. If we think this extension justified, we are logically entitled to expect a general acceptance of principles which impose themselves on minds by their compelling self-evidence. The consequence is that, so far as each individual intelligence is legislator, all must converge towards the same truths. Obeying more or less 'the impulsion of nature', individuals will tend, as private persons, to more or less virtuous actions. But as citizens and citizen-minded they will come together in agreement. The consequence is that, though there will be infractions of the laws, there will be less and less doubt about what the laws should be. That, for instance, was the view of a thinker like James Mill, whose son wrote:

> So complete was my father's reliance on the influence of reason over the minds of mankind, wherever it is allowed to reach them, that he felt as if all would be gained if the whole population were taught to read, if all sorts of opinions were allowed to be addressed to them by word and in writing, and if by means of the suffrage they could nominate a legislature to give effect to the opinions they adopted.[2]

If the extension of Cartesianism to the political and social field be well founded, it follows by logical necessity that the sentiment of James Mill must admit of empirical verification.

---

[1] See the author's essay 'Order *v*. Organisation' in *On Freedom and Free Enterprise: Essays in honor of Ludwig von Mises* (Princeton, D. van Nostrand and Co., 1956).

[2] J. S. Mill, *Autobiography* (London, 1873), p. 106.

CHAPTER 14

THE POLITICAL CONSEQUENCES
OF HOBBES

In 1651, a London bookseller published *Leviathan*, by Thomas Hobbes of Malmesbury.[1] The political thought of Hobbes was launched on the world.[2] The tercentenary, just past, deserves notice, for this book is a masterpiece and has been of seminal effect.

Hobbes has had a determining influence on political philosophy. Those who came after him, even men of the stature of Spinoza, Locke and Rousseau, followed in their reasoning the form and method worked out by him. Not only that: the postulates from which he started today underlie the principal social sciences. But I have yet another reason for evoking his name. The political principles of our time bear an initial self-contradiction; he gives me my cue for showing what it is.

THE STATE OF SOCIETY

Hobbes did not spend time in discussing the comparative advantages of the different forms of government. Rather, he went straight to the heart of the major problem of political science: how a society exists, what is the preservative principle which saves it from dissolution, what is the generative principle which makes it bear its fruits.

In the preface to *De Cive*, Hobbes set out his line of approach—analysis followed by synthesis. We must suppose human society in dissolution, and conceive of the individuals who make it up as lacking any sort of connecting link; then we must ask ourselves how they would behave under those conditions and go on to look for the means by which this behaviour of theirs could be transformed into social behaviour as we know it.

---

[1] *Leviathan, or the matter, form and power of commonwealth, ecclesiastical and civil.*

[2] His thought was, however, brought simultaneously to notice by a book written earlier, the *De Cive*. A few copies only of this were printed in 1642, but in 1651 it was published in English under a very long title beginning with the words *Philosophical Rudiments concerning Government and Society.*

The commentators on Locke and Rousseau have discussed whether their authors, in describing the transition from the state of nature to that of civil society, believed themselves to be writing history. The truth is that they followed Hobbes, who was concerned to build not a historical reconstruction but a social mechanics. Let us note in passing that concern with the past for its own sake is something quite modern; as to that, see what Bolingbroke says about the use of History.[1]

Hobbes gives a picture of individuals living each man for himself; he tells how once upon a time they gave up being each his own master and made their submission to a common authority. Whether things really went like that he does not care in the least; what matters is to realise what are the forces which, today and every day, threaten with dissolution the body social and how it is kept safe.

The reason for asking what is 'the state of nature' is in order to know how man behaves when he is no longer bound by any rule and his appetites are his only law. The interest of such an inquiry is not in the least antiquarian, for social man is always liable to return to behaviour of this kind, the motives for which still lurk beneath his social habits. Our interest in the 'state of war' is not because it is a phase through which men have passed but because it is always a possibility. Our interest in the construction of the civil state is because the work never leaves the workshop.

The fragility and the worth of the social order were both an obsession with Hobbes. For that reason he was radically opposed to the benevolent sages of tranquil epochs who took their idea of man from the most polished of the people around them and projected the gracious parties at the country place of Helvétius into the image of societies to come. Terrified by the spectacle of the passions bred by the English Revolution—passions which have kept England wise for centuries—Hobbes devoted himself to the consolidation of the social tie.[2]

---

[1] 'I have read somewhere that History is Philosophy teaching by examples.' *On the Study of History*, letter 2.

[2] In this he is like Taine who embarked on his great work under the shock of the horrors of the Commune. Taine wrote at that time to Guizot: 'Zoology shows us that man has pointed teeth; let us beware of arousing in him the instinct of the fiercer carnivores. Psychology shows us that reason in man rests on words and images; let us beware of encouraging in him wild hallucinations....History shows that governments, religions, churches and all the great institutions are the only means by which the wild animal called man acquires his little ration of reason and justice.....' (Letter to Guizot of 12 July 1873, *Vie et Correspondance de Taine*, vol. III, pp. 246–7.)

THE NATURE OF MAN

'It is essential for us', said Hobbes, 'to understand clearly what are the characteristics of our human nature; wherein it is suited and wherein it is unsuited to society.'[1] To achieve that object, he had necessarily to take away from a man's actual character all that long habit of life in society had put there—an inevitably arbitrary process. Though I may use with profit the method of introspection recommended by Hobbes,[2] it does not enable me to isolate in my make-up the part which is due to my social training and to discern what I should be like without it. Thus we see that human nature as such and in the raw must necessarily be a postulate which does not admit of demonstration. The notion that Hobbes formed of it introduced an intellectual revolution. For this nature is for him entirely a matter of what the schoolmen called 'sensible appetite'.

The Hobbesian conception is naturalistic and utterly remote from Christian ideas. Whereas Christian man both can and should subordinate his lower appetites to the higher inclination which brings him to blessedness, Hobbesian man has neither this duty nor this power. He has no freedom of choice among his various desires, and his so-called 'will' is only the desire which happens to come uppermost. There is no Sovereign Good; the various goods are such only because they are objects of desire.

But whatsoever is the object of any man's appetite or desire, that is it which he for his part calleth good; and the object of his hate and aversion, evil; and of his contempt, vile and inconsiderable. For these words of good, evil and contemptible, are ever used with relation to the person that useth them, there being nothing simply and absolutely so.[3]

It is, then, in the concupiscent energy of the heart that the essence of man resides, and therein is the source of his values. Hobbes rejects the notion of Blessedness, to be reached by the subjection of the lower appetites to the higher, and substitutes for it that of Felicity.

---

[1] *De Cive*, ed. Sterling P. Lamprecht (New York, 1949), p. 11.

[2] 'Whosoever looketh into himself, and considereth what he doth, when he does think, opine, reason, hope, fear, etc., and upon what grounds, he shall thereby read and know what are the thoughts and passions of all other men upon the like occasions.... He that is to govern a whole nation must read in himself, not this or that particular man, but mankind.' (*Leviathan*, introduction, p. 6 in the edition of Blackwell's Political Texts, under the general editorship of C. H. Wilson and R. B. McCallum. This edition contains a remarkable introduction by Professor Michael Oakeshott.)

[3] *Leviathan*, part I, ch. VI (ed. Oakeshott), p. 32.

The felicity of this life consisteth not in the repose of a mind satisfied. For there is no such *finis ultimus*, utmost aim, nor *summum bonum*, greatest good, as is spoken of in books of the old moral philosophers. Nor can a man any more live, whose desires are at an end, than he whose senses and imaginations are at a stand. Felicity is a continual progress of the desire, from one object to another; the attaining of the former being still but the way to the latter.[1]

It is this incessant outpouring of imperious desires which develops in man his essential characteristic, acquired wit.

The causes of this difference of wits are in the passions.... The passions that most of all cause the difference of wit are principally, the more or less desire of power, of riches, of knowledge, and of honour. All of which may be reduced to the first, that is, desire of power. For riches, knowledge and honour are but several sorts of power. And therefore a man who hath no great passion for any of these things, but is, as men term it, indifferent, though he may be so far a good man as to be free from giving offence, yet he cannot possibly have either a great fancy or much judgement.[2]

It is the struggle for the things desired which gives intelligence. 'For the thoughts are to the desires as scouts and spies, to range abroad and find the way to the things desired.'[3] The intellectual faculties are here depicted as born of animal needs: we see already the evolutionist thesis.

Reason is here no longer the dominie who keeps the passions in order: she is their child and their servant. Up, then, the desires, for they give us our education! If they are but feeble, they leave the man of insufficient passions hopelessly stuck in the mud of his stupidity.

The vision of man seen by Hobbes is in essence the modern view, though it is seldom that things are now put as brutally as this. Man is here the measure of his own good; the good is identified with the thing desired by each particular person, whence it follows logically that the purpose of institutions is to bring men to the realisation of their desires, whatever these may happen to be. Hobbes, as Professor Oakeshott justly points out in his remarkable introductory study to the Blackwell edition of *Leviathan*, is an individualist.

THE INSTITUTION OF THE COMMONWEALTH

The greater the pull of the desires, the greater the struggle between men. Since man's progress occurs by way of the development of

---

[1] *Leviathan*, part I, ch. XI, p. 63.   [2] *Ibid*. ch. VIII, p. 46.   [3] *Ibid*. ch. VIII, p. 46.

the passions, conflicts of growing intensity must be its logical accompaniment. Pufendorf, making more explicit the thought of his master, differentiates man from beast as being a more dangerous and less tameable animal;[1] nothing restrains him and he is stirred by appetites which follow on each other's heels. Therefore it follows that he is will to power—a will which becomes ever more aggressive.

But this man living only for himself—this *einzige*, as Stirner called him—is not alone in the world; he is for ever elbowing others whose appetites conflict with his and may bring him trouble as his may bring them harm. The number of dangers is limited only by the number of neighbours. This unbridled egoist is now threatened. Will the danger make him stop to think?

There are certain rules of conduct which it is to men's advantage to observe in their mutual relations. Hobbes enumerates them. But will men give obedience to them naturally? Hobbes doubts it. Being in essence sensible appetite, and for that reason more conscious of an immediate and definite good which appeals to their senses than of a distant and indefinite one which only the reason can appreciate, how could they? Hume was later to develop this theme with vigour.[2]

The only remedy lies, therefore, in the institution of a power to compel observance of rules which, though they are to men's

---

[1] 'Beasts sometimes contend about their food, and then it is only in the case of scarcity; sometimes again they enter the lists at the instigation of their lust, which yet has only its season of returning.... Whereas men quarrel with men, not only as excited by the stings of hunger, and by a lust so vigorous as never to be let out of season, but also by other vices and passions, unknown to beasts.... Of these, the chief are an endless thirst after things superfluous, and ambition, the most pernicious of all evils; of which, as no creature seems to have any sense, excepting man, so he has the most lively and tender sense imaginable.' (Pufendorf, *The Law of Nature and Nations* (Eng. ed. 1749 translated by Basil Kennett), Book VII, ch. I, par. iv.)

[2] 'What strikes upon men with a strong and lively idea commonly prevails above what lies in a more obscure light.... Everything that is contiguous to us, strikes upon us with such an idea...and commonly operates with more force than any object that lies in a more distant and obscure light.... This is the reason why men so often act in contradiction to their known interest; and in particular why they prefer any trivial advantage, that is present, to the maintenance of order in society, which so much depends on the observance of justice. The consequences of every breach of equity seem to be very remote, and are not able to counterbalance any immediate advantage. They are, however, never the less real for being remote; and as all men are, in some degree, subject to the same weakness, it necessarily happens that the violation of equity must become very frequent in society, and the commerce of men, by that means, be rendered very dangerous and uncertain.' (Hume, *A Treatise of Human Nature*, Book III, part II, section VII.)

advantage, men are incapable of respecting except under compulsion. But will the reason enable men to resolve even on their institution? Hume brings up a powerful objection: 'If men be incapable of themselves to prefer remote to contiguous, they will never consent to anything which would oblige them to such a choice, and contradict, in so sensible a manner, their natural principles and propensities.'[1] It is not, therefore, at the command of reason that men will sacrifice their independence but at the command of an emotion: fear.

FEAR AND WISDOM

The positive science of the twentieth century has stressed the presence of fear in man. Psycho-analysis explains to us individual behaviours by nuclei of fear deeply embedded in the sub-conscious. The picture of primitive man presented to us by anthropology is much less rose-coloured than the 'proud savage' of the *Supplément au Voyage de Bougainville*.[2] Lévy-Bruhl in particular has much insisted on the climate of fear in which, he tells us, primitive men have their being.

Here, too, Hobbes is a forerunner. He speaks of 'this perpetual fear, always accompanying mankind in the ignorance of causes',[3] and this fear he makes the womb of religion: it might be Freud speaking. For Hobbes the essence of religion consists in reducing to order, in organising as it were, the confused wretchedness of man. The irrational hopes and fears, once they have been related to a First Principle conceived as supremely rational will, have the effect of tying men down to the observance of salutary commands.

Just as metaphysical fears will be the principle of religious society, so physical fears will be that of civil. The confused fear of neighbours will be reduced to order, organised, laid at the feet of a civil authority: it will tie men down to the observance of positive laws.

The dialectic of Hobbesian thought is clear enough. Our concern is only with the individual; his development occurs by means of his passions; it is contradictory to suppose that he rises above them; his passions bring him into conflict with other men; it is to the

---

[1] Hume, *A Treatise of Human Nature*, Book III, part II, section VII.

[2] This work of Diderot's was a fictitious travel report designed to illustrate the virtuousness of the savage.

[3] *Leviathan*, part I, ch. XII (ed. Oakeshott), p. 70.

advantage of individuals in general that behaviours should be restrained to the extent that they conflict and produce a state of war; to bring that about, certain rules of conduct must be observed; these are, therefore, objectively necessary; but the recognition of their objective necessity will not make them observed, for that is not a sufficiently powerful motive; it follows that they will be observed, not from being objectively necessary, but from having been willed by a power with striking appeal to men's imaginations: God or the sovereign.

THE DIKTAT

One of the most shocking aspects of Hobbesian thought is the conception of law as pure *diktat*, which commands by right of its origin and not by right of its substance; it is, with Hobbes, an act of will on the part of the competent person, God or the sovereign, who determines what shall be good and what shall be bad. The vast majority of theologians uphold the opposite opinion, summed up by Leibniz in this striking formula: 'The just is not just because God has willed it, but because God is just.'[1]

In our time the West has slowly recovered the metaphysical sense, lost for several generations, and with it the feeling that theological disputes are of the highest importance. Even though my reader's eyes may not be open in this respect, it cannot seem to him immaterial whether Justice is represented as anterior to the decree which proclaims it, or as the mere creature of the decree. For the mind of man does its thinking by models, and the man who puts Justice second to nothing in the divine government will be disposed to put it second to nothing in human government; whereas the man who finds in God before all else power and will, will be disposed to the same view of human government.

This parallelism is not required by logic[2]—it is psychological. Occam, Jurieu and Hobbes all reproduce these two parallel judgments. Leibniz confutes Hobbes in this passage:

The justice of God, says Mr Hobbes, is nothing else than the power which he both has and exercises in distributing his blessings and afflictions.

---

[1] 'Das Recht ist nicht Recht weil Gott es gewollt hat, sondern weil Gott gericht ist.' Cited by Gierke in *Les Théories politiques du Moyen Age*.

[2] The profession is sometimes made that, since God's decree has arbitrarily determined the Good, human governments are for that reason tightly bound by this Good. This opinion is met with principally in Protestant thinkers.

Yet it is not the power of distributing them but the will to distribute them reasonably—in other words, goodness guided by wisdom—which makes the justice of God. But, says he, justice is not with God what it is with a man, whom only the observance of the laws made by his superior makes just. There too Mr Hobbes is in error, and so is Mr Pufendorf who has followed him. Justice does not depend on the arbitrary laws of superiors, but on the eternal rules of wisdom and goodness, in men as much as in God.[1]

CIVIL RELIGION

The attentive reader of Hobbes can be in little doubt as to the materialism and the pantheism of the master—a position which he was prudent enough to camouflage, but without deceiving his contemporaries. For this reason there were those who nicknamed him 'the beast of Malmesbury'.

Being obsessed with the safety of society, Hobbes could think of nothing worse than uncertainty in behaviour, and this is encouraged by differences of opinion. Though men be persuaded to live according to justice, yet, if they conceive justice differently, there is still conflict. But there is none if men are in the position of being obliged and constrained to do or not to do according to settled precepts, given out by an authority which has the last word in formulating and interpreting them and the power to make them obeyed.

This is the angle from which Hobbes conceives the civil power. And God's place in his system is, it is clear, only by way of reinforcement. The civil power has not got the last word if the subjects feel themselves bound by divine precepts which may set them in opposition to the sovereign. For this reason he requires that 'the interpretation of every law, divine as well as human, should rest with the civil authority, with the man or the council in whom the sovereign power is vested'.[2]

The aim is always the same—the escape from conflict. Hobbes distrusts diversity of opinions as endangering the structure of the Commonwealth.

THE LIBERALISM OF HOBBES

None has made authority more absolute than Hobbes did. For this reason he has, in recent years, often been named the father of

---

[1] Leibniz, *Essais de Théodicée: Réflexions sur l'ouvrage de M. Hobbes.*
[2] *De Cive*, III, xv, 17.

totalitarianism. This is an egregious blunder, rightly exposed as such by those who know him best.[1]

It is psychologically necessary to successful totalitarianism that man feels himself a mere part, whereas Hobbesian man feels himself most vividly a whole. Totalitarian man centres his affections on something outside himself, at the centre of gravity of the body social. But whom do we find advocating a displacement of this kind? The author of the *Contrat Social*, not of *Leviathan*. The concern of Hobbesian man is not to make a cult of Leviathan but to save himself from the dangers involved for himself in the unrestrained development, analogous to his own, of others.

The negative nature of Leviathan's office is brought out in a host of passages. The safety which the sovereign should procure for the individual 'is not a bare preservation, but also all other contentments in life which every man by lawful industry shall acquire to himself. And this is intended to be done, not by care applied to individuals, further than their protection from injuries when they shall complain, but by a general providence, contained in public instruction, both of doctrine, and example, and in the making and executing of good laws.'[2] The use of laws, Hobbes explains, is 'not to bind the people from all voluntary actions; but to direct and keep them in such a motion as not to hurt themselves by their own impetuous desires, rashness or indiscretion; as hedges are set, not to stop travellers, but to keep them in their way'.[3]

Hobbes is an individualist and progressive, who would like each man to develop his faculties in striving to fulfil his desires, as these are successively aroused. Only, men so employed may do each other harm. The State exists to stop the mischief which the intersection of their appetites may do them.

HOBBES, FATHER OF POLITICAL ECONOMY

It leaps to the eye that Hobbes is the father of political economy. His representation of man is identical with *homo oeconomicus*. Economic science knows no other good than the thing desired; 'goods' are for it objects of desire, and the source and measure of

---

[1] Notably by Professor Oakeshott in his introduction to *Leviathan* and by Professor Leo Strauss in an article in the International Review of Philosophy for October 1950: *On the spirit of Hobbes's Political Philosophy*. We are also in debt to Professor Strauss for an excellent book, *The Political Philosophy of Hobbes*.

[2] *Leviathan*, part 2, ch. xxx.   [3] *Ibid.*

their worth are in the appetites which they inspire. In going back to first principles, two outstanding works of political economy which have appeared in recent years go back also to Hobbesian theses:[1]

The thread of Hobbesian thought reappears in the entire web of economic science. These 'small beginnings of movement' of his, which take on actuality when the pull from without becomes sufficient, are very much the same as marginalism. What Hobbes calls indifference as between equal attractions is what are called today indifference curves. When Pareto speaks of the 'paths' along which the maximum of utility is attained, are not these paths precisely what thought, the 'scout' of desire, is seeking out in the system of Hobbes?

The Hobbesian notion that each man is the only discerner of his good provided Adam Smith with the principle that each man is the best judge of his own interest. To get himself his good, he deploys his energies to the maximum, and the whole of society is the richer for it. It matters not that the repercussions of his action may, from some other aspect, call for reprobation; to the extent that these actions advance the general wealth, they are socially good, for 'private vices profit the public', as Mandeville put it in a formula which was meant to shock.

But wait a bit! If each man acts under the impulsion of material attractions, with no other rule to guide him than his own interest as he sees it, the actions of men are going to clash. It is important for that reason that certain ways of finding satisfaction should be forbidden, so that men may have recourse only to those others which do not hurt, and may even help, their neighbours. These prohibitions, and the repression which wins them respect, are the affair of the public authority—the sovereign. The political machine acts as a filter which halts obnoxious actions and lets through those only which are neutral or useful. By means of the action of this filter, freedom is steered away from anti-social courses and is even committed to those which are social.

My neighbour's passion for horse-racing does not matter to me if this passion of his keeps him more assiduously to work which profits me too; his passion menaces his neighbour only if it drives him to theft. Close that temptation to him, and his passion will be socially useful, as is some natural source of power which clever engineers have trapped. That is the position of Hobbes.

[1] J. Rueff, *L'Ordre Social*; L. von Mises, *Human Action*.

POLITICS AND HEDONISM

Among later writers there is hardly one who has not vented his execration of the political principles of Hobbes. Yet those principles follow very logically from the Hobbesian postulates about man—and these last have been very generally accepted. If man is in essence sensible appetite, goaded to action time and again by the stimulus of desires born in succession and for ever multiplying, must it not happen that the development of the force of desire will bring in its train that of the force of the *potentia irascibilis*, needed to surmount obstacles—and which will not distinguish between those obstacles meriting overthrow and those meriting respect?

Where should it come from, the feeling that certain obstacles merit respect—as, for example, another man standing in the path? We may conceive of this moral restraint either as heterogeneous to sensible appetite or as proceeding from it.

It is possible to ascribe to man a certain natural insight into the moral law, or, more vaguely, to endow him with a 'moral sense' analogous to the aesthetic sense, as Hutcheson does. But for Hobbes neither hypothesis was open. If human intelligence emerges progressively from the exercise of activities caused by its sensible appetite, an intelligence of this kind could never rise as high as principles—only to 'maxims' in the Kantian meaning of the word.

The perception of a self-evident morality presupposes the innateness of ideas—a thing which Hobbes denied implicitly and Locke was later to deny explicitly. Both of them, in fact, rejected the affirmation of Saint John about 'the light that lighteth every man that cometh into the world'.

That denied, what is there left for turning man aside from evil actions? His long-term interest, no doubt? But the thesis of the moralisation of mankind by means of the just perception of interest does not stand up. In renouncing some immediate advantage to be had only by injuring Primus, I give myself no guarantee that Secundus will not decide to injure me for the sake of some advantage; Secundus will know nothing of and will not concern himself with my relations with Primus. Who can say that I increase in any way the probability of Secundus sparing me in turn? Hobbes himself,[1]

---

[1] As in this passage: '...contracts are made by a mutual act of trust, so that, when one is made between persons who cannot be constrained to keep their promise, the party who first carries out his side of it, knowing the tendency of men to do what pays

Rousseau,[1] Hume[2] and many others have refuted this untenable thesis.

For this reason all subsequent 'naturalists' have in the end rested moral conduct where Hobbes rested it, on the fear of repression—and on nothing else. For instance, Austin,[3] who is an avowed disciple of Hobbes, explains that the fear of punishment imposed by law is a factor in the process of weighing the desires—the process by which the act of volition is determined. It is by means of the desire to avoid the punishment that the will is made up against the prohibited act. This desire to avoid punishment forms by degrees good habits, with the result that the punishment becomes no longer present to the mind and the law comes to be obeyed from a respect now second nature. Let us note that this is to assimilate the training of citizens to the training of dogs.

NECESSITY OF POLITICAL STABILITY IN THE HOBBESIAN SYSTEM

The public authority is, then, a formidable policeman who, whether by immediate fear or by an habitual respect with distant roots in fear, checks actions that would be harmful, but allows men to do what they please otherwise, harmful actions only excepted. Hedonist liberty implies repressive authority. Thus, men give free play to their desires within the framework of certain rules. The system, as is clear, comes to grief if the power to formulate the rules is itself at the mercy of the desires which are for ever arising in the bosom of the society.

To start with, the mere fact that the rules are continually changing naturally tends to weaken the habit of obedience and to bring

them in everything, does no other than betray his own interest and hand himself over to the avarice and bad faith of the other party...' (*Du Corps politique*, II, 10).

[1] Rousseau dilates at length on this point in the famous 'suppressed chapter' of the *Contrat Social*, which answered Diderot. 'It is not true that in the state of independence Reason leads us to co-operate in the common good by way of our particular interest. So far from particular interest being in alliance with the general good, they mutually exclude one another in the natural order of things; and social laws are a yoke which each wants to put on the necks of others but keep away from his own', etc. Cf. my edition of the *Contrat Social* (Geneva, 1947), p. 383.

[2] See the earlier citation.

[3] Austin's *Lectures on Jurisprudence* are a classical exposition of the philosophy of law and the most energetic assertion of juridical positivism. They were first published in 1832 under the title *The Province of Jurisprudence defined*.

obedience back to its first principle: immediate fear. To the extent that the laws will have affected ways of life the less, the authority will have to be that much the stronger for repression. But also and above all, if the public authority is a stake in a competition, the natural result will be that appetites will seek their satisfaction by turning to their use the levers of command.

The men whom *libido*[1] stirs have lawful means of satisfying their desires. But if the satisfaction so to be had is to their thinking insufficient, within the lines traced by the existing rules, and if they have power to change those rules by seizure of political authority, are they not sure to seize it? And after them others will do it whom they have thus forestalled. And afterwards, others still!

The result will be the failure of the attempt to trap and canalise appetites in useful channels—a failure due to the opening given to these appetites when once political power is up for auction. In fact, men will find that it pays them better to achieve their desires by adapting the laws to their ends than by pursuing their ends within the hedges of the law.

From these considerations it follows clearly that a social system based on hedonism entails a political authority that can resist being used by particular interests as best suits them—an authority whose laws will be ukases from on high, not emanations of the social conflict.

HOBBESIAN MAN AND THE CITIZEN

In our own time large indeed is the number of those who accept the Hobbesian premises about man, the Hobbesian materialism and naturalism. They think with Hobbes that man is in essence an ingenious animal, whose intelligence grows more nimble from his struggle to satisfy his desires. Therein they see the principle of evolution and progress. They consider, still with Hobbes, that it is the duty of each to seek his own good where he finds it. But few indeed among those who profess his ideas have minds consistent enough to accept the political consequence of them: that is to say, the stable and very powerful authority which Hobbes made the keystone of the hedonist structure of society.

Quite the contrary: many of these same people consider that political liberty should have no limit set to it. Without being aware

---

[1] *Libido* is here used not in the restricted sense given to it by Freud, but in the classic sense, of desire in general as opposed to appetite controlled by reason.

of the fact, whenever they reason about political authority, they shift their premises and import a changeling man.

Their man, when they view him as citizen and legislator, becomes, all of a sudden, a man in whom morality is innate. The 'natural light' has been spendidly hymned by Bayle:

There being a bright and vivid light which enlightens all men as soon as they open the eyes of their minds, and which irresistibly convinces them of its truth, the conclusion must be that it is God himself, the eternal and substantial Truth, who thus enlightens us with his immediate ray, and makes us contemplate the eternal truths....This primal and universal light issues from God to show to all men the general principles of justice and to be the touchstone of all precepts and all particular laws.[1]

The idea of government by opinion and the principle of freedom of expression rest altogether on this philosophy, justly entitled the philosophy of the 'natural light'.

If there are a true and a good which are man's natural goal when he escapes from the sway of the passions, then there are centres of gravity for all intellectual discussions and all political disputes. Opinions differ just the same, but the differences occur around these centres. A government of enlightened élites would involve a smaller dispersion of opinions, but at the price of a more restricted participation in the search for the good—and that would be a pity, for this participation raises both moral and intellectual standards. Such is the essence of the thought of political liberalism.

The premises which that thought implies are entirely different from those of an exclusive naturalism. And to pass lightly from the one set of premises to the other is intellectually inadmissible. The mistake is often made by liberals, who take 'economic' man from Hobbes and 'political' man from Malebranche. That is muddled thinking: the postulates are heterogeneous.

THE LESSON OF HOBBES

Is there a practical lesson to be drawn from the foregoing considerations? There is, and of the clearest. Every time that man in society takes on Hobbesian characteristics, the irresistible force of logic makes Hobbesian solutions inevitable. To the entire extent to which men come to be ruled by their desires only and derive from them the maxims of their conduct, there cannot but come into

---

[1] Bayle, 'Commentaire Philosophique', *Opera*, vol. ii (Amsterdam, 1737), pp. 368-9.

being what Hobbes calls the 'state of war', with its uncertainties and horrors. When that day comes, the need for certainty carries it over the love of liberty.

It is the 'Augustus hour': '...*deditque jura quis pace et principe uteremur.*'[1] The miracle of Tacitean concision sums up the lesson of Hobbes in the association of two words—peace and master: the need for the one gets the other accepted.[2]

Leo Strauss has justly observed that Hobbes reasons from the extreme case. In a healthy social order its foundations stay unexamined: they get laid bare only when the order is crashing. When that happens, the merit of the public authority is not in being one thing rather than another, but simply in being. As Ihering put it: 'Impotence in public authority is an anti-social condition—the dissolution and decomposition of Society.'[3] In that event, according to the views of Hobbes, there is no safety anywhere for the individual, now threatened by all his fellows who do not respect his rights, do not observe their contracts with him, and employ against him their own natural strength—or worse still, such fragments of public authority as they have made their own.

The form of power is, then, an accident in which Hobbes disinterests himself: its substance is obedience to command.

For the prosperity of a people ruled by an aristocratical or democratical assembly, cometh not from aristocracy, nor from democracy, but from the obedience and concord of the subjects: nor do the people flourish in a monarchy because one man has the right to rule them, but because they obey him. Take away in any kind of State the obedience, and consequently the concord of the people, and they shall not only not flourish but in short time be dissolved.[4]

Beyond all question the life of a civil society would be less closely linked with the authority of the positive power in it if the members of the society all acknowledged the authority of common principles. But how could this ever be on the view of men which Hobbes has

---

[1] Tacitus, *Annals*, Book III, XXVIII: '...and he gave a new system, useful indeed to the public tranquillity, but fit only for the government of one.'

[2] So, too, Rousseau: 'It is in the heart of this disorder...that despotism, raising by degrees its horrid head...' (*Discours de l'Inégalité*). And, on a more disillusioned note, writing to the Marquis de Mirabeau: 'I see no middle way between democracy at its most austere and Hobbism at its most complete: for the conflict between men and laws, which infects a State with continual war, is the worst of all political conditions.' *Corr.* XVII, 157.

[3] Ihering, *L'Evolution du Droit* (ed. Meulenaere), p. 210.

[4] *Leviathan*, part 2, ch. XXX.

given us? Rousseau agrees: without positive power the state of society 'would be but a source of crimes and misfortunes for men, each of whom would follow his own bent only and listen only to his own passions'.[1]

It is of capital importance to grasp the link between the authoritarian conclusions of Hobbes and the premises of an absolute libertarianism. Where each man acts as he wills and his will is made up for him by his desires, this liberty of his, if it is not to engender 'the war of all against all', can be kept in being only within the rigorous framework of laws strictly applied and exactly obeyed. This framework loses all solidity if the power grows feeble; it loses all shape if the uprush of desires is for ever changing what the laws prescribe. For this reason a hedonist society must have, to maintain itself, a strong and stable government.

It looks as if the writings of Hobbes contain a serious lesson for our modern democracies. To the entire extent to which progress develops hedonism and moral relativism, to which individual liberty is conceived as the right of a man to obey his appetites, nothing but the strongest of powers can maintain society in being. The idea of political liberty is linked with other suppositions about man and with the encouragement of quite other tendencies.

---

[1] In my edition of the *Contrat*, p. 381.

CHAPTER 15

LIBERTY

Liberty is the magic word inscribed on the banners of the West, but Western men use it in very different senses. That is not surprising, for in the course of history the term has figured in a wide variety of conflicts, one or other of which has deeply affected particular sensibilities. Anyone seeking to arrive at its 'real' meaning by process of reasoning has several systems of thought to choose from. What we are going to see is that there are in effect widely different ideas of liberty; our aim will be to define them and bring to light the relations between them. What is in question here is clearly the liberty of man in society; the problems of free-will belong to a quite different order of ideas.

'THE CHAINS'

'Man was born free and is everywhere in chains.'[1] Let us note closely this metaphor of 'chains', for it enables us to see at once the great parting of the ways of our subject. On the one hand the chains I wear are a nuisance and an obstacle; on the other they are an indignity and a badge of shame. It follows that our theme admits of two possible treatments: of liberty as consisting in removal or lowering of obstacles, of liberty as consisting in increase of dignity.

The first theme is the one which, far and away, confronts the mind with the clearest images. Being impeded is a condition liable to affect every agent, with the solitary exception of God, and, correspondingly, every agent may be freed from an impediment. The horse is freed when his halter is taken off him, the river is freed when its sluices are raised—or when it breaks them itself. The physicist, a real master of precise language, calls 'liberum mobile' anything which moves unimpeded by some adverse force. Therefore a study of liberty, taken in this sense, will be a study of the relations of man with the obstacles of every sort which he encounters.

The second theme is at once more circumscribed and more subtle.

---

[1] *Du Contrat Social*, Book I, ch. 1.

An obstacle of any kind may be opposed to an agent of any kind, including man, but indignity can be inflicted only by man on man.[1] Therefore our two treatments will apply to the same subject-matter only in so far as we bring into our first theme—i.e. consideration of the obstacles encountered by man—those obstacles, and those alone, which are of man's own making, being the restraints on the force moving us which are of the same nature as that force and proceed from men like ourselves. This procedure has the authority of T. H. Green to recommend it: 'As to the sense given to "freedom", it must of course be admitted that every usage of the term to express anything but a social and political relation of one man to others involves a metaphor';[2] and Rousseau says this: 'There are two sorts of dependence: that on things, which is natural, and that on men, which is social. Dependence on things, being non-moral, does not harm liberty.'[3]

We do not question the wisdom of this advice, but what we plan to do makes it impossible for us to follow it. We are, in effect, going to deploy as far as possible the entire gamut of current notions about liberty; and some of them concern obstacles which proceed from no specifically human source. Let us begin with the first theme: being free (or being more free) is to be released from impediments.

I. *LIBERTY AS POWER*

THE CLASSICAL DEFINITION

Leibniz said: 'Actual liberty consists in the power to do what one wants to do', and Voltaire elaborated on him: 'To be truly free is to have power to do. When I can do what I want to do, there is my liberty for me.'[4] This definition, held in common by two philosophers

---

[1] Indignity of a kind can, I know, be inflicted on animals, but that is outside our theme.
[2] T. H. Green: 'Of the different senses of Freedom' in *Works of T. H. Green*, vol. II (London, 1893), p. 309. [3] *Émile* (ed. Hachette), vol. II, p. 177.
[4] As a matter of history, Voltaire was replying to Leibniz. This definition of exterior or social liberty given us by the former appears in a context in which he is contrasting it with interior liberty (which is outside our subject). Voltaire brings reinforcement to Leibniz on the first point (which is ours) while at the same time contradicting him on the second (which we do not touch on). Here are the two complete passages. Leibniz: 'Actual liberty consists either in the power to do what one wants to do or in the power to want what can be got.' Voltaire: 'To be truly free is to have power to do. When I can do what I want to do, there is my liberty for me; but I cannot help wanting what I do want.' Leibniz, *Nouveaux Essais sur l'Entendement*, vol. II, ch. XX (ed. Janet), I, pp. 136–7; Voltaire, *Le Philosophe Ignorant*, XIII.

ordinarily so opposed to each other, has a note of gay assurance about it which makes it intellectually welcome: 'cut the Gordian knot, there is my liberty, how simple it all is.' But the truth is that the definition is as ambiguous as anything can be.

Identified with the power to do what I want, my liberty wears the air of a relationship between what I can (numerator) and what I want (denominator); the relationship will be affected by all the various causes liable to affect either the numerator or the denominator. All the obstacles to my power, whether they proceed from men individually or men collectively, or from nature, or from the inadequacy of my own abilities and means, tend alike to reduce my power to a point well below the limit of my desire: they will appear as working against my liberty. On the other hand, my liberty will grow in extent with every retreat or enfeeblement of obstacles, human or natural, with every accretion to my own abilities and means, and, lastly, by the assistance in the fulfilment of my desire which I receive from the abilities and means of others. But we must not overlook the causes affecting the denominator; my power to do remaining the same, I may become more free by restraining my desire (stoicism), just as, on the other hand, with a growing power to do (a larger 'objective' liberty, if the expression is preferred), I shall be, according to this definition, less free if my desire develops faster than my power (a diminishing 'subjective' liberty, as I may call it).

We see, then, that the classical definition postulates a relationship which may be represented as a function of several variables. Leibniz realised to the full the complex and equivocal nature of the definition, and tried to simplify it: 'Generally speaking, the man with more means is more free to do what he wants; but we have in mind particularly the liberty to make use of things which are ordinarily within our power and, most of all, the free use of our body.'[1]

This classification brings with it a great simplification of the earlier relationship. Our denominator is now 'reasonable desire', equal by definition to the power which our own abilities and means give us within the limits set by the natural obstacles, and the numerator can, therefore, no longer be inferior to the denominator except as a result of restrictions of human origin (and therefore of the same nature) laid on the exercise of this power. In this system

---

[1] *Op. cit.*

of thought, which was that of the period of the classical discussions of the seventeenth and eighteenth centuries, the relationship between power and desire is, considering the individual alone, conceived as naturally equal to 'one', and liberty is regarded as checked only by the subtraction from the numerator caused by the power of other men, which limits the natural exercise of our own power.

LIBERTY AS A TRUNCATED CIRCLE

All the political ideas current up to our own time were formed in the seventeenth and eighteenth centuries, when geometry was a fashionable study. The deep impression which geometry made on Hobbes and Spinoza is well known; I seem to detect its influence in their definition of natural liberty—as a thing of like extent with the capacity of the individual in a state of independence, which is conceived as being, whether in logic or in time, his original state.[1] This definition calls up the image of a circle whose radius is determined by the power according to means—the radius of action. In the state of natural liberty, this circle is perfectly round; later, it is broken by social restrictions. Just so may we picture some wild nomad going as far as his legs will carry him, but, under social conditions, being held up by hedges. This sort of imagery is of the style of the period.

The metaphor of the truncated circle is embedded in the classical debates. The power inherent in Primus, which determined his radius of action, gave him naturally a circular domain within the limits of his radius; but the effect of social regulations is to forbid him certain regions of this circular domain—zones which are now darkened and barred to him. This causes him to lose what Beccaria called 'portions of liberty',[2] but his loss is profitable to him, for the Sovereign, who forbids Primus to enter certain zones of his primitive domain, guarantees him at the same time against anyone invading the rest of his circle—all the zones that have not been shaded in. Primus, who would lead a disturbed life as master of a complete circle, is able to lead a quiet one as master of a truncated circle. Rivarol compares this procedure to that of insurance, which involves

---

[1] Thus Spinoza writes: 'Every natural being has received from nature just so much right as he has power to live and act.... The natural right of the whole of Nature, and, therefore, of each individual, extends just as far as his power goes....', *Traité politique* (ed. Appuhn), I, 3 and 4.

[2] Beccaria, *Traité des Délits et des Peines* (Neuchâtel, 1797), p. 17.

a man in the alienation of a part of his substance with a view to guaranteeing the rest.[1] It may be agreeable to the individual that there should be no encroachment on his power to act and that his liberty should be wholly intact, but it is necessary for his own security that the power to act of other men should be restrained so as not to prove hurtful to himself. His interest is, in fact, ambivalent, and a compromise is the result—a compromise which suits each best as he gets a larger share of security for a smaller sacrifice of independence.

It should be noted that the man who is fully aware of the advantages for himself in this barter of independence for security should in reason cease to desire what is forbidden to him; if he does cease to desire it, then lack of power to get it is no longer restriction of his liberty, if liberty is conceived as a relationship between power and desire. Whether from motives which are utilitarian or purely moral (two different systems of thought), if a man's reason fully assents to restrictions on his power to act, then these restrictions are no longer contrary to his liberty. Logically, it should so work out whenever there is a perfect correspondence between the restrictions given out and the understandings of those who undergo them —and that should happen in theory if, in accordance with the democratic principle, the restrictions are given out by the very people who undergo them; but the psychological reality is, unfortunately, far removed from this abstract model. Even on the hypothesis that the imposition of the restrictions on each has been, solely and entirely, the work of the unanimous collaboration of all— a thing never yet seen—there is not a man who, at the time of encountering these restrictions, does not feel differently about them than he did when his reason caused him to promulgate them. And when they get in his way he resents them as a blow at his liberty.

Such is the despotic spirit of each individual man that he is at all times ready to plunge again into their ancient chaos the laws of society, and ever seeks, not only to withdraw from the common pool the portion of liberty which he has put in it, but even to usurp that of others; for this reason a bulwark had to be erected against this usurpation, and motives of an obvious and sufficiently powerful kind had to be provided to keep down this despotic spirit. Such motives were furnished by the penalties pronounced against law-breakers.[2]

[1] Rivarol, *Mémoires* (Paris, 1828), p. 215.
[2] Beccaria, *loc. cit.*

The system of thought just recalled has the merit of outstanding clarity; it analogizes the individual with a small sovereign state which has joined a confederation so as to guarantee its own security. By so doing it has in certain respects restricted its freedom of action and has transferred certain powers to the federal authority in which it participates. But it has kept its full sovereignty within its own boundaries in everything which has not been expressly committed to the collective authority, and it enjoys discretionary powers in its reserved domain.

In this system, no social restriction imposed on the action of the individual restrains his liberty so long as the restriction in question is voluntarily accepted by him. For on this condition whatever is no longer lawful for the individual is no longer desired by him. The classical thinkers considered that this acceptance by the will was procured by the mediation of the understanding. Four possible positions may be distinguished. First, the restraints seem unjustified, in which case the understanding does not strive to get them accepted by the will and even exerts itself against them. Secondly, the restraints are justified on grounds which the understanding should acknowledge itself and induce the will to acknowledge. Thirdly, not only are the restraints so thoroughly justifiable that the understanding should accept them, but the will too has public-spiritedly assented to them of its own accord and stands pledged to their observance. Fourthly, even though the understanding finds no clear grounds on which to justify the restraints, the will has assented to them.

In the last three cases the reasonable man should not regard the restraints on his action as diminishing his liberty, for he is in principle unable to desire what is not allowed; his understanding (the second case) or the prior assent of his will (the fourth case), or both together (the third case), are a theoretical obstacle in the way of his actual will acting in defiance of the restraints. Yet his actual will may well differ greatly from the will which his understanding or the will's prior assent should inspire in him, with the result that he will in fact feel these restraints as a limitation of his liberty. And there is much more real validity in this last point of view than in the others.

LIBERTY AS MEANS

In the nineteenth and twentieth centuries, the problem of liberty came to be treated very differently. We said earlier that, if liberty was defined as a relationship between power and desire, this definition justified taking into consideration natural obstacles no less than human obstacles. The classical discussions of the subject had ignored these former variables, and had treated them as so many basic limitations laid on the will of the subject.

This was the line inevitably taken in days when 'the natural man' —a being who necessarily meets with inescapable natural obstacles— was the starting-point of philosophers, who pictured social organisation as laying restraints on the exercise of natural power. But nineteenth-century minds were particularly impressed by the gains in human power over nature brought about by social organisation. The social state was bearing fruits far richer than had been thought possible by the philosophers of an earlier day, who regarded it mainly as an association for mutual guarantee between men living autonomous lives.

Experience attests that disputes about distribution take on an added sharpness in times of growing wealth; there is, therefore, nothing surprising in the fact that they have reached a crescendo during the last century and a half, the more so as political power was in process of devolution to the masses during the same period, that is to say, inevitably, to the poorly endowed. Social conflicts as such are outside the scope of our present subject. They link up with it only because our own time has taken to thinking of liberty as a function of the variable, 'the means of each'.

In the quotation given earlier, Leibniz said: 'Generally speaking, the man with more means is more free to do what he wants'; but, though uttering it, he ignored this complication and put this aspect of his definition to sleep. It is the return to waking life of this factor which has given a dynamic character to the previously static definition. Anatole France said somewhere that the law is equal for all because it forbids rich and poor alike to steal bread and sleep under bridges. We may give this sally positive form and say that the poor are as free as the rich to go to the Balearic Islands on holiday. It may be objected at this point that the unequal distribution of individual means in a society is a quite different problem from that of liberty. I do not dissent, but it remains true that the two questions have become inextricably confounded in most people's minds and that the definition of liberty now in vogue gives ground for this confounding of them.

If I picture my liberty as my power to do what I want, my libertarian restlessness may as easily rebel against the narrowness of my means as against the restrictions laid on my actions. It all turns on how the imagination reacts to the stimulus of circumstances. The obligation of military service does not strike me as an encroachment on my liberty, because I am used to it, whereas the re-introduction of compulsory labour, though quite as justifiable, would seem an encroachment contrary to my habits. If I feel closely linked to a milieu within which, generation after generation, those like myself have had the same opportunities, I shall not chafe against the existing limits on my power to act, because they will seem to be 'natural'; I shall not regard them as a prison. They will come to seem to me a prison only if, in the society of which I am a member, the limits beat a rapid retreat before technical progress, and if social mobility on a considerable scale presents me with the spectacle of one man after another enlarging his means on no clear principle of distribution. I shall begin to feel, if not in a prison, at any rate confined within a stagnant pool from which, if I try, I should be able to make my escape.

We live in a dynamic society where human action changes both things and human situations—a society which stimulates hope and imagination, so that wishes go ahead even faster than realities. Voltaire would have thought it ludicrous to say: 'I am not free to fly.' But in proportion as the impossible of yesterday becomes the possible of today, the mind loses its sense of the distinction between dream and wish. In this condition of optimism, *libido* (in its true sense of desire) finds for support some concrete foundation or other on which to raise the vision of what should be possible for me. The means possessed by another provide me with this base; 'what I want to do is what Primus has the means to do'—which is not necessarily what he does. My wishes being based in this way on the means of Primus, his greater means seem to me a denial of liberty to myself, and I do not stop to consider that I am forming a quite heterogeneous mental image, in which the larger means of Primus are associated not with his obligations but with my own. I do not necessarily envy him what he does, but I think of what I should do were I—but only as regards his means—in his place. It is the thought of what I should do were I he and were I not he simultaneously on which my vision of my liberty is formed; for it is, as Plato observed,[1] natural for man to think of all the fine things he would do if he wielded such power as he sees in the hands of another, knowing nothing of the mortgages upon it.

The logical fallacy implied in envy of this kind is immanent in the conception of a man's liberty as a domain determined by his means—a domain cut into by the requirements of the Sovereign, but, except for that, given over to the arbitrary will of the individual, who is the absolute master of it, free from all moral and social obligations. If there ever was such a domain, there could be no justifying its not being equal for each of us; and the more a man uses his domain after this fashion, the stronger becomes the argument for equal domains. But this is getting away from our subject.

MEANS AS SOCIAL GRANTS

Whenever it is linked to the feeling of power, the idea of liberty undergoes big ups and downs by reason of social transformations. At the time of the classical doctrine it was a case of enfranchising as far as possible the individual's own domain from social burdens, and this point of view was in accord with the economic conditions then prevailing. The mode of life of the vast majority of the population was then that of a peasantry, and for that reason the peasant's mode seemed the normal one. In a situation of that kind, what belongs 'naturally' to the individual[2] gives rise to little argument. It is, first, his natural forces; next, the plot of earth which these forces enable him to till;[3] lastly, the whole of the fruits which he derives from the application of these forces to this plot. When he is master of his natural forces, has an adequate plot of land to till and is left in possession of the fruits won from it, the individual has as much in the way of power and means as he can hope to have, and his liberty (looked at from the angle of power) consists in the defence of these possessions against the requirements of other people. This power of his stays intact whenever the individual is left to use his

[1] Plato, *Laws*, III, 687.
[2] It would be better to speak of the family than of the individual, but the classical exponents thought in terms of the individual.
[3] It was possible to regard the soil as something which did not, in the nature of things, have to be paid for, at a time when demographic pressure was low and the poverty of working appliances narrowly limited the acreage which a single individual (or family) could profitably exploit.

natural forces as he thinks fit, whenever he is not denied access to so much soil as he is able to till, whenever nothing is taken in dues from the fruits which he wins. On the other hand, his own domain is invaded to the extent that his natural forces are required of him for feudal or public tasks, that access to natural resources is impeded,[1] that he is forced to hand over some part of his fruits to his overlords or to his sovereign.

This image never deserted the writers of the classical period; they had ever before their eyes an autonomous agent, who hopes for nothing but what he can win for himself by his own efforts and asks for no more than to have this minimum guaranteed him at the price of the smallest possible sacrifice. There is, let us note, a close relationship between the political idea of liberty as exclusive power over my own domain, and the social idea of it as title to the entire produce of labour. The man who is left to do his own work in his own way, with no-one checking his activities or levying dues on his profits, obtains the entire produce of his labour and has no just complaint against anyone but himself or fortune if his fruits are smaller than his neighbour's. That man is 'free' who, in his government of his domain, gives nothing away but what he has agreed to give.

Different indeed is the social state in which a man no longer has either autonomous activity or produce of his own issuing therefrom, where his activity is pooled and his share allotted to him from the pool, where in consequence his way of life is no longer visibly dependent first on himself and next on the dues he has to pay, but derives immediately, as appears to him, from the allotment he receives.[2] In such a state his concern is no longer the defence of his own but rather an offensive operation by which to increase the grants which seem to him to depend on another's decision.

Under these conditions, the sharp dividing line drawn by the classical thinkers between the activities open to Primus by means of his own capacity and what is forbidden (or ordered) him by society tends to disappear; for Primus owes what is his own not to himself but to society. He cannot, therefore, regard society as merely opposing a hindrance to certain of his desires and acting in restraint of his power to act, but must also see it as bestowing on

---

[1] The place occupied by protests against sporting rights at the time of the French Revolution is characteristic.

[2] It will be noted incidentally that so fruitful a thing is social co-operation that it gives each participant more—indeed, much more—than the entire produce of his autonomous labour.

him the satisfaction of his desires and supplying him with the very idea of what he needs. And this leads to the obscuring of the distinction between the obstacles which Primus meets with from men and those which the meagreness of his resources and the general lay-out of things put in his path, for now both his resources themselves and the lay-out of things also seem to him to turn on other men; the result is that his power to act is no longer merely a possession which he defends but an indeterminate claim upon the means of society, and the relationship between his power and his desire slides into the relationship between what he actually gets and what he would like to get.

HOW LIBERTY LOSES ANY COMMON MEANING

What has just been said explains why the word liberty is liable to be invoked in contrary meanings. It is not, or it is no longer, an idea with a meaning common to all, as it was in the seventeenth and eighteenth centuries.[1]

[1] Understanding of this idea may be seen in a highly developed form in Sieyès' draft of a Declaration of Rights:

'Art. v. Every man should be sole owner of himself. He may hire out his services or his time, but he cannot sell himself. This primary possession is inalienable.

'Art. vi. Every man should be free in the exercise of his personal faculties, provided that he refrains from injuring the rights of another.

'Art. vii. For this reason no-one can be held to account for his thoughts or his feelings; every man has the right to speak or keep silent; no method of publishing his thoughts and feelings should be forbidden to any man; and, in particular, each man is free to write, print and have printed what seems good to him, always on the sole condition of not injuring another's rights. Lastly, every writer may sell his works or have them sold, and may have them freely circulated by post or in any other way without ever having to fear any breach of trust. In particular, letters should be treated as sacred by all the intermediaries between the writer and the recipient.

'Art. viii. Every citizen is equally free to use his muscles, his industry and his capital resources in the way he thinks good and useful for himself. No species of work is forbidden him. He may manufacture and produce what pleases him; he may keep and transport at will every sort of merchandise, and sell them at wholesale and retail. In these various occupations, no man and no association is entitled to trouble him, still less to stop him. Only the law may lay down the limits which must be set to this, as to every other, freedom.

'Art. ix. Every man is equally his own master as to going or staying, entering or leaving—even as to leaving the Kingdom—and as to returning, when and as it seems good to him.

'Art. x. Lastly, every man is his own master in disposing and using his property and income in the way he deems advisable.

'Art. xi. The liberty, property and security of the citizens should be under a social guarantee, which is removed from all possible attack.'

Déclaration des Droits de l'Homme en Société, by M. l'abbé Sieyès, at Versailles, issued by Baudouin, Printer to the National Assembly (1789).

Liberty was then conceived as the 'seigniory' which each man exercises over his own domain—his person, his actions, his property —and it was assumed that each man was equally concerned for the preservation of this seigniory, so that all were naturally in league against any unjustified aggrandisement by the suzerain's rights on this private seigniory. And the struggles for liberty in the seventeenth and eighteenth centuries were directed to the enfranchisement of the private seigniory.

The situations in which men find themselves are, however, very diverse. The result is that a measure conceived in general terms against private seigniory as such, in whatever hands it rests, may, if it affects adversely only a minority, be regarded by a majority as advantageous; it may even wear in their eyes the guise of an increase of liberty. For instance, the whole complex of measures which has in France today deprived landlords of the right of effective dealing in their property—in the case of commercial premises the deprivation is of the most explicit kind—would have been regarded by the men of the eighteenth century as beyond all question a blow to liberty. But this legislation has produced for tenants—especially commercial tenants—a capacity to deal effectively in the premises occupied by them; this capacity constitutes a real enlargement of their domain, so that, if liberty is power, it has increased their liberty.

Speaking more generally it may be said that all legislation which, in forbidding an action which is open only to a minority, simultaneously facilitates an action which is to the taste of a majority, is liable to be represented as an addition to the sum total of liberties.

If, in the same law, foreign travel is forbidden and holidays with pay are established—there will never in practice be any difficulty in finding plausible reasons for linking the two provisions—the law will bring a curtailment to some and a new right of enjoyment to others; the latter being more numerous than the former, the law will be both represented and felt as an addition to the sum total of liberties. And as everything which the law makes possible and forbids is made possible to and forbidden to all, it will be possible to urge that equality before the law is left intact. But it will be equally possible to turn upside down Anatole France's sally and say that this law, which is equal for all, forbids sculptors no less than dockers to visit the public galleries of Italy.

Intellectuals often feel surprise that, in the twentieth century, it has been possible to abolish freedom of intellectual expression and freedom of discussion in so many countries. But it needs to be noted that these rights, though they may be regarded as beneficial for all, have an immediate and actual value only for the tiny minority who put them to effective use. (I mean here not only those who debate and write but those also who follow assiduously the course of intellectual and political discussion.) Contrary to every prediction, the reign of universal education has brought no corresponding addition to the 'enlightened public'. If *L'Esprit des Lois* appeared today, its sales would be little greater than its sales in the eighteenth century—and would they even be as great?

If, in consequence, this liberty to publish and read what is published has nothing more to it than the power to do something which it is desired to do, this something is desired by so small a number of persons that resolute governments find it easy to abolish it, always provided that, when destroying a faculty which is prized only by a few, they simultaneously furnish the majority with a faculty which it likes.

These observations bring out the fact that, whenever liberty is regarded merely as the power to do something which it is desired to do, the tyrant need only base himself on the desires of the masses to suppress the liberties cherished by a few. But can anyone fail to see that the very concrete problem here posed is the problem of the maximisation of satisfactions, and not the problem of liberty at all? How, then, has it come about that we have drifted away from what we were discussing? This is the very definition of liberty which we allowed as our starting-point. Its development makes it clear that the thing discussed does not merit the fair name of liberty.

It is certain that every man desires addition to his power and chafes at the obstacles which stand in his way; it is also certain that the quest for a power which is wider binds him to a growing dependence on other men; it is certain, lastly, that this dependence creates a growing tendency to quarrel about distribution. All that is important, but it is the story not of liberty but of human imperialism. And whoever thinks to see the essence of liberty in the power of man is utterly lacking in any true feeling for liberty.

II. *LIBERTY AS DIGNITY*

'NO MAN IS AN ILAND'

The figure which we chose for representing the classical conception was a circle whose radius was the length of a man's power; this circle had been cut by shaded areas representing the sacrifice of portions of his liberty which he must make. Human co-operation results in successive extensions of the radius, but it also necessitates, as the condition of these extensions, a growth of the shaded areas which must be conceded. The free space can, for all that, be looked on as growing; and the white patch which it constitutes is like an island whose irregular outlines are determined by the concessions made to the public authority. According to the classical conception, man is the sovereign master of this island and does with it as he pleases. But this is a misleading metaphor, for no man is a self-contained island.[1]

This conclusion is brought home to us when we consider the definition of 'the island' given by John Stuart Mill: 'all that portion of a person's life and conduct which affects only himself';[2] it is permissible to wonder whether this portion is not so unimportant as to be insignificant. The whole of a man's life, whatever society he lives in, is passed in never-ending contact with his fellows; there is not a single action or even word of his which may not prove obnoxious, there is not one which is completely devoid of consequence for someone. On a true view it is impossible for us to exist at all without continually affecting others; sometimes we help and improve, sometimes we injure and worsen. Unawareness of mutual influences is the mark of the brute; awareness of them is the mark of self-conscious man. And for that reason there is no such thing as a reserved enclave where a man may behave himself as he pleases; more truly, he is subject to the feeling of obligation at all times and in all matters. Therefore, the problem of liberty does not present itself as a delimitation of the frontier between a domain in which orders must be obeyed and a domain in which fancy rules; far from it. In sober fact a man is never free from obligations, but some he appreciates himself and some are formulated for him by a superior in power. He is a free man in so far as the formulator of his obligations is none other than himself. Herein resides his dignity.

[1] 'No man is an iland, entire of itself.' J. Donne, *Devotions*, XVII.
[2] J. S. Mill, *On Liberty*, Introduction.

ON OBLIGATIONS

The famous battle-cry, 'Man is born free,' is the greatest non-sense if it is taken literally as a declaration of original and natural independence.

Man is born and remains throughout his life in dependence. At his birth he is completely helpless; unable to subsist by himself, he has to be nourished and guarded by his parents, and his state of utter dependence on them lasts much longer in the case of the young human being than in that of the young of any other animal—indeed it continues the longer the more advanced and admirable is the society into which he is born. Man arrives at adult age and puts on the characteristics of a finished man only by means of the prolonged efforts of others; thereby obligations are created for him of which he will be the more sensible the more he deserves the name of man.

A man's dependence does not cease when he enters adult life. Thanks to the habits and to the store of knowledge and skills which he has received from others, he is able to take his place in an association where his activity, just because it fits into a whole, is able to assure him fruits of every kind—fruits which, unassisted, he could not get himself. Society furnishes him with a wonderful gamut of delights, ranging from his daily bread to a Vivaldi concerto, and human activity reinforces even the pleasure conferred by the beauties of nature, which are appreciated the more when seen through the eyes of painters. Neither what we have nor what we are is ours in fee simple or is due only to ourselves. Man is in essence an heir entering on the accumulated heritage of past generations, taking his place as a partner in a vastly wealthy association. That individual must be blind indeed and presumptuous to the point of folly, who does not recognise how wretched in every respect his state would be had he no part in this organisation and this wealth, how small and insignificant is his own contribution to them and how utterly he depends on them.

For this reason every individual with a spark of imagination must feel deeply indebted to these many others, the living and the dead, the known and the unknown. So logical is this piety as regards human association that it is found among peoples incomparably less advanced than our own; and it is a major folly of modern times to fill the individual with ideas of what society owes to him rather than of what he owes to society. The wise man knows himself for debtor, and his actions will be inspired by a deep sense of obligation.

Man is, first and foremost, a debtor. And his debt is, no doubt, the greater the more richly that, culturally or materially, society has endowed him.[1] But the differences between us in this respect are small indeed if we compare the median situation in our own society with that prevailing in lower human organisations.

If every man is a debtor, then the feeling of obligation, so utterly incompatible with using our powers as we please, should never leave him. Not for a moment is he completely out of debt. His energies and his time are pledged to those countless associates by whose services and collaboration he lives as he does live, and to that smaller number who are directly dependent on him, whose potentialities it is for him to actualise, even as his own were actualised. How can he ever feel himself free? Never, if freedom consists in exemption from obligations. But it is in fact something quite other.

A man is free when and to the extent that he is his own judge of his obligations, when none but himself compels him to fulfil them. A man is free when he acts *sponte sua*, spontaneously, as the executor of a judgment passed *in foro interno*, in the forum of his own conscience.

THE FREE MAN AS VOLUNTEER

Primus loves his work, thinks himself well treated and gives satisfaction. One day his employer sends for him and suggests to him that so good a workman ought to go to mass. Primus takes offence and leaves his job; he resents the claim to substitute an outside judgment for his own. This feeling of his is the feeling for liberty. He will react with just the same anger if his mates put pressure on him to get him to join a union when 'he thinks he ought not to do it'. In this last phrase are found the essential elements of the question. When what guides my actions can be called 'what I think I ought to do', then I am free. And anger and revolt against a suffered indignity perfectly describe the feeling called forth by pressure to make me act in a way contrary to what I think is right. There are no grounds for anger when it is only a question of what I want to do being thwarted.

---

[1] 'Do you know what is nobility? It is the advances made to you by your country on the security of your ancestors, until such time as you are able to honour their bonds.' Marmontel, *Bélisaire* (1767), p. 52.

Secundus has made willing sacrifice to finance an establishment for religious instruction. This institution is nationalised, irreligious instruction is substituted, and the public authority requires of Secundus the continuance of his support; he must, in other words, go on doing what his own judgment had once led him to do, even when his judgment has turned against it. Secundus takes offence.

Tertius patriotically enlists for a war which seemed to him just. After it is over, he is kept on in the service for a colonial expedition of which he disapproves. Tertius takes offence.

Every man takes offence whenever, in a matter in which he once acted voluntarily in accordance with his own sense of obligation, an attempt is made to force on him a different action, based on an outside judgment. He is conscious of injustice because, whereas his own judgment found a certain action just, the other one thrust on him seems to him unjust. Also, he feels humiliated because it is sought to make him act in accordance with this outside judgment; this feeling of humiliation is experienced by every man of the least elevation of character, even when all that happens is that an action which he formerly took voluntarily of his own free will becomes a legal obligation—for in that case the quality of his action suffers a degradation.

From what has already been said it emerges that the free man is in essence the voluntary executive of his own moral judgment.

LIBERTARIAN HARMONY

The actions which I take voluntarily in obedience to my own judgment may or may not coincide with what others, whom these actions affect, think that I ought to do.

Let us suppose that Primus, inspired by the sense of his obligations, acts in such a way that at every moment each of his actions fits the expectation of each single person affected by it. Nothing, clearly, need be forbidden to Primus, and, if society consisted of Primuses, edict and constraint would be unnecessary. Is this ideal state possible? The first point that strikes us is that, since the different peers of Primus have different interests, there must be those of his actions which can only be fully agreeable to one of his peers by being less agreeable, or actually disagreeable, to another. That being so, these peers of his must be wise enough not to appraise the actions of Primus from a purely subjective standpoint.

This carries with it the admission that what his fellows expect from him is not the conduct which gives each of them the highest measure of satisfaction possible but rather that which is the best possible in itself. (This is pitching the requirement rather too high; let us rather say 'the best that can reasonably be expected from a man in view of our imperfect natures'.) Let us, then, put it like this: that within this society of Primuses each looks to each for such action as can reasonably be expected of him. If the judgments as to what is reasonable of the doer and the person affected by the deed happen to coincide, then society will achieve perfect harmony in a state of complete personal liberty.

This is, in fact, the libertarian Utopia which never loses its attraction for the minds of men. It is not a complete absurdity, for more often than not the action of each of us answers the expectation of those affected by it; if it did not, any society would collapse, for all societies rest on expectations being answered regularly. But experience also teaches us that it is not so with every action. If, always and in all respects, it could be so, it would be the reign of libertarian harmony.

We are now in a position to advance the following propositions: first, that liberty for the individual consists in his acting voluntarily by reference to his own sense of his obligations; second, that men are entitled to be left free, and not to have their actions prescribed to them, to the extent to which the sense of their obligations inspires their actions; third, that a society of completely free men implies that each of its members acts after this fashion and, further, that all have the same idea of their obligations.

All the builders of Utopias have imagined a paradise of liberty, and every political action based on these foundations has led to tyrannical regimes. The contradiction is easily explained. Hypotheses of this kind postulate in every citizen an internal principle of action which is the same for all and sways completely the conduct of each. Since, in reality, this principle is constantly found wanting, the step is but a short one to forcing everyone to behave as if he was influenced by it. The result is a structure which is the very opposite to what its builders claimed for it. Instead of a society in which every action is voluntary, a society arises in which none is: terror takes the place of liberty.

Utopias in the real are, beyond question, always abominable, but Utopian dreams also tend invariably to a certain degeneracy. The substance of such a dream ought truly to be so great a 'charity' (in the Pauline sense) between the members of an association that, whenever one of them speaks and acts, the others, under the spur of their affection, gather round in silence, ready to applaud what the love felt for themselves by the man in question is about to prompt him to say or do, being something which, thanks to the ingeniousness of love, will be in every respect exactly what was required—and yet original. Nor is such a description wholly divorced from reality; for the relationships between a well-loved king and his people, between a virtuoso and his audiences, between lovers, really do answer to it. So it is also in a circle of philosophers when human vanity fades out before the thirst for knowledge, when the desire of each is to hear from his neighbour the word which will throw light on new ways of thought.

The dream turns to dross when external opinion is no longer one of hopeful confidence as regards our fellow, when we are no longer ready to welcome the unpredictable excellence of Primus's next move, when, on the contrary, the limit of our demand on him is that he obeys the conventions. Seldom are we inclined to praise Primus for what he does. His conduct ordinarily follows prescribed lines which expectation has discounted. Convention, not love, is the cement of such a harmony.

This conventional harmony plays a large part in the life of historical societies, which could not go on without it. A certain model of behaviour for any given situation completely dominates Primus and those affected by his conduct. Primus feels obliged to do exactly what others consider him obliged to do, and for that reason does it voluntarily and freely. These 'models of behaviour', however, when they are no longer the expression of active beliefs and living affections, become fossilised; in the end, they are seen as shackles—the shackles of custom, the prison of conformity.

OF ARBITRARINESS IN LAWS

There would be no need for laws at all if each separate ego could be trusted to live by the inspiration of love, or at least by the authority of custom. He cannot so be trusted; therefore behaviours must be prescribed and intimidation must play its part in enforcing them. It was long believed that laws were only the formal declaration of the just and necessary. Then the idea grew that what the law does is not to command what is just, but to make just what it commands. This is an important difference from the point of view of liberty.

If my view is that the law is declaratory and does no more than make me aware of a justice which I should have been able to find and realise for myself, then in obeying these laws I make no sacrifice of my liberty, for I am acting in conformity with the feeling of obligation within me which the lawgiver has clothed in a new light. This is an attitude which presupposes one of two things: either that I accept entirely the beliefs which underlie these laws, so that my feeling is the same as that of the legislator; or that I acknowledge in the legislator a moral authority which inclines me to allow as just and good whatever he tells me is just and good, even though, left to myself, I should not have reached that conclusion.

The first point sufficiently explains why laws which, like those of Sparta, seem to us anything but liberal, did not in the least offend the feeling for liberty among those who were subject to them: they represented completely their private beliefs. It is no less clear that any faction which is closely tied to a given system of beliefs will see nothing contrary to liberty in a system of laws answering to those beliefs, though the system may seem odiously tyrannical to those with different beliefs.

The second point explains why the laws put forward or defended by moral authorities whose judgment was accepted have never been found contrary to liberty.

But when a dispersion of beliefs occurs in a society, when judgment becomes an individual matter and the public authority is stripped of its various prestiges—phenomena all associated with ageing civilisations—conflict shows itself between the judgment of the public authority and private judgment. The legislators, having themselves lost any deep sense of beliefs held in common, will no longer present the rules of their making as objectively just; henceforward they will invoke only the subjective right committed to them of formulating laws—laws which have power to bind not by their substance but as the emanations of legitimate authority.

No amount of legitimacy in the legislator can ever legitimatise laws which offend my moral judgment. Whether he owes his place to heredity and coronation or to popular election, a law which my own conscience does not recognise as just and which runs counter to my private judgment is for me illegitimate, and whenever I find myself constrained to govern my actions by it, my liberty suffers loss.

THE INTERNAL TENSION WITHIN THE INDIVIDUAL

Politics is, on a true view of it, one of the moral sciences, for the most serious political tension is that which arises in our own breast whenever our will swings undecided between our private judgment and the judgment of others. No doubt it is always faintly absurd to represent what goes on inside us as a play with several characters; but anyone who has looked inside himself even a little finds illuminating a representation of this kind.

Man, we say, swings undecided between internal and external judgment. Is it his duty to consider the external judgment right and his own erroneous? We demand that of him. Liberalism has gone some way already when all that is demanded of the individual is that he conforms his actions to the judgment of others, for there have always been times when the desire of these 'others' was that Primus not only should act conformably to their judgment but should also admit that their judgment was right and his erroneous. Not only must Joan of Arc wear female clothes again; she must admit that she now sees them to be the only suitable ones for her to wear and that her former opinion to the contrary was wrong. The external judge requires, in short, that Primus comes into line not only as regards what he does but as regards what he thinks; he must be punished for nonconformist action and he must disown his private judgment. Here we see the deep instinct for the extraction of confession, a process which has in all times resulted in a variety of barbarous treatments. The 'guilty man' must condemn himself out of his own mouth, he must agree that the internal principle of his actions was bad; not only his actions but his conscience itself must be put to rights. This requirement, which is the cause of shocking cruelties, is a sort of monstrous homage paid to the necessary coherence considered to exist between a man's actions and his private judgment. A man is felt to have been treated as unfree when he is forced to take an action of which his private judgment disapproves, or when he is put to death for a crime which he does not regard as such. Conscience feels easier when his private judgment has been conditioned to find the action desired of him good, the action which he has committed bad, and the execution to which he is brought just.

The spectacle of an individual defying this external imperative is seen at its supreme in the case of Socrates. I consent, said he, in the forum of my conscience to my execution, for I hold the view that it is right for a citizen to be subject to the judges established by the laws of the city for the purpose of applying these laws; but I refuse to admit that my action was unjust, or that the judgment of mine which inspired it was ill-founded. And the persecutors of Socrates proved themselves infinitely superior to many another, past and present, in that they were content with this attitude, and did not torture the philosopher with a view to extracting from the weakness of the flesh the repudiation of his inner inspiration.

Whenever laws no longer manifest the just for all to see, the fact that they are not presented as the necessary expressions of justice, but as rules whose only claim to obedience is that they have been commanded, may be regarded as an advantage. Then indeed obedience to the laws—in itself a good and useful thing—no longer involves the disavowal of my private judgment, though still the laws must not command me anything which my private judgment condemns so strongly that obedience becomes sin.

In such a state of things, the laws seeming to me to be merely the arbitrary decisions of others, my wish will naturally be that they will not push their claims on me too far.

LIBERTY AS PARTICIPATION AND AS ISOLATION

To a conscientious man in whom the sense of obligation is much alive laws are never a limitation on his liberty in so far as they prescribe only what his sense of obligation, whether immediately or on reflection, makes him think justly due. It can never so work out completely, but the less laws answer to his sense of obligation the greater is his concern to defend a domain of his own into which the law does not enter. In my own house, where no outside authority comes, I act according to my own sense of my obligations—I am free there. I should be no less free in the market-place and in the forum if the behaviour which my private judgment causes me to adopt was regarded as good by others. The importance of a frontier is in proportion to the disparity between my judgment and that of others.

The more pronounced this disparity and the more I find myself constrained to act in conformity with the judgment of others, differing from my own, the more do I prize the domain in which I can act according to my sole judgment. I am irked by the conformity which is imposed on me and clogs my liberty; I prefer the part of my life which is lived away from this imposition. Though I defend my own domain, though I enjoy it and increasingly take refuge there, I still deplore the heterogeneity introduced into my life, which now has two principles: in some things my own judgment, in others the judgment of others. The discomfort which this situation causes leads me to dream of another state of things, in which my own judgment and that of others would coincide. There are at present two men inside me, the private man subject to his own judgment and the burgher or citizen subject to the judgment of others. In a different state of things these two men would be reduced to one. The thought of both Plato and Rousseau becomes clearer if we see in them men out of sympathy with their own times, whose lives are in consequence remote and isolated from the real city which they know. This separateness they feel as a reproach; therefore they dream of a city in which coincidence of judgments would be so great that a man—Plato, that is to say, or Rousseau—would be as joyfully and spontaneously himself in the forum as he is in his own retreat.

It is not unreasonable to project pictures of this kind into the past. It is quite conceivable that, where personalities are still somewhat undeveloped, the feeling for liberty can be fully satisfied in a state of very close social interconnection. Men have then, so to speak— I must not be taken too literally—only a single conscience; some can easily make seem good to others what they find good themselves. That there could be unanimity in the forum is attested by the researches of anthropologists into primitive communities; we receive from them the picture of a society in which the suggestion of one man sweeps the others off their feet, just as we see happen today in crowd phenomena where the individual is seen at his most primitive.

But just as this unanimity comes apart in proportion as the warmth of the crowd is dissipated, so it is bound to fall to pieces in proportion as a human grouping becomes more complicated, as it absorbs disparate elements and, above all, as the personalities of individuals become more marked. For this reason Rousseau was right in regarding the decomposition of the primitive harmony as an inevitable result of the course of evolution. That was the lesson he taught in his much misunderstood book, the *Contrat Social*. It almost passes belief that this great work should have been taken as affirming the absolute right of a majority, when its message so obviously is that the only morally valid foundation for collective command is the collective unity of judgments, when it describes so clearly the inevitable loss of this unity in proportion as a city departs further from an ignorant and rustic way of life. No-one has praised with greater enthusiasm the liberty brought by the spontaneous convergence of ethical judgments; but no-one has asserted more unmistakably that convergence of this kind does not and cannot happen in advanced societies—a flat contradiction this to the post-Cartesian notion that it advances in step with education.

Rousseau's advice regarding existing societies was that which he gave to Emile: it was to keep aloof, to escape as far as possible from the sway both of the sovereign and the prevailing opinion, to defend the private judgment against the pressure of the judgments of others. Though he styled himself 'citizen of Geneva', Rousseau was no active citizen, and behaved more and more like a perpetual refugee in the society of his time. By way of compensation, he cherished the vision of a city of which he could be wholeheartedly a citizen. This analysis of Rousseau seems exactly applicable to Plato; it is what emerges from the study of Plato given us by David Grene.[1]

The thought of the two philosophers can be put in the form of an 'either—or': either our city is bound together so well that it is the natural home of unanimity of moral judgments, from which it follows that each single man, in giving himself completely to the city's service, is free and happy—completely free because everything commanded him is everything he considers good; or ours is a degenerate and corrupted city, in which the public judgments, whether they issue from an authority or from opinion, not only do not strike the individual mind with any feeling of necessity, but even offend his notions—and in that case every man's desire must be to live as private a life as possible. Plato, while keeping aloof from the Athenian polity of his time, toyed with the illusion of building the perfect city at Syracuse. Rousseau had more of the historical sense, and his relative freedom from illusions shows itself in his affirmation that Corsica alone was capable of being made into the perfect state.

The vision of a city in which spontaneous harmony abounds comes, no doubt, more naturally to minds the more sensitive they are to psychological strife, and is the more enthusiastically received by a society the less this spontaneous harmony can find a place in

[1] Cf. D. Grene, *Man in his Pride* (Chicago, 1951), and my edition with commentary of the *Contrat Social* (Geneva, 1947).

it—where every common basis for judgment has been ruined by such a climax of disagreement as arises in every ageing culture. It is a very dangerous vision because the moral disintegration of a large, highly developed society is a condition favourable to the development of small sects displaying the moral and psychological unity which our philosophers pronounced so desirable; these sects then regard themselves as perfect societies whose mission it is to remould the large society in their own image—in fact they will embark on the conquest of it, reducing to moral slavery those whose beliefs differ from their own.

BABYLON AND ICARIA

Let us take for consideration a large and complex social whole, far advanced in civilisation; for convenience we will call it Babylon. Its economic development is such that every sort of activity and a wide variety of ways of life are to be found in it. Religious orthodoxy has been in decline there for some time, and incessant discussion has favoured the dispersion of beliefs. In a first stage of intellectual emancipation, the metaphysics of earlier beliefs had been called in question; they had been repudiated or abandoned by a growing number of members. In a second stage, the ethical rules linked to these metaphysics also get called in question; more and more frequent and various contacts with other societies have brought a knowledge of different moral systems. Agile intelligences then find themselves confronted with different notions of right and wrong. Foreign ideas of morality at first astonish the philosophers of Babylon, who come in time, however, to use them as critical missiles against the traditional morality of their own country; it dawns on them that, if foreign systems of morals strike a Babylonian as absurd, no less absurd can the Babylonian system be made to seem when looked at from the point of view of a foreigner. As the result of these critical exercises the ethical system of Babylon comes to be regarded by the most advanced thinkers as based merely on custom. The philosophers next spend some time looking for an entirely rational system of morals, but in the course of their hunt opinions come to diverge so much that the only result is very different views as to what is commanded by Reason.

As the result of this long-drawn-out intellectual crisis Babylon presents to the onlooker a great diversity not only of ways of life but also of beliefs and opinions; Babylonians differ very much in what they want to do as individuals, but also (what is much more serious) they hold very different notions of what they ought to do—what is seemly, what is moral, what is just, what is owing. The Babylonian society continues, however, to function satisfactorily, thanks to a system of laws of pragmatic inspiration, which forbids actions of a kind harmful to the social organism and commands behaviours necessary to social prosperity. These laws do not draw their authority from a common pool of moral beliefs; they make no claim to embody what is good in itself but only to safeguard what is useful to the preservation and development of the whole. As they do not draw their authority from a common pool of beliefs, what makes them respected is, essentially, the fear of punishments induced by a strong government. In short, the laws are legitimate, in Austin's sense, as the emanation of a recognised authority which makes itself obeyed: the principle of government is Hobbesian.

Every citizen feels an authority of this kind as a restriction on his liberty—and so indeed it is. For he abstains from the actions which are forbidden him not because he thinks them bad but because they are forbidden, and he executes the actions which are commanded him not because he thinks them good, but because they are commanded. The idea of repression is ever-present to his mind to keep him from doing not only what his own judgment forbids him to do, but also things which his own judgment either would not forbid him or would actually encourage him to do. In this state of things, laws and the power which sees to their execution seem onerous to the citizen. Some of the citizens will then come naturally to think that it would be a great and fine reform to shake off the burden which weighs society down—or, to speak more precisely, which weighs down each single member of society—and to replace this arbitrary rule which finds no echo in the conscience of each with the inspiration of a system of commands which gives expression to the imperatives of the individual conscience.

To me, Primus, a reaction of this kind is very natural, for I am keenly aware of a feeling of obligation which encourages me to certain actions and forbids me others. How easily borne and natural is the yoke of conscience compared with this foreign yoke of the laws to which I am subjected! Let them but make obligatory the system of commands which rules my heart; I shall have no difficulty in keeping them and I shall feel myself free under ukases of that kind!

And there are other citizens who feel as I do; like me, they detest this burdensome government whose laws are in contradiction to the ethical beliefs which are common to them and me. Thus, they yield themselves easily to the fascination of the vision which I put before them—of a society in which there would no longer be an apparatus of repression because there would no longer be need for one; the reason being that this society would have adopted as its system of obligations the one which we feel to be just, whose excellence is proved by the fact that we obey it voluntarily.

The only flaw in our argument then is that the system of obligations which seems natural to us, to which we, my companions and I, give spontaneous obedience, is peculiar to our group or sect, and is not shared by all the citizens of Babylon. When I ally myself with others who share my beliefs down to the last tenet, what actually happens? In effect, we reconstitute a small, primitive society in the heart of the large, highly civilised society. This group is a tribe in the true sense, capable of a spontaneous harmony of behaviours; and the small society which we form between ourselves is a *societas perfecta*. All that we have to do now is to seize the reins of government and make our principles the rule of the entire society. In that way we shall have a society which is good and free for all, for all will follow willingly imperatives which partake of immediate self-evidence.

Unfortunately, matters will not go like that, because the system of values of my group is not the system of all the citizens of Babylon. Were it so, Babylon would not be Babylon but a quite different society which we will call Icaria. In Icaria the unity of principles and the spontaneous harmony of behaviours hold the field. That is not the case at Babylon, but it is the case with us, the members of a conspiratorial group of Icarians, and in so far as we apply the rules which we have in common only as between ourselves there is no actual need for repressive constraints. But as soon as we aim at imposing our rules on the rest of the Babylonians who do not share our beliefs, we are led to enforce them on them, because these rules are alien to the conscience and the will of others and, in consequence, have to be upheld by punitive methods.

And at that point we find ourselves, to our great surprise, no longer content to use the apparatus of repression already in being in the service of neutral laws, but led on to enlarge this apparatus enormously—for it is now our task to bend the rest of the Babylonians to a system of rules which is coherent, rational and complete. Then we shall hear those of the Babylonians who do not share our beliefs complaining bitterly that their liberty has been reduced as compared with what it was before, and even that it has been lost completely. We shall think these complaints absurd; on the contrary, the Babylonians are now free, liberated. For now they are entirely free to do all the things which are good in themselves—which we do voluntarily and joyfully. All that they are forbidden to do are bad things, which we do not want to do, and which consequently, as being bad, they ought not to want to do either. So convinced are we of the rectitude of our principles that the resistance of our fellow-citizens seems to us to proceed merely from their unenlightened state. Ours is an essentially free society composed of free men, because all that is commanded in it is what a free man should choose to do voluntarily, and nothing is forbidden in it but what a free man should not want to do. If the apparatus of constraint which we have to employ is heavier than ever it was, it is only an accident due to the moral laziness of our fellow-citizens. As soon as their consciences have been aroused, we shall be able to liquidate this apparatus. Let us hasten the coming of this happy moment! and to that end, let us not allow false opinions to retard the real awakening of conscience, the grasp of the only true principles. In consequence, just as we have had to make the apparatus of repression much heavier, so also we must suppress utterly liberty of opinion. But these are but accidents in the march to total liberty, which will be attained as soon as all the citizens of Babylon have made their own the principles which animate us, the Icarian society.

Such is the dialectic of tyrannical sects. It is useless to point out to them that their design is absurd at the source, for, if the principles which they find self-evident had the transcendent value which they ascribe to them, the citizens of Babylon would subscribe to them without outside help. It is useless to try and bring home to them that they are trying to brand a civilised society with the unity of a savage society—an attempt which results in their practising systematic cruelties. All objections of the kind come up against a profound and instinctive inspiration. The dream of Icaria is for ever being born again spontaneously in the heart of Babylon. For men never resign themselves to Babylon being Babylon. It will be no use the lawyers pleading that the laws of Babylon are not the expression of a moral rule but only the means by which Babylon can be kept together. It is so natural to man to think of laws as the expression of a moral rule that in the forum of his conscience this is the light which illuminates the judgment of each of us. And since there is no longer in our society sufficient moral unity for the law to reflect this light, since there is, on the contrary, a dispersion of personal judgments, the legislation taken as a whole will always seem to each private judgment in some respects unjust. This general feeling of injustice will serve the end of any coherent group with a nostrum for making institutions entirely just, though reflection would show that they will be just only by reference to the beliefs of this particular group, and cannot be just by reference to the beliefs of all, seeing that by hypothesis these latter have suffered dispersion.

The conspiratorial struggle of Icarians is a psychological product of the Babylonian situation; its constant recurrence is in the nature of things. Though it finds its most perfect expression in totalitarian regimes, it is continually at work in the democratic process as well. Our western societies are not subjected to the strong, neutral government which we postulated at Babylon, but their legislative system fluctuates at the mercy of pressures exercised by the dominant wills. Some of these pressures, certainly, spring from nothing but interests of groups—a phenomenon which has been fully studied but is not the one which concerns us here; for those who, to advance a partial interest, bring pressure on legislators are perfectly aware of what they are doing and are handicapped in their action by the feeling that it is immoral. Those, on the contrary, who think to impose on society the 'good' system of restraints, which will for that reason one day find itself obeyed by all without constraint and will re-establish between men that spontaneous harmony of be- haviours which remains ever the libertarian ideal—whose leader, moreover, embarks its champions, by the dialectic described above, on tyrannical action—those have a moral fanaticism to uphold them.

It will have been noted that the idea of dispersion of beliefs and the dream of return to unity play a vital role in our present discussion. Therefore it is of great importance to examine the various possible hypotheses concerning the evolution of beliefs—their convergence or divergence, their oscillations between one and the other, or their partial convergence and their partial divergence.

CHAPTER 16

LIBERTY OF OPINION AND NATURAL LIGHT

Liberty of opinion is the basic principle of the political institutions of the West. It is an obvious mistake to regard majority decision as the criterion of the regimes which we call 'democratic'. So far from massive majorities in favour of a government and its policy giving us a feeling of the excellence of a regime, they render it suspect to us; we get the suspicion that so much unanimity is the result of hindrances placed in the way of the expression and propagation of adverse opinions, and these hindrances, we think, deprive of all significance the majority obtained. For this reason majority decision derives its virtue in our eyes from the liberty of opinion which precedes it.

It is liberty of opinion which animates what is called the dialectic of democracy. Out of the free clash of opinions a majority view emerges and commands. But its right of command can never obstruct the free play of liberty of opinion; the latter continues as before and in time issues in a different majority view, which commands in its turn. Interrupt this process and you take leave at once of the regime of liberty. Majority opinion derives its authority not from majorities alone, but from majorities formed in a climate of liberty of opinion.

Such is the principle of our institutions; it is accepted by all but a few and is never invoked in vain. The belief in the virtue of this liberty of opinion is general in our civilisation; it is one of the few points on which nearly all agree.

For this reason the principle seems to make a wonderfully apt starting-point for an inquiry into the implicit postulates of our political discussions. All or nearly all of us hold it. But why is this so? This visible emergent belief has no other authorisation than the hidden underlying beliefs which we are going to find in the course of our inquiry. Thus we may hope to arrive at certain fundamental axioms of our political reasoning which it is important to bring to the light of day.

WHAT IS CALLED LIBERTY OF OPINION IS
A FREE CLASH OF OPINIONS

When we say that opinion should be free, we do not mean that every man should be free to think as pleases him in the forum of his conscience. This would be pointless, for there are no practical methods of violating this inner sanctum, or at any rate none were known before some horrifying practices were discovered in quite recent times.

Everyone agrees, however, that this liberty of the private conscience is an incomplete thing, passively and actively. Passively, because there is a dearth of options when no opinions from without find entry. Actively, because an opinion of its very nature seeks expression. What the expression 'liberty of opinion' suggests to the mind is liberty to propagate opinions, the right of initiative and enterprise in the dissemination of the opinions which are dear to us.

Society may be pictured as a sort of paddock of receptive and selective consciences into which are loosed all the opinions that ever were. In actual fact, this clash of opinions is necessarily imperfect by reason of the existence of the various material channels of propagation—pulpits, despatch boxes, newspapers, parties, etc.; the opinions which get the benefit of these channels have an immense advantage over others. And this poses the problem of the right of access to the various instruments of propagation. In our own times, complaint is sometimes heard, in the name of liberty of opinion, that certain views cannot be put forward, either on the radio or at universities, that there is thus a preliminary selection of opinions allowed to compete for popular approval.

Some selection of the kind seems in fact inevitable. For example, no university faculty could permit anyone, under pretext of liberty, to teach that the earth is flat. The obviously false is ruled out, and occasionally it happens that a mistake is made. The obviously wicked is also ruled out, and here our only guide is the moral opinions we profess ourselves. But these limits, we may note, are in our own time exceedingly relaxed, and in any case only circumscribe the use of certain instruments; certain opinions are forbidden certain collective platforms, but propagation by way of individual energies is for all that not generally prevented. There is, in general, reluctance to put obstacles in the way of a new and disquieting opinion; the feeling is that it must be given its chance.

This attitude implies an almost unlimited confidence in the selective capacity of the public, and confidence on this scale is a thing immanent in our society. We must try to discover what are its foundations.

THE HISTORICAL ORIGINS

Our ancestors felt very differently. Their view was that men live well when their beliefs are healthy, and they made a point of propagating and upholding these healthy beliefs by teaching them and not teaching others.

The West started on its career under the sway of Christian beliefs, forming an organised body of doctrines, of which a visible body, the clergy, was the repository. It was then thought that among the things of which men ought to be convinced there were some which could be apprehended by their reason and others which they could not apprehend and must believe on the guarantee of a weighty and unimpeachable authority. Opinionativeness was then considered dangerous; it was a phenomenon which St Augustine defined as 'imagining one's self to know what one does not know'.

The Reformers shared these views. They did not aim to introduce a new version of the Christian verities, but to correct a deviation which had, according to them, been brought about. This feeling persisted; thus, towards the end of the seventeenth century, Jean Claude was still comparing the deviation of the Roman Church with that which occurred at the time of the Arian heresy and had then too, according to him, engulfed the bulk of the church, leaving the true believers in a minority. Alongside this argument he put forward another, implying a very different system of thought. He compared the condemnation by the Roman Church of the Reformers' views with the condemnation by the Jewish Church of the teaching of Christ himself: 'If the first Christians, who were Jews, could not hearken to the doctrine of the Son of God, nor accept his miracles without violating their duty towards the church which had condemned him, what must the state of scruple be into which is cast everything in the world today that calls itself Christian?'[1] In other words, if the Arians were mere deviationists as regards an already revealed truth, our Lord, on the other hand, had introduced a new law transcending the old; in such a comparison the idea of truth advancing by way of abrupt mutations is clearly visible.

[1] J. Claude, *Défense de la Réformation*, I, VIII, 7.

Whether the Reformers considered that they were bringing back the truth from which most had gone astray, or that they were introducing a new understanding of it to which most were still in a state of rebellion, they regarded the truth itself as the one, sure truth than which none other was worthy to be taught. At first, at any rate, they were keenly alive to those differences between themselves to which Bossuet called attention—differences which in early days seemed to them, as to Bossuet, to carry presumption of error.[1]

For two whole centuries, until the seventeenth century was well advanced, the dispersion of fundamental beliefs was thought a terrible evil, and the aim of each and all was the restoration of unity, naturally along the lines of his own set of convictions. Each sect hurled its own anathemas, and it was only *raison d'état* which brought about toleration. It is worthy of note that the starting-point of toleration was expediency, not an idea of justice. The primary virtue found in it was restriction of political damage.

Only at a later date did its positive virtues find their eulogists, among whom the most famous advocate was Milton in his *Areopagitica*. The great poet expounded even at that early date what was to be the central theme of the Age of Enlightenment: that the intellectual reflections of individual men and women, being struggles towards the truth, are entitled to have their utility presumed, and that a pious people, which makes the reading of the scriptures its study, is in a sufficiently robust state of health to separate the good seed from the tares, both of which must be permitted, as in the parable, to grow up together.

We may ask ourselves whether propositions of this kind, so far from being revolutionary, were not really a reversion to the early state of Christendom, for it is amply attested that different authorities put forth different readings of the Christian verities and that a great liberty of interpretation was the prevailing rule. We are sometimes

---

[1] 'When variations in the exposition of the faith have appeared among Christians, they have always been regarded as a mark of falsity and incoherence in the doctrine expounded. The Faith speaks simply: the Holy Spirit spreads its pure light abroad and the truth which it teaches is clothed in a language which is always the same.... Tertullian said long ago: "Politicians make varying regulations; each of them thinks himself entitled to change and modify what he has received, seeing that it is by means of his own spirit that the founding father of the sect has built. Heresy never loses its proper nature of incessant innovation; in that respect the thing continues as it began." ' Bossuet, *Histoire des Variations des Églises Protestantes*, preface, pp. 2–3.

tempted to wonder whether a sharper clash between the notions of orthodoxy and liberty may not have been precipitated by the invention of printing, for divergences between things said made much less impact than those between things printed. The coming of a new medium of instruction raised the question of access to its use —in fact, the most modern of all problems.

OPINIONS AND BEHAVIOURS

After Milton, apologies for liberty multiplied apace, though the arguments were always the same. First in order was a negative argument. You cannot force beliefs; it is a case 'of producing in the soul certain judgments and certain movements of will.... Violence is incapable of persuading the mind.'[1] There is no refuting the argument, but it does not justify the propagation of opinions. To justify this, we must return to the parable of the good seed and the tares—to the impoverishment of society which would ensue on attempts to suppress the harmful and on the sacrifice of the salutary which would inevitably result.

Our apologists emphasise to a remarkable extent the absence of danger to the public order in diversity of thoughts. It is by attempts to terminate this diversity and unify thought by force that the public order is troubled, that 'the inevitable war of all against all' breaks out. It is Bayle who talks so.[2] If the sovereign eschews this folly himself and forbids it to his subjects, the diversity of opinions, being now respected, will cause no harm. So says Spinoza in his *Traité Théologico-Politique* and Bayle repeats the assertion more forcibly and more fruitfully. Both these great writers express a horror of seditious opinions, such as excite to turmoil in the state, and express themselves thereon in the strongest terms; but both seem to think that the modification of beliefs is without influence on actions.

On this theme, indeed, their respective arguments are as different as their respective metaphysics. In his *Traité Politique*, Spinoza makes the sovereign the arbitrary judge and master of human actions; he stamps as criminal every action contrary to the rules laid down by the sovereign, while holding that there should be freedom to change individual beliefs, changes in which will never be reflected in acts which, so long as the sovereign has not modified his rules,

[1] Bayle, 'Commentaire sur le Compelle Intrare', in *Opera*, vol. II, p. 371.
[2] *Op. cit.* p. 438.

would themselves be culpable. This total dichotomy between thought and action is certainly surprising.

Bayle's argument is different. He too would authorise the nonconformist thought but not the nonconformist action. If in his view there is little likelihood of the latter, the reason is a postulate which runs right through his thought—that difference in beliefs cannot be reflected in different conceptions of moral duty. For him, as for his pupil Voltaire, morality is one, necessary, universal, independent of metaphysical beliefs. Sometimes he seems to say that the only needed condition for feeling morality is not to be an atheist; sometimes he says that even for atheists it is no different.

In other words, Bayle divorces metaphysics and morality, just as Spinoza divorces thought and action. Spinoza seems to hold that whatever a man thinks will not make obedience to the laws harder for him. Bayle puts the line of demarcation at a higher level: whatever each believes, all will be in agreement on the same moral truths. This hypothesis of Bayle's is of the highest importance and has the most serious consequences for the political order. We are now going to consider where it leads and on what philosophical foundations it rests.

THE POSTULATE OF CONVERGENCE

If we run over the thinkers who have asserted and won acceptance for the excellence of democratic regimes, we find at the root of their convictions the idea that the greater number judges well in matters of moral import and will know how to discern what is just. It is not occasional decisions, called for by passing circumstances, which they sought to remit to the arbitrament of the greater number. They recognised that decisions of this kind must stay with the actual rulers, guided as they are by an exact acquaintance with the facts and trained in the difficult art of collective management. What it was right to remit to the people were decisions in principle, bearing a moral character. That was a subject-matter in which all were less likely to go astray than some.

The postulate behind this opinion is, clearly, that in the formation of general judgments there is a moral self-evidence to which the judgment of men is bound. In some this self-evidence may be obscured by the murk of the passions, but this does not happen with the citizens in the mass, always provided that, at the time of consultation, each of them proves able to forget himself in considering the problem—as though it were a problem set to the citizen of some other country where he had no personal interests.

Where is the guarantee that matters will work out so? Bayle has formulated it clearly:

There is a vivid, natural light which enlightens all men from the first moment that they open the eyes of their minds and convinces them irresistibly of its truth. From this we must infer that it is God himself, the essential and substantial truth, who then gives us this direct enlightenment and causes us to contemplate in essence the ideas of the eternal truths.... But why should He do that as regards certain truths only, why should He thus reveal them inescapably in all times and centuries, to all the peoples of the earth, in return for a little attention? Why, I say, should He thus deal with man, unless to give him a rule and a criterion for judging the other objects which come continually under his observation?... God's will has given the soul an unfailing resource for discerning true and false; this resource is the natural light....

And the just is discerned in the same way as the true:

All moral laws without exception must be tried by this natural idea of equity which, no less than metaphysical light, illumines every man coming into the world.[1]

This passage is of capital importance. It emerges clearly from it that the reason why opinions should be free is that they gravitate naturally towards truth and justice. What folly to try to hinder their disorderly movements when this disorder joins inevitably with the recognition of order!

No less clear is the source from which the assertion comes; therein is shown the deep Christian feeling of a much misunderstood philosopher. This natural light, which is at the heart of his work and gave its name to the Age of Enlightenment, is the light spoken of in the Gospel of St John, 'the true light which lighteth every man that cometh into the world'. Cartesian thought had rested on the same pivot: 'God is no deceiver.' It is too often forgotten that it is this postulate of the participation of man in the intelligence of the Creator which underwrites Reason and justifies its use.

If the postulate of some kinship between the human mind and the divine intelligence is accepted, with its corollary that truth is the naturally desired food of every mind, it logically follows that error is basically precarious. Let us bring out clearly this important point.

[1] Bayle, 'Commentaire Philosophique', *Opera*, vol. II, pp. 368–9.

In the system of thought under consideration, truth is conceived as the centre of a target at which all aim. Interest and passion may largely deflect my personal aim, and therefore what I call true may be very wide of the mark. And the same interest and passion may very likely cause the same deflection in the aim of a majority of my fellow-seekers. But it is improbable that, as time passes and trials multiply, all of us will continue subject to this single interest and passion. The powerful cause which, for a time, made us concur in a particular error will in time dissolve, and we shall return to our more normal condition, in which each is misled in his own way by his own specific interest and passion.

As soon as we envisage not one common cause of error simultaneously infecting minds in general, but a large number of causes variously affecting each individual mind, the picture presented by the sum of individual judgments changes fundamentally. It is now not one of agreement on some quite untrue conclusion, but of a considerable dispersion of judgments. And the more numerous and individual the causes of error, the more random the dispersion. As we have assumed that the striving towards truth is, however weak and obscured, common to all men, this dispersion of individual judgments is bound to occur around the centre of the target. They will bunch towards truth, however wildly they land all around it. This, I believe, is what Rousseau meant by a phrase which has always been accounted obscure.[1]

This reasoning, it may be noted, while trusting to 'the voice of the people', does not lead to the kind of majority decision now commonly practised, but to that practised every day by men of science when, out of many trial measures of a quantity, they work out its most likely value. There are, in fact, alternative notions of majority. The ordinary man will say that, if a country contains more adult males under five feet eight inches in height than over, then the majority of adult males is made up of those under five feet eight inches. But a scientist will be more prone to think of the median height of adult males and to construct his majority out of those classes of height which deviate least from the median. And this second mode of thought is, I believe, implied in the system of thought under consideration. The modern notion of a 'trend of opinion' is probably far nearer to the original thinking on the

---

[1] 'Mais ôtez de ces mêmes volontés les plus et les moins qui s'entre-détruisent, reste pour somme des différences la volonté générale.' (*Du Contrat Social*, Book II, ch. III.)

subject than is our practice of weighing packages of opinion against one another, as must, of course, be done if a plain Yes or No is called for.

THE POSTULATE OF DIVERGENCE

Let us suppose an all-powerful legislator, such as the eighteenth-century writers loved to imagine. Let us suppose that an angelic intelligence is at his elbow when he plans his laws. And let this intelligence say to him:

'The men of your city will, as time goes on, tend to behave in conformity with their particular opinions. If you impose on your city from the start common beliefs of great persuasive authority, the conduct of each, though inspired by his own judgment, will answer the expectation of others, for then his judgment coincides with theirs. Furthermore, all will agree on the rules appropriate to their life in common—rules which will be the necessary outcome of the convictions they hold in common.

'But this harmony will come undone if you permit or favour the introduction of aberrant beliefs. The first batch of new beliefs will be presented as a complete substitute for the old, meant to be held by all as the former were. But they will fail in this total conquest and win only a limited adherence. After this first wave, another will succeed; it too will have a very incomplete measure of success. Thus, in time, as a consequence of successive introductions of new beliefs which receive only a limited acceptance, the dispersion of the beliefs held by the members of society will go on increasing; and efforts to reunite all the associates either under the original system of beliefs or under an eclectic system will fail. The conduct of each, being now the product of his private judgment, will fail more and more the expectations of all those others who judge on different principles; at the same time, there will be less and less agreement on the general rules of social life, with each sect seeking to make its respective principles the criterion.'

With this warning in his ears, our hypothetical legislator would feel greatly alarmed for the future of the city, and he would seek to provide against the envisaged situation by taking some precautions.

First, he would think it absolutely necessary that the laws, whatever their origin, should grip the citizens in the tightest possible vice; in this way individual behaviours would be subjected to an order without which the society would dissolve. But, since there is no belief on which to rest respect for laws—for the citizens are by hypothesis unable to unite in any belief whatever, even belief in the virtue of legality—repressive force must do the work of respect for the laws. And this is in substance the doctrine of Hobbes, Spinoza, Destutt de Tracy and Austin.

But, secondly, our legislator may also reflect that in the prevailing disorder of opinions it will not be easy for the citizens to come to terms for the purpose of legislation. The disorder of factions will complicate the task of law-making, even if the laws, once promulgated, are executed with such severity as to provide an escape from the disorder caused by private behaviours. Inevitably, moreover, disorder in making them will react unfavourably on their execution. Laws which are a stake in embittered public conflicts do not inspire much respect, even among those who execute them; the latter may fear that they may soon be reproached with having executed too rigorously edicts which were to prove short-lived. Therefore our legislator would ask himself whether it would not be better to remove from the arena the actual making of the laws, and to entrust it to some authority whose decision, though it would not necessarily be the best, would have the advantage of exemption from debate and change.

In this way our legislator would, by rigorous execution of the laws, have prevented individual behaviours from plunging into disorder, and would also, by instituting a supreme and unchallengeable authority, have escaped the dangers of political disorder. Even after he had thus chained up the men of the city, however, the disorder which it was his aim to forestall would smoulder out of sight and would, in the end, break out, for political institutions cannot maintain themselves in being for ever without consent, and the dispersion of opinions makes agreement impossible as to the worth of these institutions. Our legislator would, therefore, find it simpler to strike at the disorder at its source and prevent, if he can, the future dispersion and clash of opinions, instead of having to make continuous use of the police to keep in check those wanting to behave differently and having to maintain unpopular laws by force.

If the assumption is made that the historical tendency of opinions is in fact towards an indefinite dispersion, then the legislator will reason in the way we have described; he will proceed from rigorous control of behaviours by the laws to the removal of the laws from the arena of debate until he comes in the end to the prohibition of intellectual novelties. These three degrees of authoritarianism, taken together, constitute precisely the system of Hobbes.

None can fail to see, however, that our legislator will find this authoritarianism necessary only if he is trying, *a posteriori*, to put together again a chain of causes and effects which has come undone —to return, in other words, to the start of a historical process; we are supposing his task to be that of re-establishment and reparation. But if at the very start he is aware of the consequences in store, he need do no more than prevent, if he can, the inauguration of government by clash of opinions; and that by itself will prevent disputes about the laws and incompatibilities among individual behaviours. For this reason the system of Hobbes strikes us as violating the principle of economy of action. The result he seeks could be just as well achieved by the maintenance of unity of belief, and that is what Rousseau saw so clearly. The whole of his large stock of political wisdom consists in contrasting the dispersion of feelings in a people morally disintegrated by the progress of the 'sciences and arts', with the natural unity of a people in which disassociation has not occurred. Among unsophisticated peoples judgments tend to be unanimous—the rule of the general will. Among highly developed peoples there is dissension and 'the general will is dumb'. Whenever the general will makes its voice heard easily, because beliefs and sentiments are deeply felt in common, it is possible for men to live under the sovereignty of laws which are not felt as a burden because they correspond with the personal judgments of the subjects. When, on the other hand, the process of disassociation has set in, the only expedient left is 'Hobbism at its most complete' (Letter from Rousseau to the Marquis de Mirabeau, 1767).

That is why Rousseau links his vision of a democratic city with silence on the part of the philosophers. There is a strange refusal to see the central position occupied in his thought by the *Discours des Sciences et des Arts*, and to understand that the *Contrat Social* needs to be read in the light of this discourse, which the *Dialogue de Rousseau avec Jean-Jacques* forcibly underlines. The necessary and sufficient condition for the effective working of Rousseauesque democracy is the exclusion of beliefs from discussion. Rousseau attaches so much importance to the unity of beliefs that he goes so far as to say, notwithstanding his protestant outlook, that the introduction of protestantism into France should, if possible, have been prevented—in his mouth a most revealing statement and one whose significance has been insufficiently realised.

His system can only be understood if he is recognised for an enemy of calling beliefs in question. It is true, no doubt, that no intellectual can be consistently the enemy of an activity which is natural to him, so that contradictions appear in his work, but it is, even so, a striking fact that in Rousseau's unsophisticated republic matters proceed much as they do in Bossuet's infallible church—in the sense that the citizen who has advanced a particular opinion contrary to that of the majority must not only submit but formally recognise that he was mistaken. In the same way Bossuet's Christian must not only 'sit lightly to his own thoughts' but must 'prefer to his own sentiments the sentiment felt in common by the church'. (Bossuet in the preface to his *Histoire des Variations*.)

THE PRINCIPLE OF DISPERSION

Everything that has gone before is a discussion of the consequences of and the remedies for dispersion. We do not say that a regime in which beliefs and opinions are freely introduced must necessarily lead to the indefinite dispersion of opinions. We are considering only how the problem of social harmony presents itself on the hypothesis that this dispersion will occur.

In doing so, we have, we hope, made it clear how fundamental is the cleavage in political philosophy between those thinkers on the social order who choose the postulate of convergence and those who choose the postulate of divergence. Earlier, we pointed out that the postulate of convergence rests on a metaphysical conception—natural light. We are now to look for the different philosophy which leads to the postulate of divergence.

Let us resume the imaginary dialogue between our legislator and the pure intelligence advising him. Alarmed at the prospect disclosed to him, this Solon of ours asks the intelligence why it is that opinions, once set going, are for ever diverging further.

The reason is [answers his adviser], that the primary beliefs are nothing more than superstitions buttressed by custom. They are, moreover, different in different places, and their social virtue is derived not from any truth which they embody but merely from their unifying power. Their only defensive weapons against the sceptical reason are the inertia of minds and the power of routine. But no more has Reason which attacks them any certain criterion by which to establish other beliefs and social norms, for there is no such thing as an absolutely true belief or norm. Those which a man propounds are valid only for himself, and, being wholly subjective in their root, are nothing but 'mystifications' due to interests and 'derivations'[1] due to feelings. Now, as a society grows in range and complexity, the diversity of situations grows too; a growing diversity of situations causes a growing diversity of interests and in the end results, inescapably, in a growing diversity of judgments.

Found in sociology, this is the language of the materialist and relativist school. Found in theology, it is the language of the Prince of Darkness. Few of the learned men who use it recognise that its very logic assumes an ever-growing disorder; this disorder must either be stopped dead at the source by means of a ban on discussion, or, once its effects have begun to show themselves, it must be held in check by despotism.

It is logically inadmissible to adopt this standpoint of root-and-branch scepticism, and yet continue as the champion of unfettered intellectual innovation and political liberty.

THAT MORAL RELATIVISM CANNOT LEAD TO TOLERATION

One of the strangest intellectual illusions of the nineteenth century was the idea that toleration could be ensured by moral relativism. In our day too we still find those—and men of distinction too—who explain toleration in these terms: 'If I do not believe in the absolute value of truth and justice as I see them, then, and only then, shall I not seek to impose my values on you. But, were I too strongly convinced of them, then I should want to force you to adopt them and enter what is the only true system: *Compelle intrare.*'

This line of thought infers a collective attitude from an individual attitude in a way which is wholly illegitimate. To an intellectual who takes no active part it may be a matter of indifference whether another intellectual, who also takes no active part, holds moral opinions very different from his own. But the possibility of active social groups being guided in their behaviour by irreconcilable moral judgments must always interest the state.

After all, the abstract proposition that moral opinions as such are devoid of absolute value does not in the least imply that they do not answer the imperialist requirements of those who adopt them—

---

[1] Pareto's term.

whose interests and feelings they serve. They are necessary for the man of the group which champions them even though they have no absolute necessity. And the more he vaguely suspects that they are not absolute and universal, the greater will be his hurry to impose them by pressure and violence. Haste would be pointless if he was assured of the contrary conclusion, that everyone would, in longer or shorter time, reach inevitably the same goal.

The nearer to earth that the source of opinions is put, the more clearly they are seen for vague shadows and the less reason there is to respect them. The relativist tells us that the man professing opinion A ought to respect opinion B, because his own opinion A has no more intrinsic value than B. But in that case B has no more than A. Attempts to impose either would be attempts to impose what had no intrinsic value; but also suppression of either would be suppression of what had no intrinsic value. And in that case there is no crime, no sin against the spirit, in the suppression of contrary opinions.

The great utilitarian value of unity of opinions cannot be disputed; yet to preserve it by throttling inspirations which partake of the divine seems monstrous. But if what is in question is the rationalisation of a group interest—a rationalisation wearing the bright colours of an intellectual fantasy which suits this interest well—divine inspiration does not come into the matter at all: and then where is the harm in suppressing an opinion which keeps men divided?

The idea so commonly found that scepticism leads to toleration arises from considering the effects of scepticism in the intellectual who takes no active part—not its effects in the man of action. In the man of action, moral relativism and scepticism as to the absolute and universal value of his principles are no obstacle to fanatical belief in their immediate value as regards his own clan at the actual moment; they do not weaken in the least his will to impose his principles. How should he glimpse a soul of truth in the principles of others, entitling them to respect, when he does not believe in noble origins of this kind even for his own principles?

PANORAMA

It is customary in writing the history of liberty of opinion to distinguish two periods: that of orthodoxy and that of liberty gradually parting company with orthodoxy and triumphing ever more completely. Our own classification is very different.

Granted a first period in our western culture in which it was held for certain that there were beliefs which correspond to truth and opinions which correspond to justice. Within this period may be found two subdivisions. In the first, it was thought that the apprehension of truth was beyond the powers of an unaided individual, who was presumptuous even to try; truth had, therefore, to be in the collective keeping of the organised body of the church. In the second, it was believed that this organised body, because of its very weight, had come to stand between the individual mind and the light shining directly from God. Throughout this period in both its subdivisions it was felt that nothing compared in importance with the apprehension of truth. Our ancestors, though much poorer than ourselves, rated the increase of material wealth much lower than we do. For them Truth was the all-important value.

Still confining ourselves to this first period, it is clear that, if the repository of truth is a body, this body must for that reason be the just and necessary adviser of those who govern, to keep them informed as to what they should and should not do. If, on the other hand, every mind is equally capable of grasping the same truths, then it is the business of all to pronounce on moral issues. In the first case the role belongs to the hierarchy, in the second to the assembly. What we are saying here recalls the diametrically opposite constitutions of the church and of the kirk—of the original presbyterianism. And it is on this point that the battle has raged which has torn the church to pieces. The democratic principle is, it is clear, nothing other than the triumph, in the political order, of the presbyterian idea. It is even banal to say so.

But what needs stressing is that the new function of the *populus* was essentially an ecclesiastical function. It is as a church, and in the spirit of a church, that the people got its title to pronounce, being assumed to possess adequate 'light' for the purpose.

Let us note at once that many, if not most, of the political questions calling for decision are of a kind in which exact acquaintance with the special facts plays a much larger part than the discernment of ethical imperatives. If these questions too are subject no less to decision by the assembly, as was the case in the small reformed churches, the reason must be the generalisation of a practice which, on the hypothesis of diffused moral illumination, should logically be confined to general decisions of a moral character.

Whether some decisions are morally indifferent is a question which has much agitated philosophers; the Stoic doctrine that no issue whatever is morally indifferent has often led to abuses. If there are ethically neutral decisions, they may properly be taken in the light of mere personal preference, but it is clear that in that case consultation with the people takes place on a new and quite different footing; the question now put to those consulted is not what they consider good absolutely, but what they find good for themselves as individuals. The form in which consultation occurs remains the same, but its principle and ethos are entirely reversed.

This duality in the expression of the people's voice seems not to have been sufficiently perceived. Expression of the second kind progressively gained ground on expression of the first kind, and in the end entirely supplanted it without anyone noticing.

This occurred in what I propose to call the second period of our culture. It is a period characterised by the dissolution of morality in the true sense. It was thought at first that morality could support itself by, so to speak, its own weight, without the help of metaphysical principle—that it was both universal and necessary. But it was later observed that the presumed agreement of all peoples at all times about moral principles had no real existence.

This discovery was favoured by the voyages of travellers and the reports which they brought back of moral beliefs very different from our own. The Jesuits insisted, with much force of conviction and much ingenuity of exposition, on the fundamental similarity which they claimed to find beneath accidental differences. They have for that reason been the great inventors of the democratic philosophy of natural light; it is strange that they are so seldom given credit for this.

The more favoured thesis was, however, that of the fundamental diversity of moral systems, which has given rise to the sceptical outlook of Montaigne and Pascal. Montaigne is the great mocker of ideas of natural law. It is vain, he says, to seek in human institutions the similarity of rules which it is considered ought to be there. On this subject he has written pages which Pascal has only reproduced, though Pascal's are the better known.

If, in fact, 'the only rule our duty has is fortuitous' (Montaigne), if it is 'the caprice of chance which has sown human laws' (Pascal), there is one consequence which flows logically from this absence of *consensus gentium*: the putting to debate of laws and general institutions will not result in a single conclusion which is inscribed beforehand in the fabric of human nature. The most that will emerge are the various preferences. The ultimate consequences of this point of view could not take effect in an age that was deeply religious. But they emerged more and more with every weakening of the religious tie and every consequent growth of materialist beliefs.

In a materialist vision of the world, moral imperatives are no longer a projection from on high, as they are in a theological vision; they have become the mere idealisation of the desires of our nature, now regarded as essentially carnal—they are the dreams of the flesh. Therefore they are, as is the case with all dreams, in the first place relative to the dreamer, to his condition and to the impressions which he has received and which stir him, and secondly, they are unreasonable. That being so, where is the guarantee that they will accord with one another? There is none.

Acceptance of these premises carries with it two conclusions. One is that there is neither necessary accord nor, in this diversity, necessary predominance of the opinion which best conforms with justice (or even with utility). The other is that there must be some means of ensuring an artificial convergence, if not on a 'just'—a word which has now really lost all meaning—at any rate on a 'useful'.

What means are proposed to ensure this convergence? There are two of them. The first is that of the utilitarian liberals. Only certain measures, they say, procure for the members of a society the maximum of utility. And by the education of the intelligence individuals can be brought to see that the adoption of and respect for these measures conform to their own interest. But it is much harder for an individual to see the distant and uncertain relationship between his own interest and the general interest—it presupposes a long chain of reasoning of which few are capable—than it should be for him to perceive, in the system of natural light, the moral evidences imprinted in us by God. For this reason, the utilitarian liberals have always drawn a distinction in fact between minds capable of such an effort and minds incapable of it. Sismondi openly distinguished between those able to have an opinion and those unable. Thinkers of this school prefer a limited franchise to a universal franchise, though in recent times they have hardly dared to publicise this preference.

It is a historical fact too little stressed that universal suffrage has been installed nearly everywhere in Europe against the wishes of a liberal left of the utilitarian brand. And that is very logical. Nothing authorises us to affirm the equal capacity of men to make the long calculations needed to reconcile the public and the private interest; nothing authorises us to deny the equal capacity of men to feel moral truths. In this respect, it is materialism which is inegalitarian and spirituality which has no right to be.

The second means proposed for healing the divergence which is, as we have seen, bound to occur under the pressure of needs according to a materialist system of thought, is that of Marxist socialism. It relates the requirements of men to their situations, and deduces from this that their requirements would be the same provided only that all were in the same situation. It lays down, in principle, that members of the proletariat are all in the same situation, and concludes from this that there are certain specifically proletarian requirements as to which all proletarians are, by an absolute determinism, necessarily agreed. It regards democratic regimes, in which liberty of opinion is the rule, as furnishing these requirements with the opportunity of pressing hard; should they come to press with an irresistible weight, the proletariat will impose them as the rule of the entire society and generalise its own situation. As the situation of the others will then have changed, their requirements will follow suit, and will become uniform with those of the original proletarians. Consequently, the same rules will in the end be desired by all, because all will be in the same situation. This will be the orthodoxy of materialism—an affair not of light but of needs.

GENERATING LINES OF VARIOUS SOCIAL PHILOSOPHIES

In a dualist philosophy, the aim of freedom of the mind is the perception of a truth which participates somewhat in the Divine essence; the pious quest for it is man's noblest endeavour. A dualist system must necessarily separate this endeavour, which belongs to the city of God, from the turbulence of the desires and tastes which confront the city of men with its specific problems. Whatever pertains to the celestial order transcends the simple needs of the temporal organisation and merits respect absolutely. In the temporal order, individual preferences have their rights, but must yield them to what the city needs for survival; at this level, then, opinion lacks both the self-evident dignity and the absolute right which array it in the first order.

In an idealist monism, the two orders are confounded and the opinion which it is thought—against the evidence—necessarily embodies the ideal inspiration never lacks a transcendent right.

In any sort of materialist monism, there is no guarantee that the dreams of the flesh will converge, nor that any substantial part of them will coincide with what is salutary for society. Utilitarian liberalism would seem often to have wished to forget this consequence of its basic affirmations; in this it is helped by its logically untenable affiliation to the liberalism of natural light. The facts have spoken. The political experience of liberal democracies has shown that, in everything pertaining to the order of material interests, it has never been possible to effect a spiritual union; accord on any scale has never been seen except when the moral sentiments were involved.

Just as the facts have contradicted the liberal branch of materialism, they have contradicted more violently still the Marxist branch. According to this school, spiritual union was to come about as soon as uniformity of situations had been established. In principle, therefore, control of opinions would no longer be needed as soon as situations are controlled; but this relationship has been proved false and minds must be narrowly controlled even when situations are already narrowly controlled.

The movement of opinions in the age of liberal democracy would be a most useful study. It would enable us to verify empirically the postulates of convergence and divergence and to observe the class of case in which each is applicable. We must be content ourselves to have brought out that confidence in a natural ability to choose the just and the true is narrowly linked to the idea of natural light—of human participation in the Divine essence. When that is no more believed, the whole edifice collapses.

CONCLUSION

In the French original there was no concluding chapter, and this lack accorded with my understanding of the book as suggestive rather than didactic in purpose. I felt that my investigation had proceeded fan-wise into territories which I was as yet unable to map. I have been, however, urged to attempt a summing-up, and helped thereto by the invaluable criticism of Professor Michael Polanyi, Professor J. J. Chevallier, Professor Carl J. Friedrich, Mr Chester Barnard[1] and my distinguished translator, Mr J. F. Huntington. At my urgent request, both Professor G. C. Homans and Mr T. E. Utley have done me the great kindness of preparing illuminating statements of the gist of the book, as they saw it; thanks to their contributions, I have realised which points, important in my eyes, stood out with sufficient clarity, and which did not. No author could have wished for a more fruitful dialogue.

With all this help, I embark upon my task. But still not without diffidence. It is in the very nature of a conclusion to be more peremptory than my taste and the exploratory character of my work incline me to be. I hope that fellow political scientists who may not like the conclusion will not be deterred from accepting the concept of group-building as a factor tending to unify the fields of sociology and politics. I hope that some will agree that Political Science needs a more ambitious programme and a more affirmative attitude than is now thought proper.

POLITICAL AUTHORITIES NOT THE SOLE SUBJECT OF POLITICAL SCIENCE

I was taught that Political Science deals with public authorities. Political theory justifies the existence of a right to command, states now that this right is immanent in the People, explains that its exercise has to be delegated, and enunciates the process whereby it must be delegated and allocated in order to remain the same

---

[1] Mr Chester Barnard's writings offer a brilliant demonstration that Political Science thrives on its connection with responsible decision-making. Thinking about his function leads this author to contribute greatly to the advance of science. It is to be regretted that there is too little in academic Political Science of this thinking about the executive function, in terms which might help decision-makers to formulate their problem.

essence throughout these modifications and specifications. Those commands are lawful and deserve obedience which have been lawfully enacted from those seats of power set up by that agent in which, or in whom, sovereignty inheres. Political theory, in short, deduces consequences from a source of sovereignty which is premised; it is mainly deductive. Practical Political Science is mainly descriptive; it describes the actual operation of these agencies which political theory justifies. It is fashionable to regard political theory as a thing completed, and to deal with it from an historical angle only, relating by what successive achievements of the mind it was built up.

It is then left to sociology to study men's behaviours in so far as they are left indeterminate by legal commands. In other words, the use which men make of their civil freedom, understood as the indetermination of conducts within the bounds set by legal obligations, and even the impulses which, in the exercise of political freedom, they transmit through the fabric of public agencies, pertain to sociology rather than to Political Science, when it comes to explaining them.

Observation and introspection have convinced me that, even in our times of numerous and detailed laws, men are in fact ruled much less by laws than by compulsive internal images of what they should do—behavioural models; that their conduct is not a matter of personal fancy within the limits set by legal obligations, but gravitates around their behavioural image, which itself alters over time; that, even though public commands become both more frequent and more specific, behaviour and action are governed in the main by suggestions without legal force; that these phenomena are more important than those usually denominated 'political' and are in fact basic to so-called 'political phenomena'. Men can in fact be moved to certain actions and behaviours by means lacking all legal authority and power of constraint no less well than by the public authorities; that being so, the more general case surely includes the more particular.

Every already established form of co-operation rests upon a confident expectation of performance by the other man. How is such a confidence fortified? Every new form of co-operation results from a process of suggestion and response between one man and another, or many others. How can such a process of suggestion be encouraged, how can injurious suggestions be weeded out, and how can the novel behaviours so generated be reconciled with the postulated necessity that habitual expectation should not be disappointed?

Suggestions give rise to goal-directed groups of action; the stability of conditions necessary for men to function confidently calls for regulating factors. The interplay of forces driving and forces regulating, and the many human organisations arising therefrom, constitute a complex in which public authorities are only one element.

What I regard as Political Science covers a wider ground. To me it is the study of all agencies tending to establish and develop the conditions of fruitful co-operation between men. The formation of groups and organisations of any kind, and the resolving of conflicts arising within and between these bodies, that is Political Science. Obviously such a science must be empirical in its method; conditions conducive to fruitful co-operation can be observed and appreciated in terms of more or less. And the science is normative as to its goal; from it we can learn how to foster fruitful co-operation.

It is immediately obvious that the conditions of fruitful co-operation do not hang merely upon the fidelity with which the public magistrates reflect the will of the sovereign body, for other men exert simultaneously a non-governmental authority. Again it is obvious that men are amenable not only to enacted laws but also to moral imperatives. Further, neither the behaviour of those in government nor the quality of the enacted laws are uniquely determined by the procedures whereby the offices are filled and the laws passed. Therefore political theory, if centred on the latter procedures and objects, covers only a minute part of the field, and this involves the danger that the part should be taken for the whole.

THE RULE OF LAW: WHAT IT MEANS

I was taught that the Rule of Law obtained when the men in public office merely executed the laws of the realm and saw to it that these were obeyed by citizens. Such a view leads, in my opinion, to two erroneous assumptions. The first is that the men in office have to solve no problems of choice since the laws tell them what to do. This is an obvious fallacy, upheld however by the formula: 'A Government of Laws, not Men'. There can be no such government, least of all in a society undergoing a process of ceaseless transformation. Men in positions of responsibility have to make decisions,[1] with

---

[1] That the 'Executive Power' cannot and should not evade the obligation to make decisions is admirably brought out in President Truman's farewell address from which I quote: 'The greatest part of the President's job is to make decisions, big ones and

necessarily inadequate information—decisions which, therefore, have the character of bets on the outcome. Political Science cannot, as I see it, evade the obligation of teaching them how to bet as wisely as human ignorance and fallibility will allow.

The second erroneous assumption is that citizens are induced to obey enacted laws mainly because there are agencies of enforcement, but partly also because they trust the process whereby laws are made.

As I see it, the Rule of Law is a natural phenomenon. Men are inhibited from doing certain things, and offended when such things are done, by reason of shared feelings as to what is right and proper. Upon those feelings, the content of which changes over time but the nature of which is unchanging, rests the possibility of social co-operation. The actions of individuals, puny or powerful, the decisions of those in office, and enacted laws themselves, are subject to these deep-lying convictions. That such convictions should be held strongly, and that they should be shared, constitutes the essence of the Rule of Law, which is actualised by the expression of moral approval or disapproval. This is certainly no new idea: it is perhaps the oldest of political ideas. But the problems which it raises today are of extreme urgency. Is there any contradiction between the freedom of suggestion and the necessity of common beliefs? If there is, how can it be resolved?

THE INITIATIVE: WHERE IT LIES

I was taught that the chief problem of Political Science today lies in the relationship between the state and the individual. I believe that the figure upon which Political Science should focus its attention is the Initiator, the Promoter, and that the chief problem of the science is to study the conditions of dynamic balance between the driving forces and the adjusting factors.

Wherever I look in society, I find the self-same process at work: the rallying of individuals at the call of some person who has suggested a goal to be achieved in common. Such a rallying of individuals builds up through the adding together of their energies 'a power'

small ones, dozens of them almost every day. The papers may circulate around the Government for a while but finally they reach this desk. And then there's no place for them to go. The President—whoever he is—has to decide. He can't pass the buck to anybody. No one else can do the deciding for him. That's his job.' (From *The New York Times*, 16 January 1953.)

in the simple and immediate sense of the word: a power capable of doing 'work' which no individual could do by himself. This is the basic social phenomenon; as we find this process going on at all times, everywhere and in all fields, it is convenient to think of this catalysis as caused by 'a force' of which the initiator is the bearer or agent. This force I have called *vis politica*, and the agent or bearer *dux*.

The concept serves to link up the separate fields of social progress and political conflict. The catalytic agent is the fount and origin of both conflict and progress; the *duces*, by assembling human forces, multiply the efficacy of human action, but their competing bids set them at variance, while possibly their ends may be incompatible.

We should not, I believe, regard the *vis politica* as a 'quality' inherent in the *dux* and therefore capable of producing more or less effect according to the responsiveness of the particular society; rather it should be thought of as a relationship in which suggestion and response are part of a global process. With the concept so understood, we can say, by definition, that the quantity of movement in a society will be a function of the *vis politica* at work. There will be little in a quiescent society, and few *duces*. There will be much in a vigorous society, and many *duces*.

THE OPPORTUNITY TO GENERATE A GROUP

Focusing attention upon *duces* will bring into sharp relief the character of a society and the nature of its government. A society is a *class* society when only those born in certain families can be *duces*. It does not matter whether the others are excluded by formal legislation, or are so lacking in status that they can obtain no response to their call for followers, or are bereft of the necessary daring or of the necessary education; it is enough that they lack the opportunity, for whatever reason.

A government is despotic which claims the monopoly of the function of the *dux*, whether it uses this monopoly to exercise this function alone, or whether it uses it to make the exercise by others of the functions of *dux* dependent upon its own grant.

The essential freedom, as I see it, is the freedom to create a gathering, to generate a group, and thereby introduce in society a new power, a source of movement and change.

'REX': THE STABILISER

It is obvious, however, that every new movement injected into society tends to disturb pre-existing conditions. It is a cause of uncertainty. Each man lives in a behavioural environment and must assume, as near as no matter, its stability. On this assumption depend both his feeling of safety, without which he tends to become an asocial being, and his ability to make rational calculations, without which he cannot exercise his liberty. It is the basic paradox of liberty that my right to alter my course can be put to purposeful and intelligent use only if I expect little change in ambient behaviours, which are, notwithstanding, those of men enjoying the same freedom which I claim.

I regard it as the essential function of the sovereign to ensure the reliability of the individual's environment. This can be done most easily in a society where individuals are chained to their routines. But that would be the very opposite of the society we want. We wish to encourage initiatives which make for change. Therefore the problem posed to the sovereign becomes very difficult; the social universe must be at the same time fluid, responsive to new initatives, and a solid ground to which the individual may trust. The unexpected must be allowed to happen and legitimate assumptions must not be belied. An adequate degree of stability must be achieved in the face of change.

In the course of this book it has been amply noted that, while this task of adjustment and stabilisation is the essential duty of the sovereign, there are many factors and processes in society which contribute to the adjustment and stabilisation and so take a large part of the load off the sovereign's shoulders. Society offers in fact an intricate texture of *duces* and *reges*. It is the sovereign's business to see that the *reges* operate to repair the insecurity caused by initiatives, not to preclude them; and it is his duty to intervene to the extent necessary for the adequate fulfilment of the function of *rex*.

STATE ACTION: A COMPANION TO
INDIVIDUAL INITIATIVE

The importance here granted to initiative suggests a classification of political attitudes: there are those who are in general distrustful of initiatives making for change; there are those who are very much in favour of such initiatives but want to see them centralised in and monopolised by the public authority; finally there are those, among whom I count myself, who like initiative and want to see it very widespread. This last may serve as a definition of Liberalism.

But it is the tradition of Liberalism that the public authority is the natural enemy of widespread initiative. This tradition should be replaced by the historical observation that men in authority have a tendency to stifle or supersede individual initiatives. A government which backs the dead-hand of established interests against nascent initiatives stifles the latter. A government which claims the monopoly of initiative, though its intentions are different, also stifles initiatives; in time it is inevitable that its claim to exert *vis politica* to the exclusion of others results in there being far less exerted than would have been the case otherwise. However 'advanced' a government which monopolises initiative deems itself to be, in the end it will be found that it has assumed the character of a dead-hand. These are the incontrovertible lessons of experience.

The activity of the sovereign is necessary, however, to foster the conditions under which initiative will flower; and as these initiatives generate change, disturbance and conflict, it seems logical that the greater their dynamism and variety, the greater the problems of adjustment which the sovereign must meet. Nor can these problems be solved by the mere application of general laws; for these assume unchanging issues and the issues are forever changing. Therefore, there must be in government a perpetual capacity for novel situations and an inventiveness to deal with unforeseen complications.

The progressive character of society is here conceived as arising from non-governmental initiatives, but the necessary stability requires that a government should be that much the more active in resolving problems as the citizens are active in creating them. It follows that an ever-increasing activity of government in the performance of its essential function must be expected. This intensification of governmental activity in the performance of its essential duty is not to be confused with the extension of the governmental label to functions which need not be performed by government; the latter are an unnecessary burdening[1] of the governmental machine, injurious to the performance of its proper duty.

---

[1] It may indeed be mentioned that, where the government assumes many functions which are non-essential to its character, either these functions are only nominally performed by the government and are performed in fact by agencies which become autonomous, or the government, obsessed with these functions, loses the character of *rex* and acquires traits in character with the functions.

THE UNFREEDOM OF GOVERNMENT

Now comes a critical point. If society is so run as to allow individuals great freedom of initiative, and if by the enjoyment of this freedom individuals have exhausted their elbow-room, then they are not free to demand that the government do some one thing or another, irrespective of the circumstances created by their own use of their freedom. The argument is quite a simple one although its conclusion may be unpalatable.

The gist of the foregoing exposition is that initiatives should be allowed, encouraged, fostered, but that they pose problems which the government must solve if it is to fulfil its natural mandate— the preservation of security in the course of change. The more abundant and vigorous the initiatives, the more difficult are the problems arising for the public authority, and the more delicate, therefore, the process of working out adequate answers. These answers are to a considerable degree determined by the data, resulting from the actions of the citizens, and by the imperative of equilibrium, resulting from the universal need of citizens for stability. Or, to put it otherwise, the solutions of problems must be sought by statesmen under constraints which narrowly limit their liberty to pick the solution of their choice. If, then, measures are demanded from the government which lie clearly outside these limits, and are thus outside the range of feasible solutions, a conflict arises between the will expressed by the demanding body of citizens and the duty of government.

This may be deemed an argument against democracy; it is not; it is an argument against irresponsibility. Whether the law of the land grants to all, to many or to a few the right to participate in the exercise of sovereignty, the attending obligation is ever the same; the obligation incurred by the participant is to address himself to the problem arising for the sovereign. He is entitled to manifest his own preference, but within the bounds set by the problem itself. Whether this participant is a peer of an oligarchy or the party-liner of a democracy, he equally disqualifies himself when he expresses his particular will without regard to the problem which the sovereign, as such, has to solve.

The idea here advanced is not new; it is fundamental to Rousseau's *Social Contract*.[1] Even this genius, however, failed to make it under-

[1] See mainly Book IV, ch. I.

stood. Chastened by this example, let us spare no trouble in stressing it.

Everyone grants that the more free are the citizens, the less free can the government be. But in the relationship so stated, some terms are dropped. One implies that the government of free men is not free, because it must be obedient to the political wishes expressed by the citizens. But I say that government is not free even to practise such obedience, because, by reason of its very purpose, it must solve the problems posed by the social actions of free men, and this essential task may be incompatible with deference to the demands of citizens for a given action by itself.

No conclusions follow therefrom as to the form of government. The conclusions to be drawn concern the spirit of government and the spirit of citizens. The public spirit, in short, consists in awareness that the sovereign, as such, is unfree to do anything not consonant with the performance of its function.

In Rousseau's terminology, the command of the citizen addressed to the government partakes of the character and dignity of General Will in so far, and in so far only, as the citizen seeks to answer the problem which is posed to the sovereign; it loses this character and dignity when the citizen is unaware of, or indifferent to, this problem. Obviously such a fault can be committed not only by the citizen but quite as easily by the man in political office, and is then far more grievous. The foregoing remarks should not, then, be mistaken for a plea of greater political independence for those in office. What they stress is that the performance of the function of sovereignty depends upon the public spirit.

THE CHARACTER OF POLITICAL SCIENCE

And here we come to the moral of this book. It is a trite one: Political Science is a moral science. While all our several interests are completely dependent upon social co-operation, social co-operation does not rest upon our inadequate understanding of our interests, but essentially upon our moral feelings. Montaigne truly said[1] that the generalisation of lying would, by itself, dissolve human society.

The statement that Political Science is a moral science has been

---

[1] *Essais*, Book I, ch. IX: 'Nous ne sommes hommes, et ne tenons les uns aux autres, que par la parole'; and Book II, ch. XVIII: 'S'il nous trompe, il rompt tout notre commerce, et dissout toutes les liaisons de notre police.'

greatly abused by some who have used it to stress a contrast between it and the natural sciences, and to build it up as an *a priori* system, deduced from simple assumptions about Man—a system exempted from confrontation with ascertainable facts. For purposes of clarity I should, then, say that Political Science is a natural science dealing with moral agents.

The elementary political process is the action of mind upon mind through speech. Communication by speech completely depends upon the existence in the memories of both parties of a common stock of words to which they attach much the same meanings. In like manner, the influence of man upon man, which is the elementary political process, completely depends upon there being, in the consciences of both parties, a common stock of beliefs and a similar structure of feelings. It would be foolish to ignore that men are disposed to action by their subjective interests, but just as foolish to forget that these interests themselves are conceived within a framework of beliefs and feelings.

Even as people belong to the same culture by the use of the same language, so they belong to the same society by the understanding of the same moral language. As this common moral language extends, so does society; as it breaks up, so does society.

The analogy may be pressed further. The security of communication with our fellows rests upon a clear common understanding of the terms in use, but the enrichment of communication calls for the coining of new terms which, through the backwardness of many minds, give rise to misunderstandings. Let us hope that the tensions in our society are of a similar nature. And let us in any case cherish the simple terms which are capable of moving the hearts of all men.

INDEX

Achilles, symbolism of human activity in his shield, 51

Adonijah, 50

advertising, as example of the prestige of the leader, 75

Aegeus, 48

Aegidius Romanus, *see* Colonna, Aegidius Romanus

Age of Enlightenment, Christian significance of the term, 282

aggregates, conditions for founding and stability, 22–5

their study essential to political science, 25

Aguesseau, H. F. d', and 'fortunate powerlessness' of the king, 204

allegiance, as counterpart to *vis politica*, 24

ambitus (Roman candidate's canvassing tour), 103

Anne of Austria, 186

Antaeus, as symbol of nostalgia for primitive closed society, 135

Ariadne, 48

Arianism, Claude's parallel with Roman church, 278

Aristophanes, on 'Laconomania', 135 n.

Aristotle, as illustrating *rex-augur* association, 46

his definition of justice, 140

on justice as equality of proportions, 151

association, explanations of rejected, classical, 26–8; by conquest, 29

the *auctor* as founder, 29–30, 31–2, 71

various types of, 33–4

primary social forms, 56–64

the domestic unit, 57–9

the 'milieu of existence', 59–61

the 'team of action', 62–4; as transforming human existence, 62; criterion of its success, 63; as Hobbes's model for political society, 63; the leader ('man of the project'), 64–5; the leader as master-builder, 66–7

apathy of the majority, 67–8

conditions for and necessity of discipline, 68–70

the social state a matter of degree, 113–14

natural, not artificial, 113–14

as enlargement of the circle of trust, 115

dependent on trust, 119–21

harmony in the City: modern rejection of Plato's and Rousseau's conclusions, 123–6

contrast between historical process and Plato's view of harmony, 124

Plato's view of immutability of the City rejected, 125–6

nostalgia for narrow close-knit society, 135–6

charity as the basis of perfect association, 265

see also society

Assyria, its religion compared with modern nationalism, 131

astronomy, its aptness for human speculation, 42

auctor, as builder of aggregates, 22–5

his part overlooked in classical explanation of association, 28

Augustine, St, on liberty of opinion, 278

Austin, J., 272, 285

on fear of punishment as determining the will, 242 and n.

authoritarianism, three degrees of, 284–6; *see also* Hobbes (his authoritarianism)

authority, properly considered in light of *auctor*, 21

defined, 29–30

as cause of association, 29 ff.

functions and virtues, 30–1

distinguished from power, 32

not opposed to liberty, 33

reasons for decline of in the state, 33

reasons for assent to, 35

positivist and poetical attitudes to, 36–8

its services outbalance its cost, 37

as creator of the social tie, 39

dual function of, 40

metaphorically portrayed by Bridge of Arcola and Oak of Vincennes, 40

as preservative, in primitive societies, 43; in advanced societies, 52–4

good (*cont.*)

subjective view rejected, 107–9

difficulty of identifying with particular good of individuals, 109–12

conflict between, and difficulty of defining, personal goods, 110–11

consists in the social state itself, 112–14

problems of in a mobile society, 121–2

danger of equating with social friendship, 123–8

difficulty of reconciling change with avoidance of disturbance, 126–9

and collective social interest, 128–30; importance of the distinction, and attempts at definition, 128–9

contradiction between trust as original basis and later development of relations, 134–6

government, judgment of the goodness of its acts neither unnecessary nor impossible, 6–11

justification for belief in its influence on public fortune, 35–9

see also authority, law, sovereign

'grands politiques' as builders of aggregates, 26

Green, T. H., on freedom as relating only to man-made obstacles, 248

Grene, D., on Plato's attitude to his own society, 270

Grouchy, Marshal, 218

Guizot, F., 213; on the sovereign will as reason, 210

Hampden, John, and royal right of taxation, 186

harmony in the City, conflict between Plato and Rousseau and modern views, 124

hedonism, necessitating dictatorial authority, 241–5

Helvétius, C. A., 232

Henrietta Maria, Queen, 187

Henry I, King of France, 5

Henry III, King of France, 205 n.

Henry VIII, King, and extension of royal power through Parliament, 178

heredity, from maternal uncle to nephew, and consequent grievances, 52

Hervey Islands, *see* Mangaïa

Hitler, A., 222

Hobbes, T., on subjective judgment of the good, 6 and n.

his explanation of association criticised, 35

on the action group as model for political society, 64

on the sovereign's supremacy to law, 89–90

on artificiality of association, 113

his view of the just criticised by Leibniz, 148

his justification of absolutism, 190

and the individualist approach to political science, 196–8

his attitude to legitimacy of command contrasted with the Christian, 201

his view of the good implies arbitrary rule, 210–11

Leviathan, 231

his approach to the study of society, 231–1

his view of human nature contrasted with the Christian, 233–4; its modernity, 234

his individualism, 234; its progressive nature, 239

on fear, not reason, compelling obedience, 235–7, 242

his views on fear echoed in Freud, 236

on law as commanding by right of origin, 237

on the power of will necessary to enforce rule, 237

and human government viewed as model of divine, 237

on the supremacy of civil power as necessary for avoidance of conflict, 238

his materialism and pantheism, 238

on the negative nature of Leviathan, 239

as father of political economy, 239–41

on the sovereign as guiding self-interest, 240

paradoxical rejection of his political principles and acceptance of his view of man, 241, 243–4

his implicit denial of innate ideas, 241

his lesson for modern democracies, 244–6

on the form of power as an accident, obedience as substance, 245

his authoritarianism drawn from libertarian premises, 246